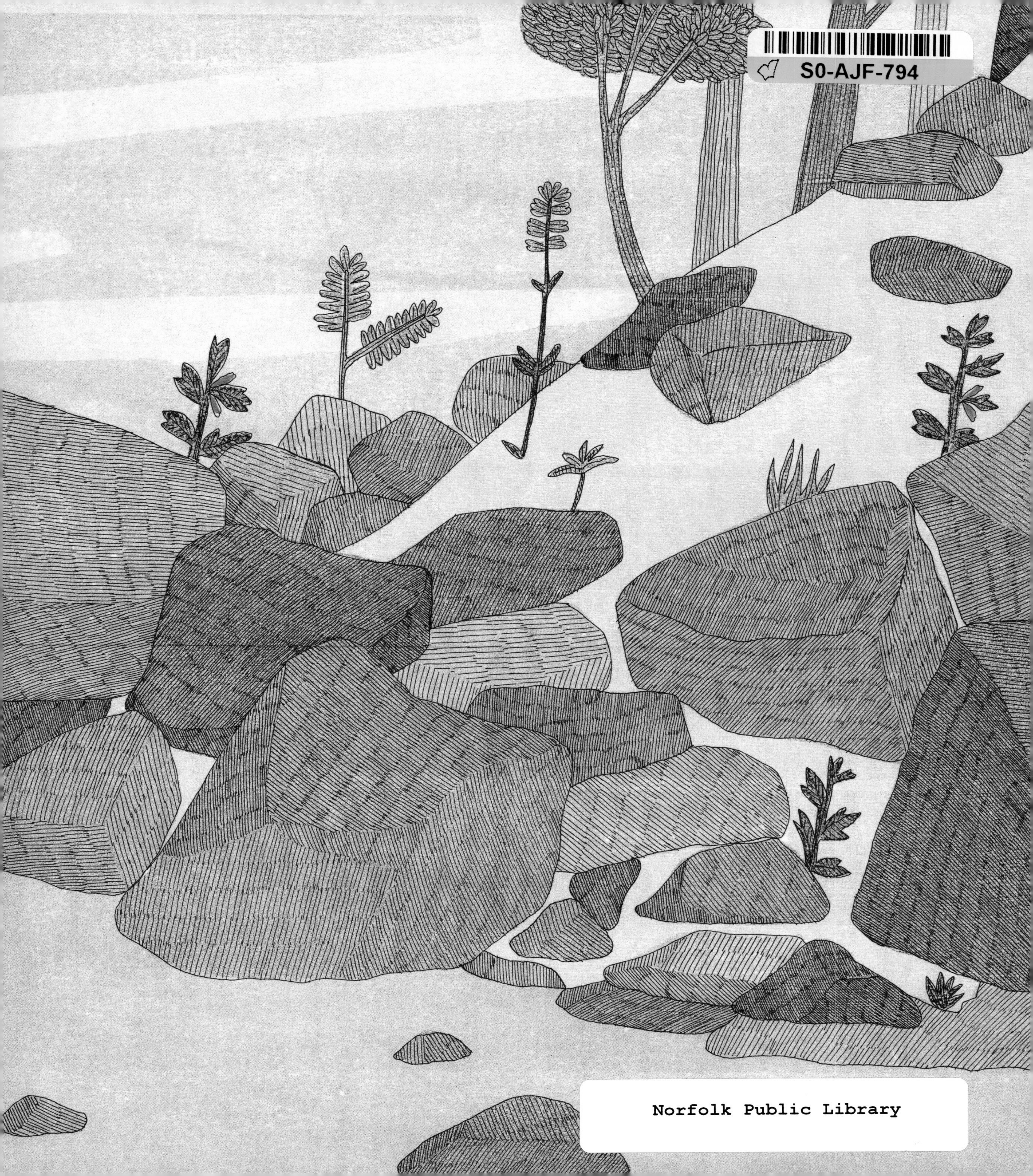

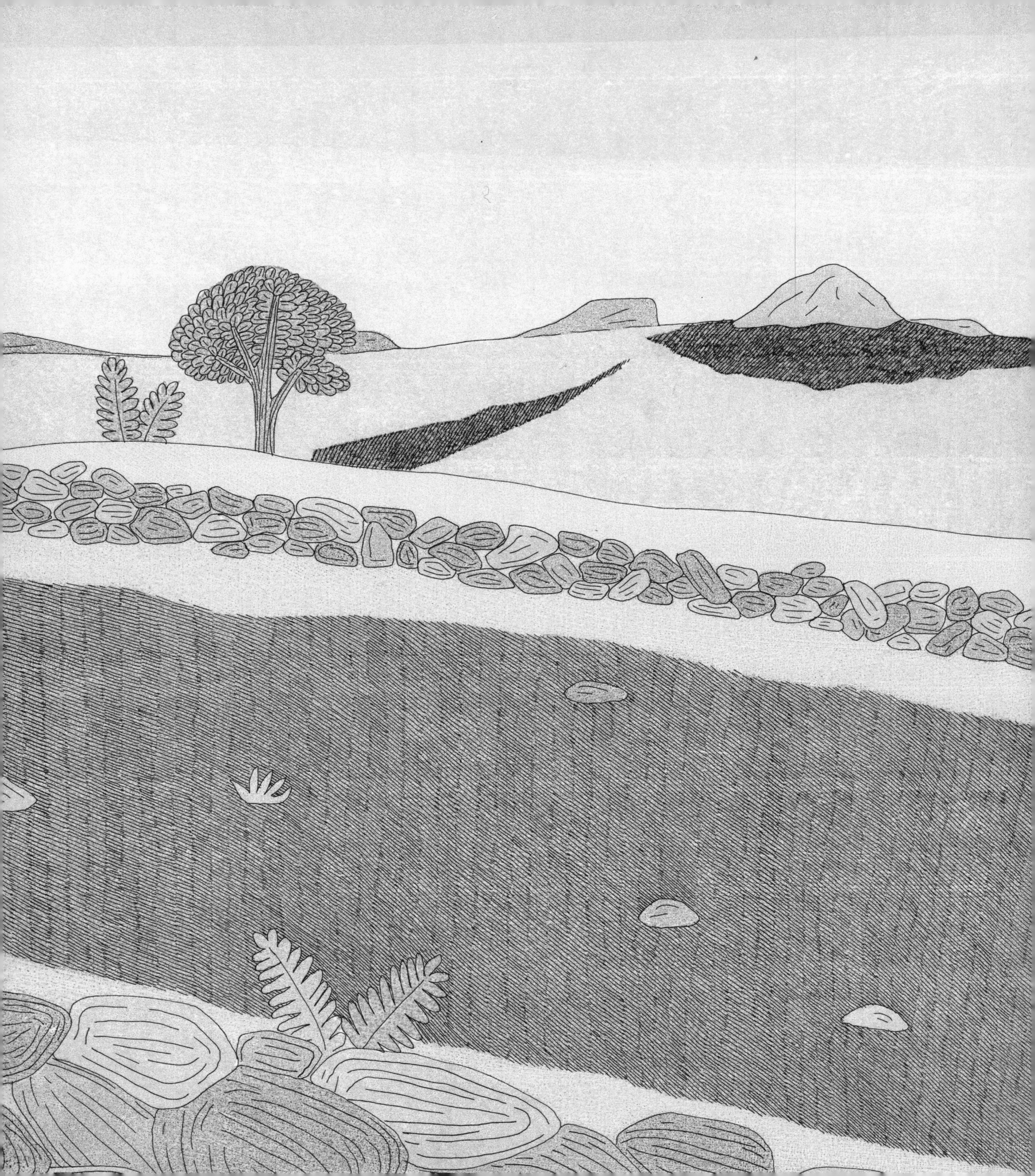

a book by marion fayolle

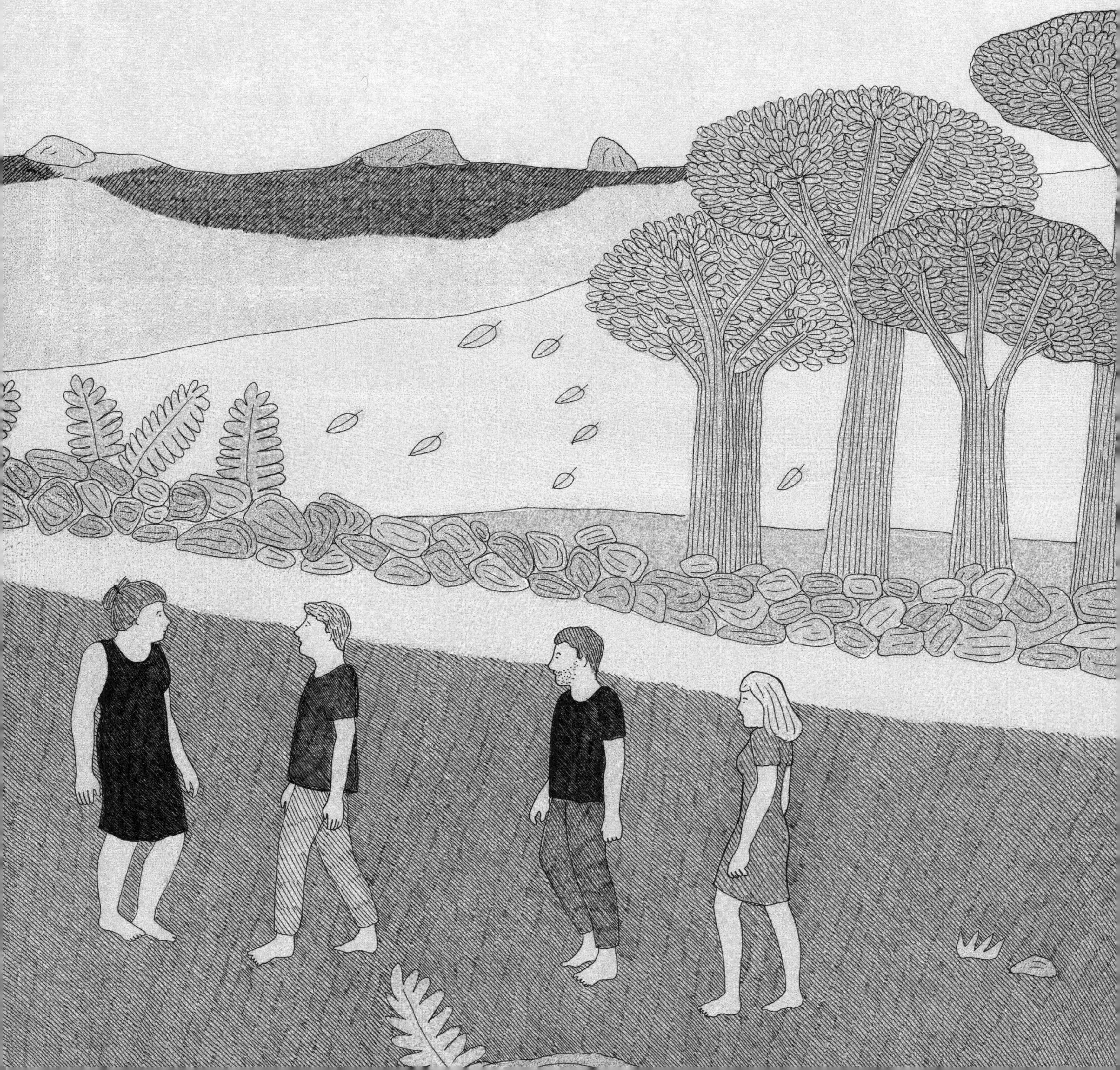

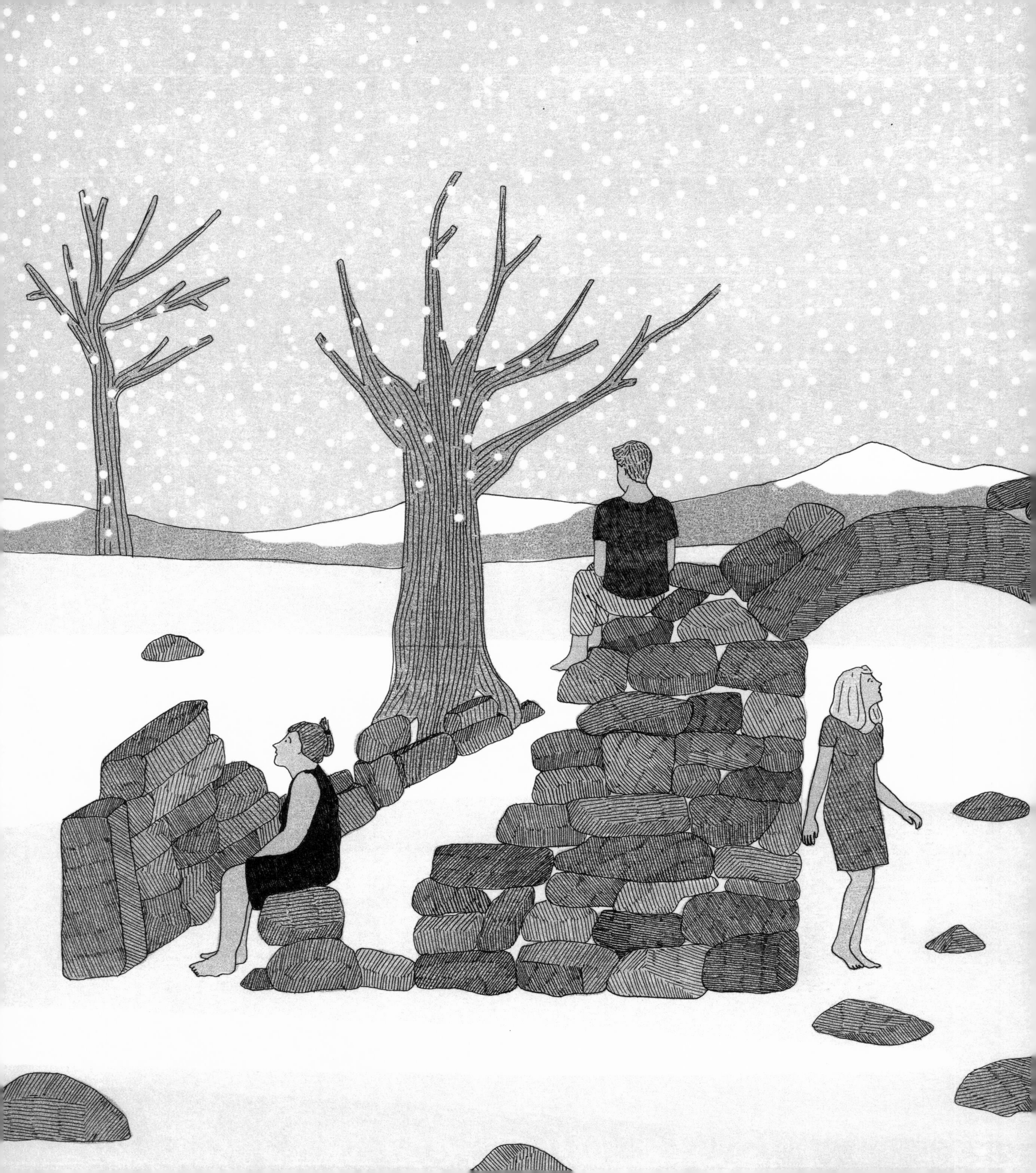

the tenderness of stones

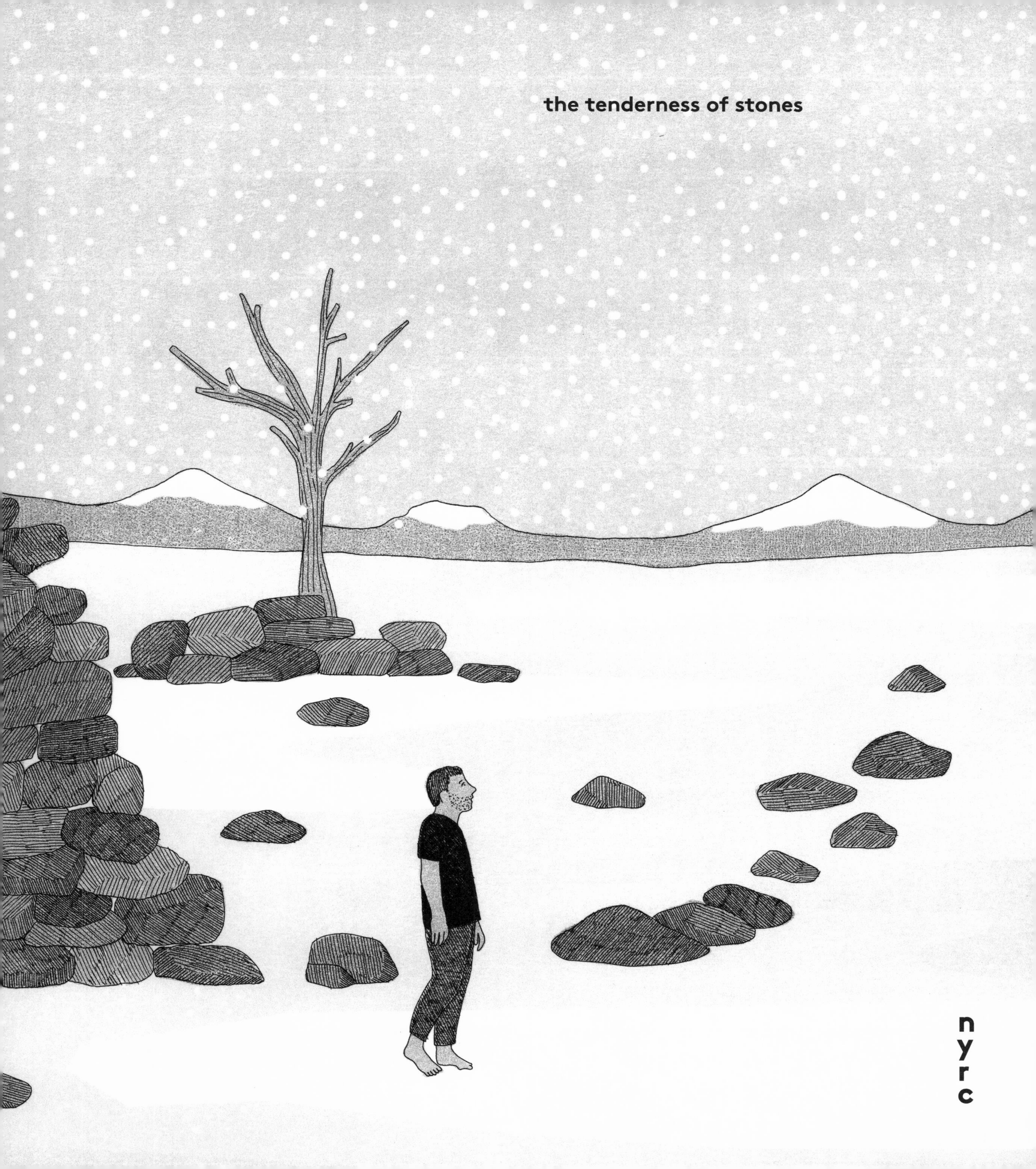
nyrc

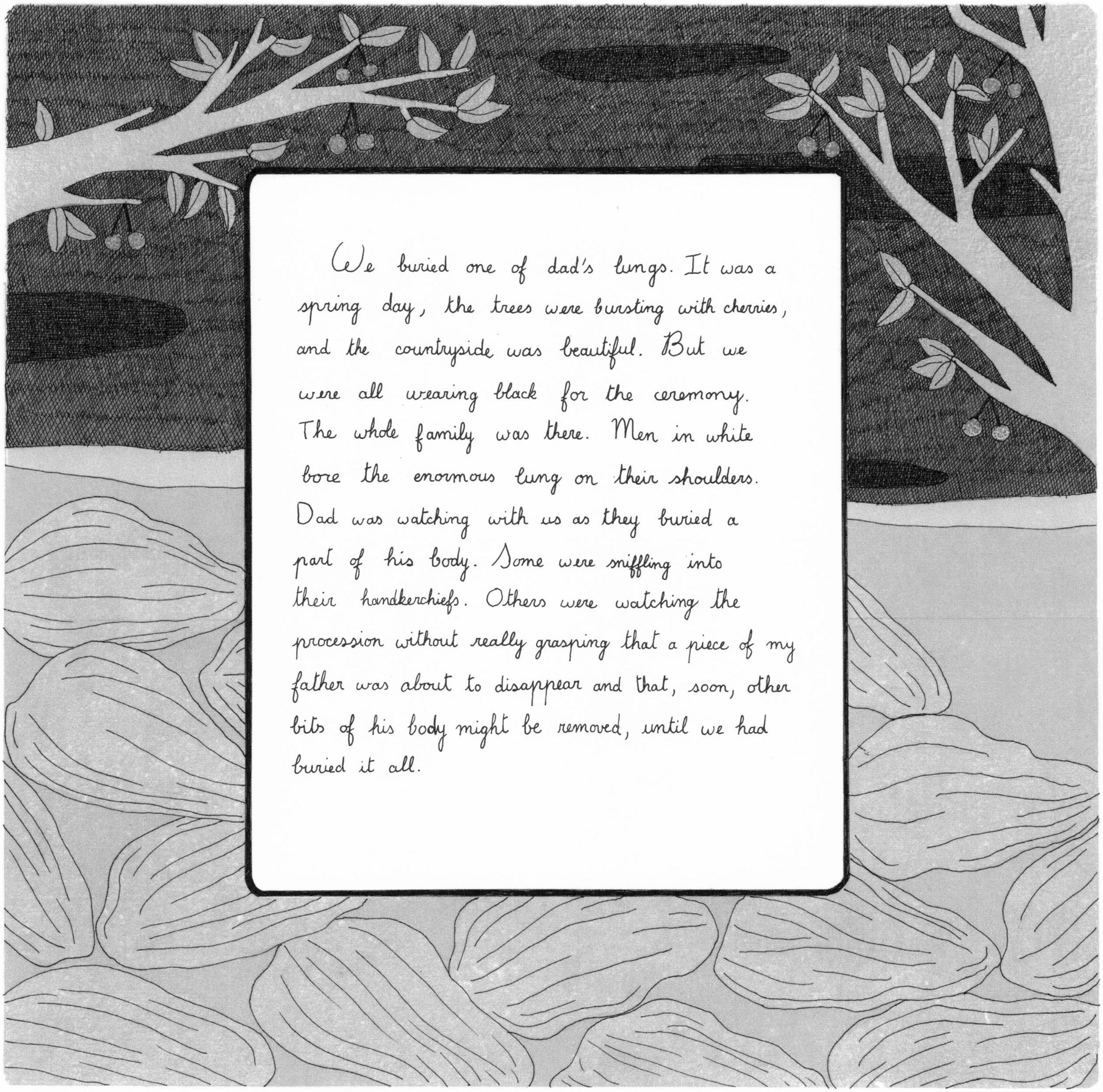

We buried one of dad's lungs. It was a spring day, the trees were bursting with cherries, and the countryside was beautiful. But we were all wearing black for the ceremony. The whole family was there. Men in white bore the enormous lung on their shoulders. Dad was watching with us as they buried a part of his body. Some were sniffling into their handkerchiefs. Others were watching the procession without really grasping that a piece of my father was about to disappear and that, soon, other bits of his body might be removed, until we had buried it all.

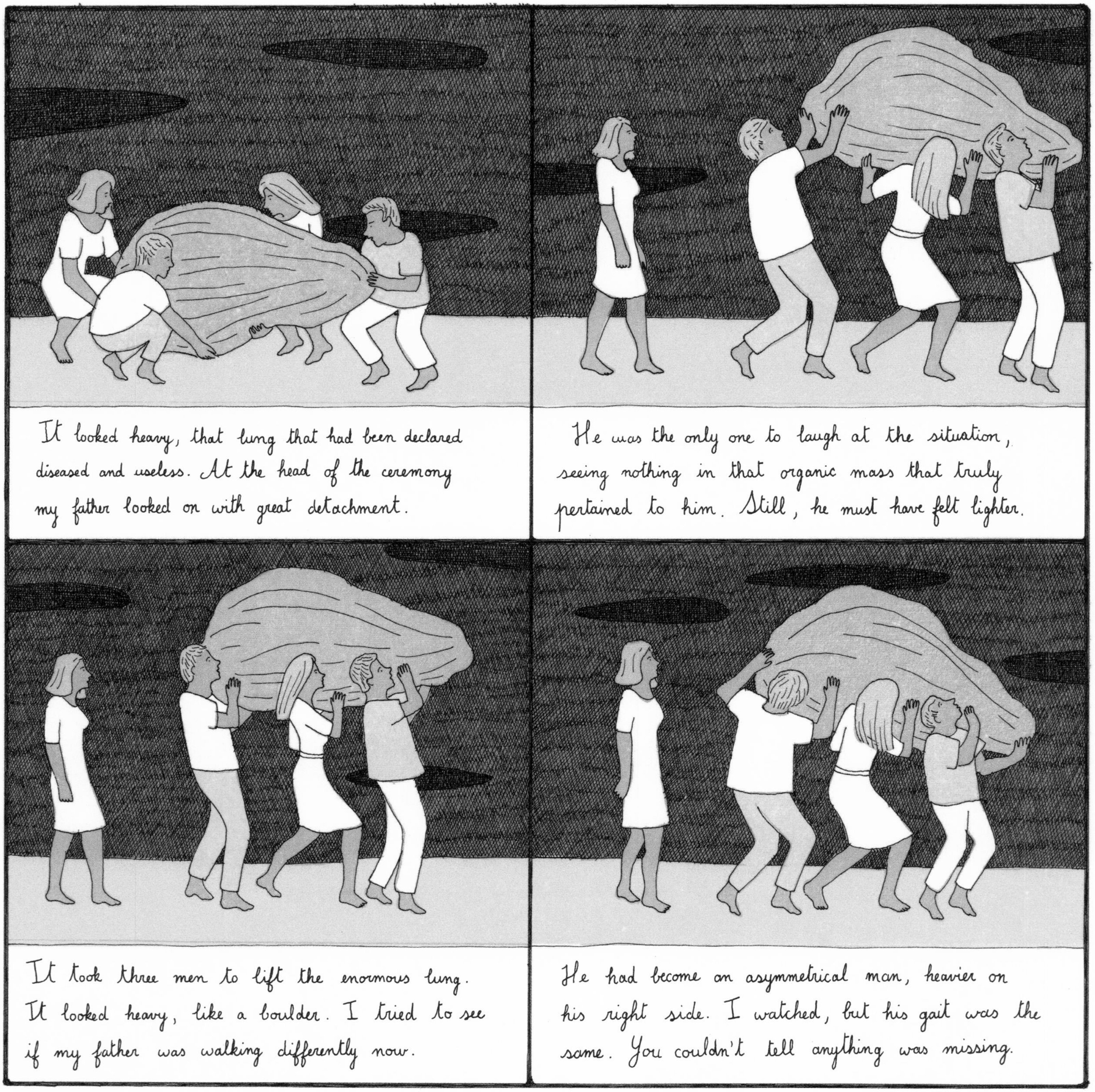
It looked heavy, that lung that had been declared diseased and useless. At the head of the ceremony my father looked on with great detachment.
He was the only one to laugh at the situation, seeing nothing in that organic mass that truly pertained to him. Still, he must have felt lighter.
It took three men to lift the enormous lung. It looked heavy, like a boulder. I tried to see if my father was walking differently now.
He had become an asymmetrical man, heavier on his right side. I watched, but his gait was the same. You couldn't tell anything was missing.

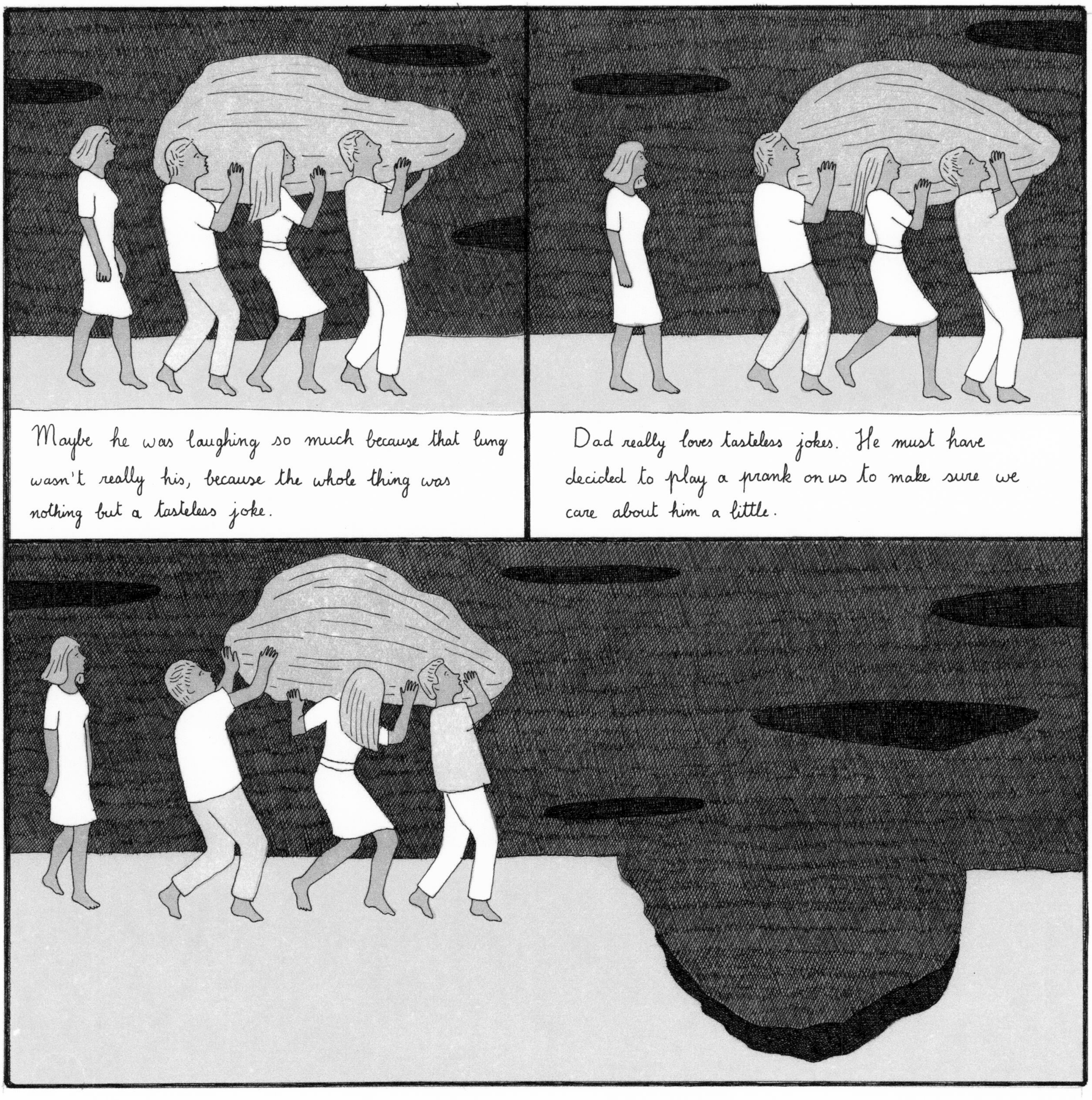

Maybe he was laughing so much because that lung wasn't really his, because the whole thing was nothing but a tasteless joke.
Dad really loves tasteless jokes. He must have decided to play a prank on us to make sure we care about him a little.

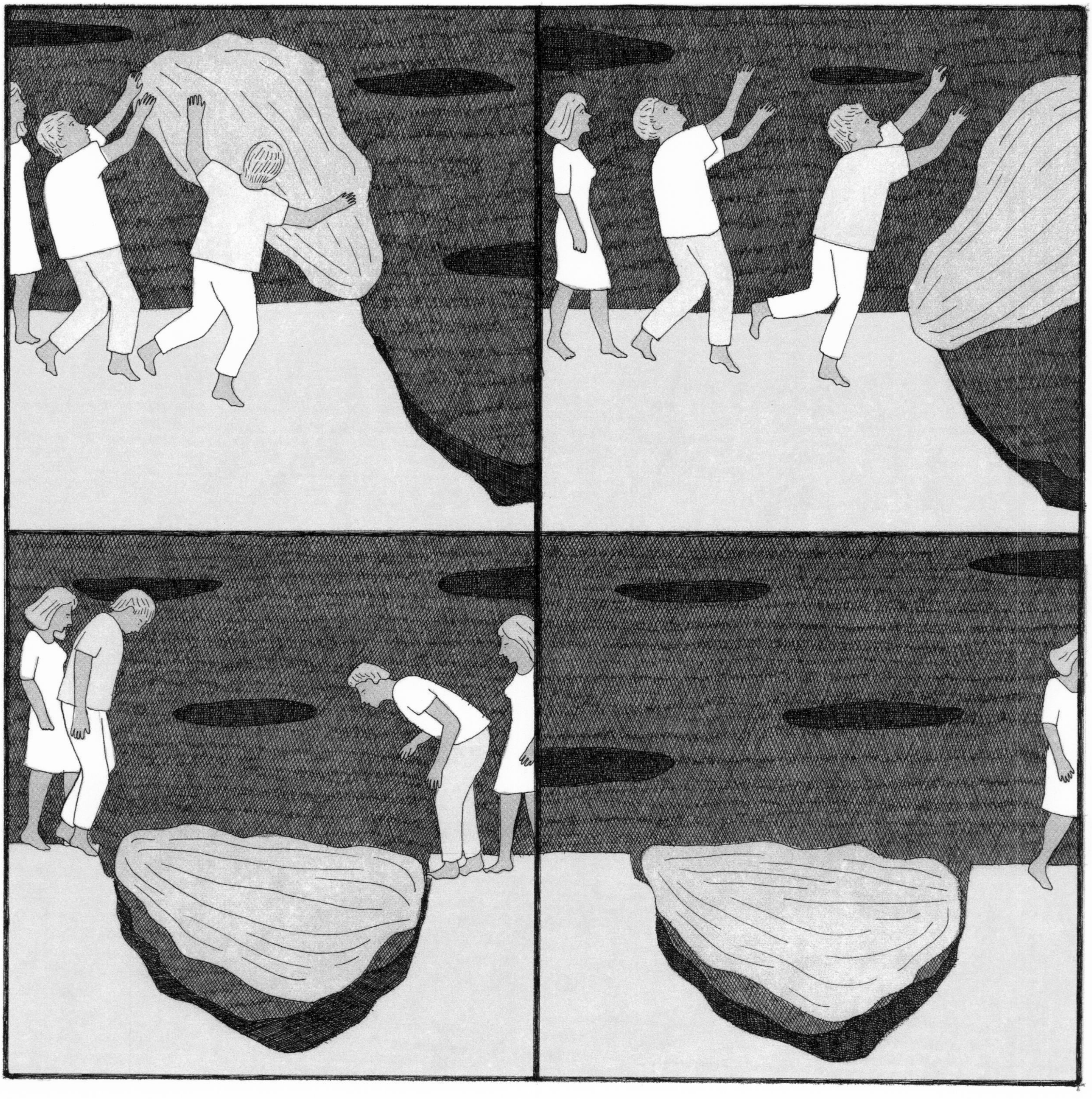

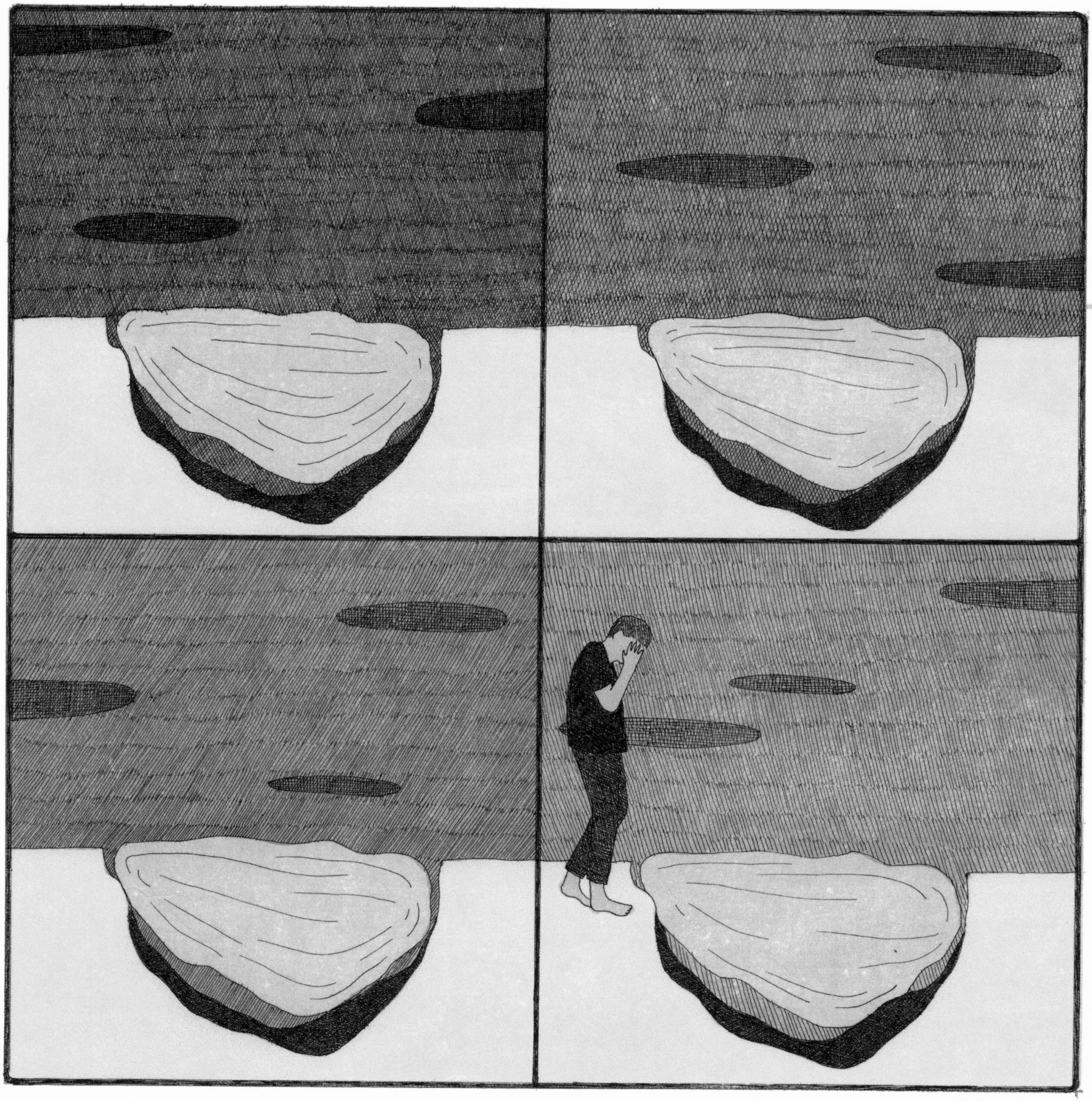

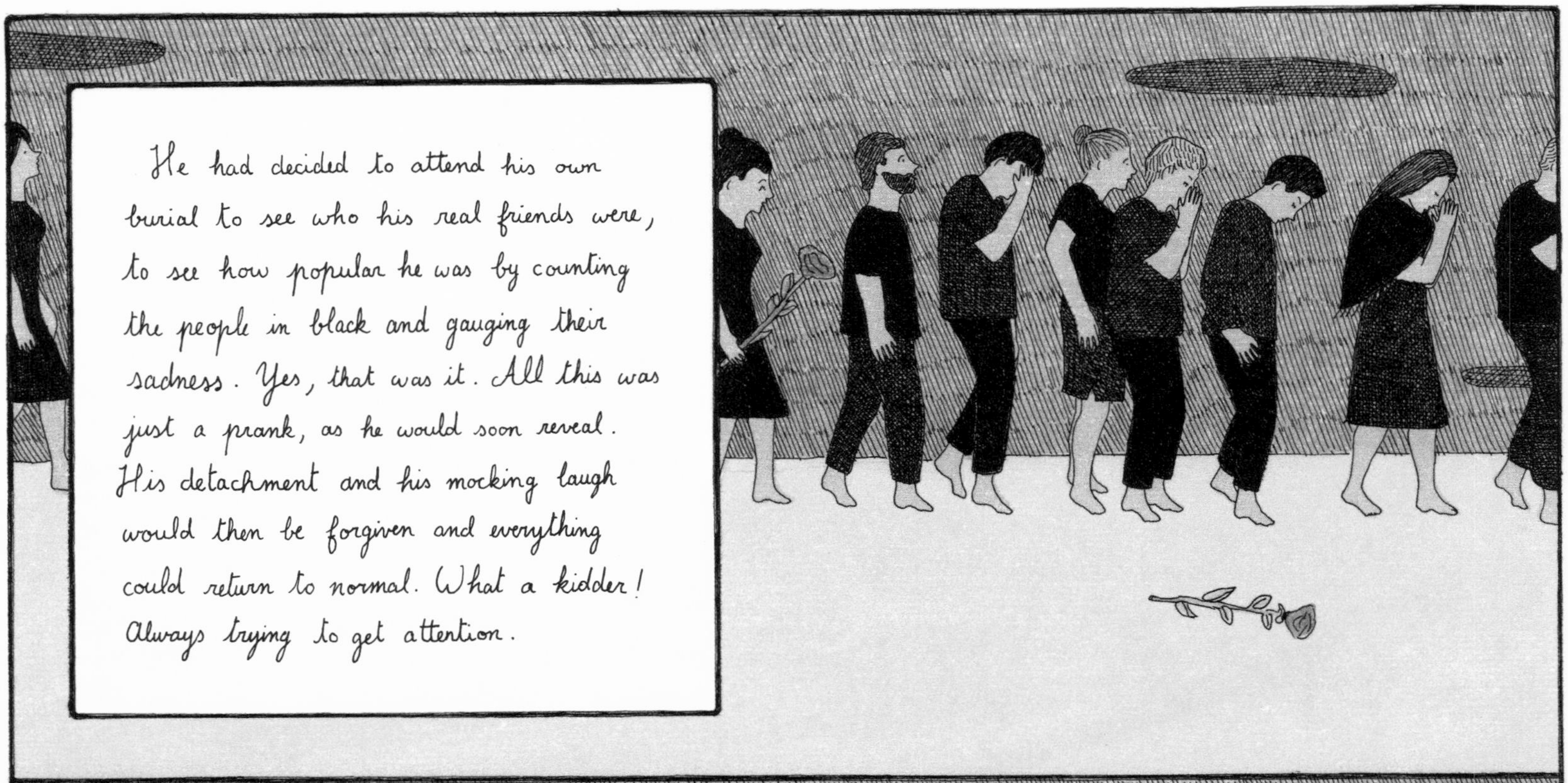
He had decided to attend his own burial to see who his real friends were, to see how popular he was by counting the people in black and gauging their sadness. Yes, that was it. All this was just a prank, as he would soon reveal. His detachment and his mocking laugh would then be forgiven and everything could return to normal. What a kidder! Always trying to get attention.

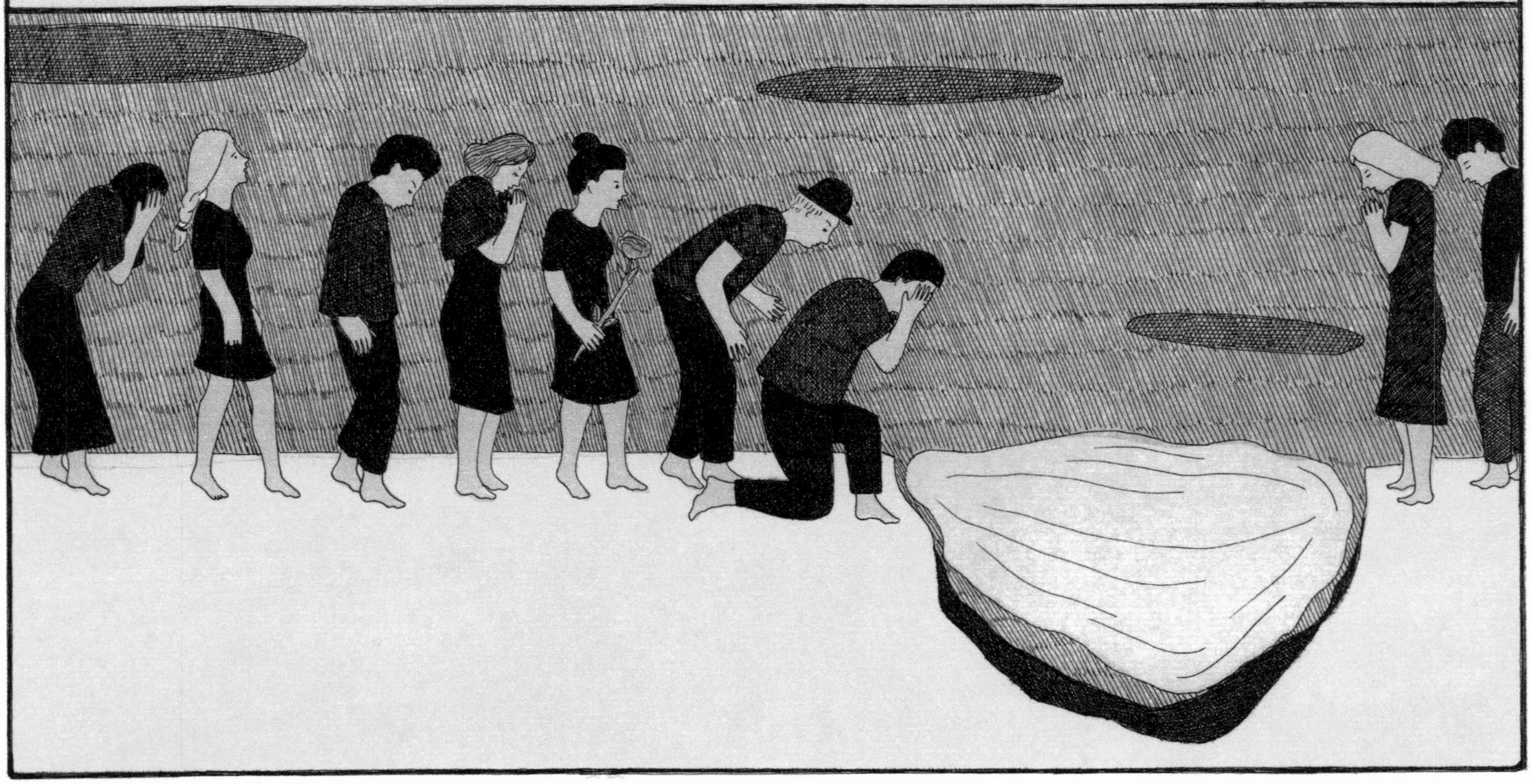

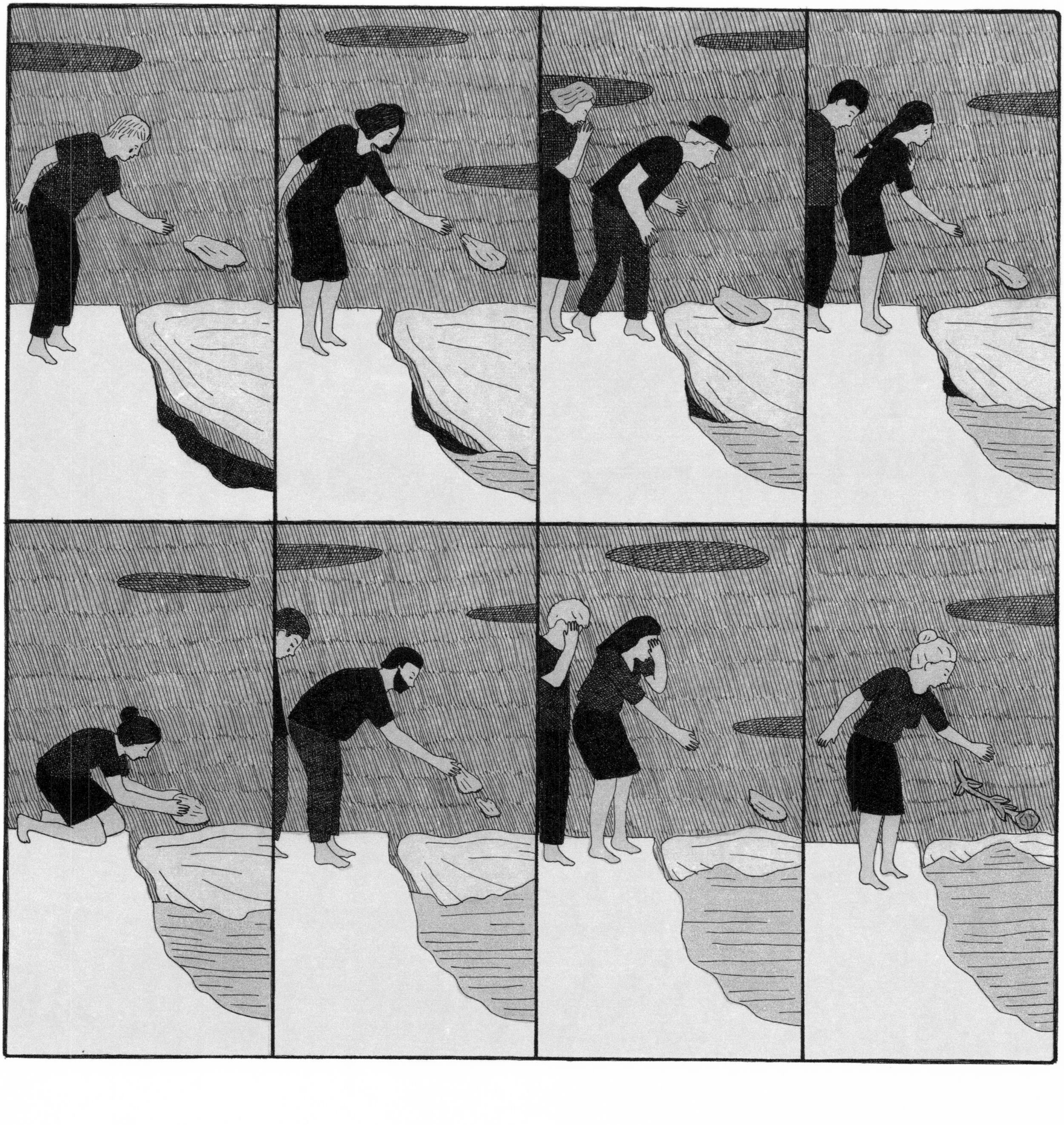

One by one, people came to say farewell to a piece of my father. His stunt had worked and he could rest assured. There was much embracing and everyone was emotional.

Now it was time to reveal the joke. It wasn't going to be easy, he had gone much too far. I felt like his accomplice and wouldn't have wanted to be in his place.

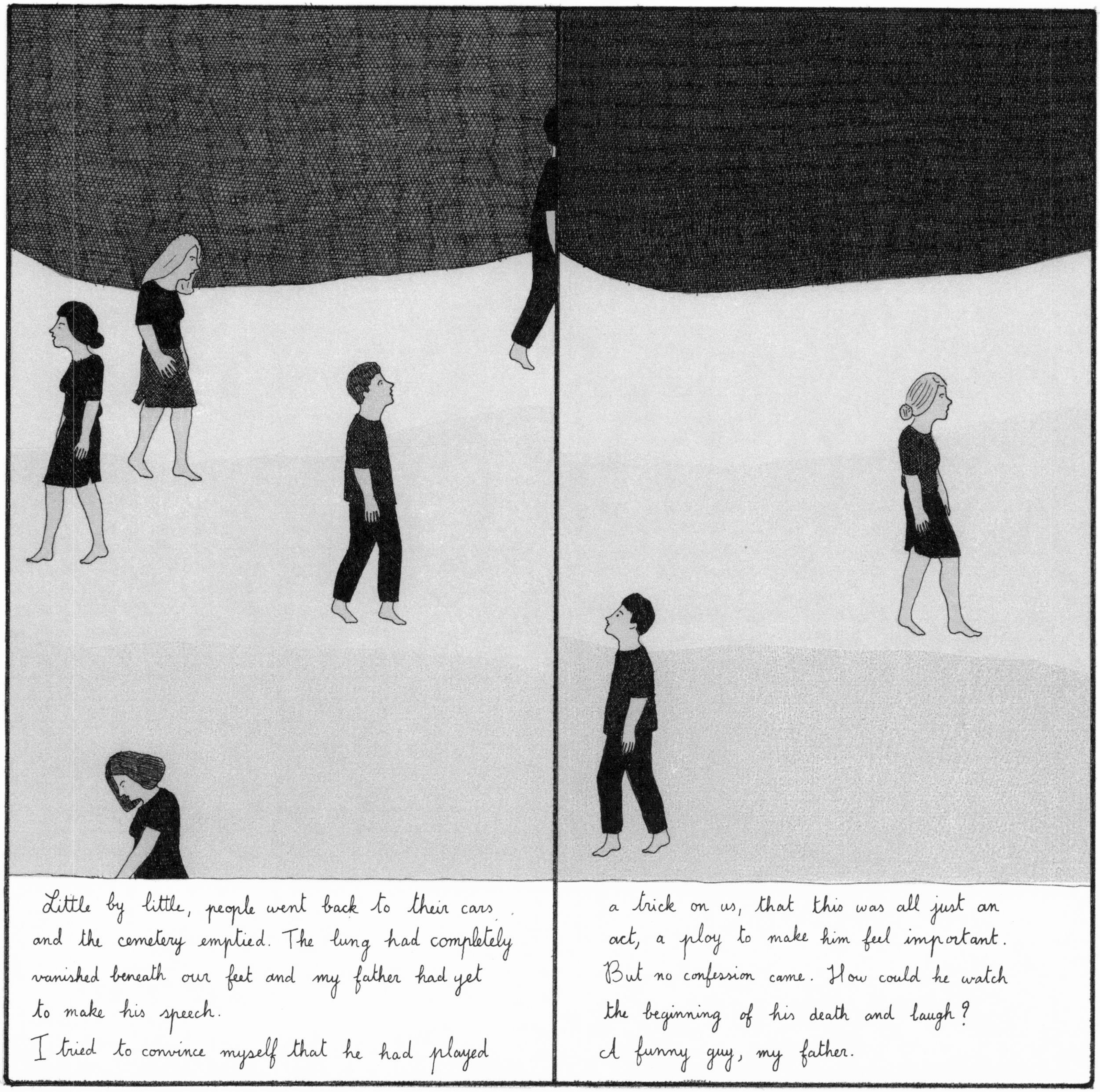
Little by little, people went back to their cars and the cemetery emptied. The lung had completely vanished beneath our feet and my father had yet to make his speech.
I tried to convince myself that he had played
a trick on us, that this was all just an act, a ploy to make him feel important.
But no confession came. How could he watch the beginning of his death and laugh?
A funny guy, my father.

I

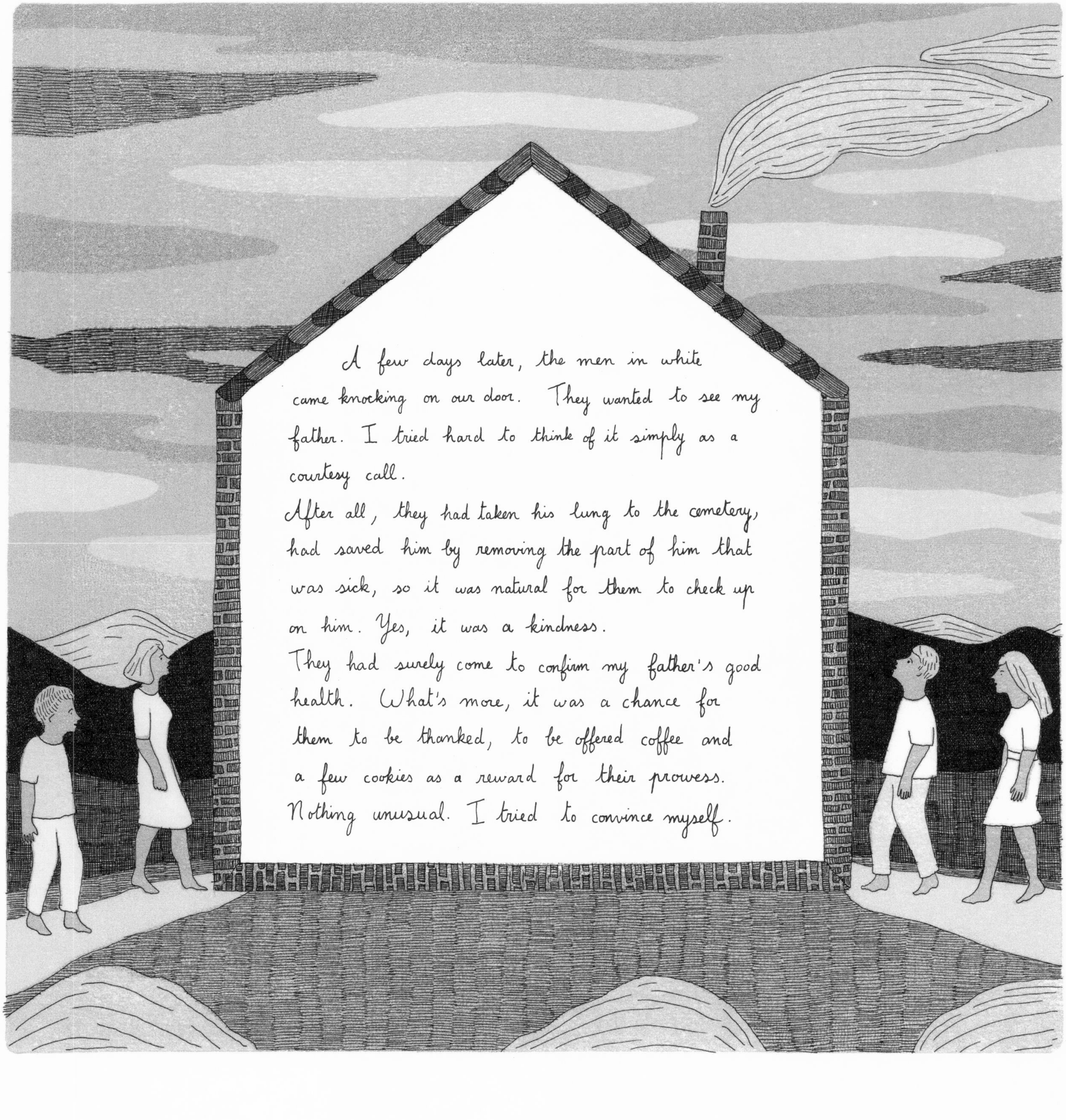
A few days later, the men in white came knocking on our door. They wanted to see my father. I tried hard to think of it simply as a courtesy call.
After all, they had taken his lung to the cemetery, had saved him by removing the part of him that was sick, so it was natural for them to check up on him. Yes, it was a kindness.
They had surely come to confirm my father's good health. What's more, it was a chance for them to be thanked, to be offered coffee and a few cookies as a reward for their prowess.
Nothing unusual. I tried to convince myself.

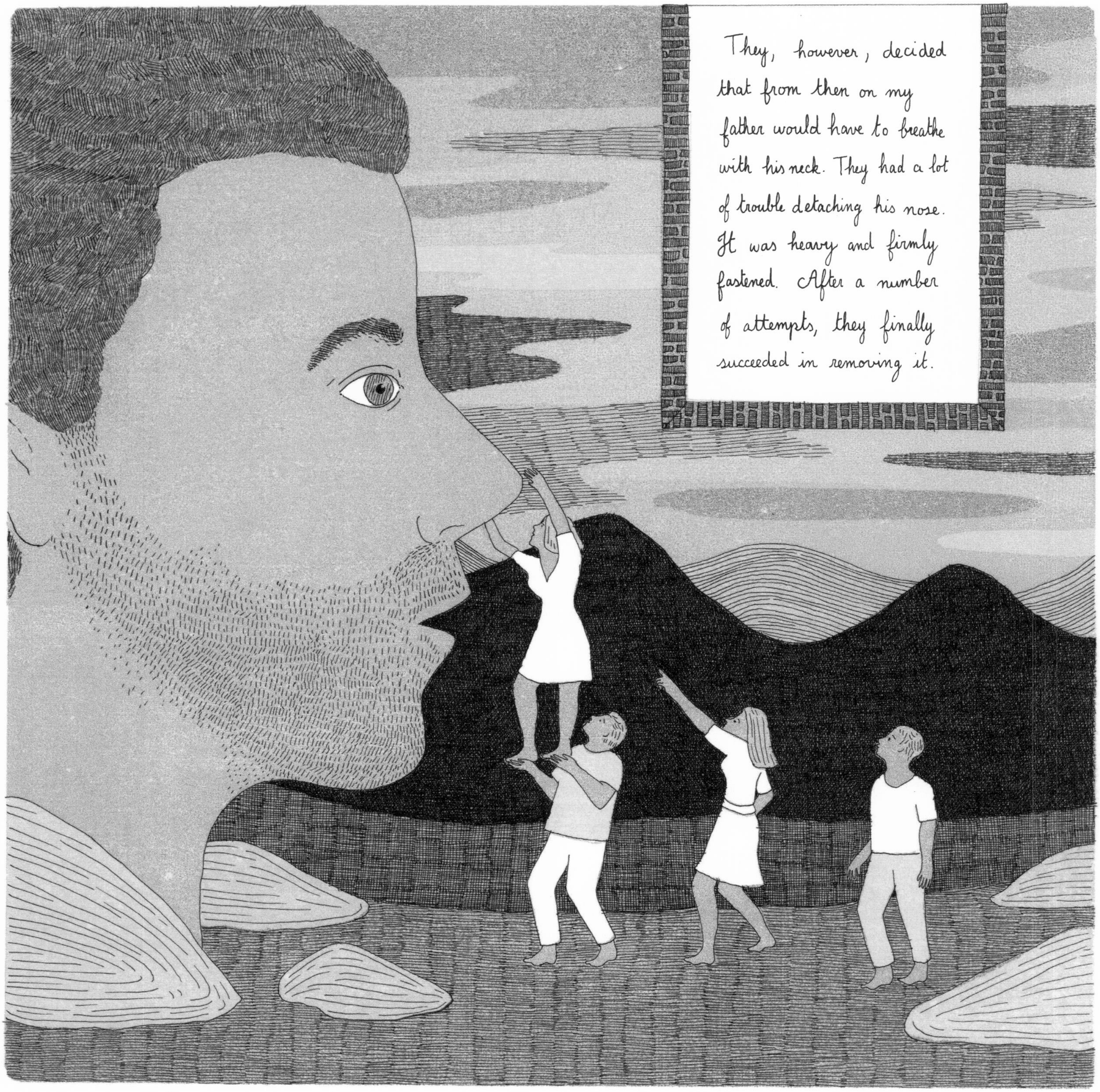
They, however, decided that from then on my father would have to breathe with his neck. They had a lot of trouble detaching his nose. It was heavy and firmly fastened. After a number of attempts, they finally succeeded in removing it.

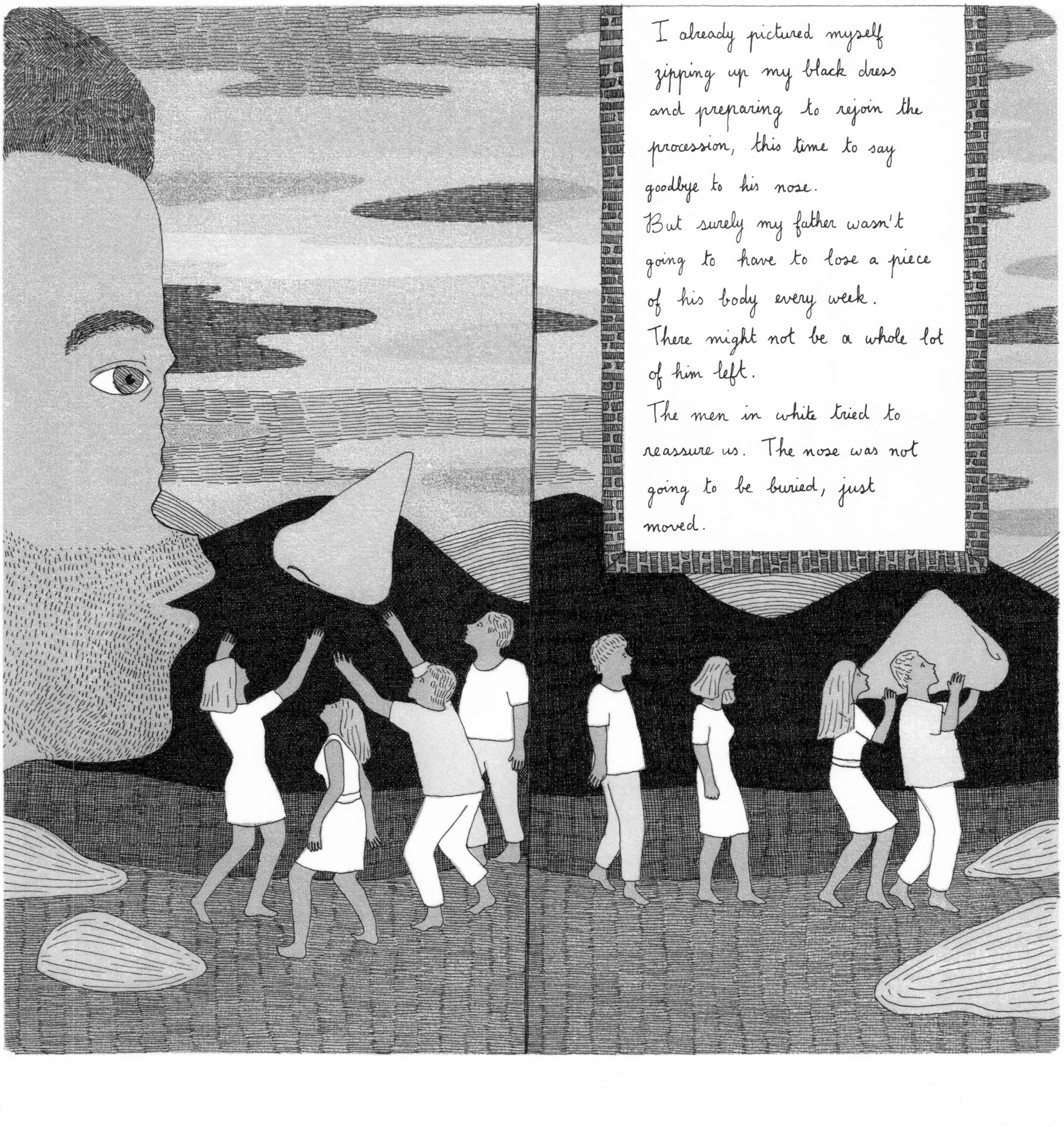
I already pictured myself zipping up my black dress and preparing to rejoin the procession, this time to say goodbye to his nose.
But surely my father wasn't going to have to lose a piece of his body every week.
There might not be a whole lot of him left.
The men in white tried to reassure us. The nose was not going to be buried, just moved.

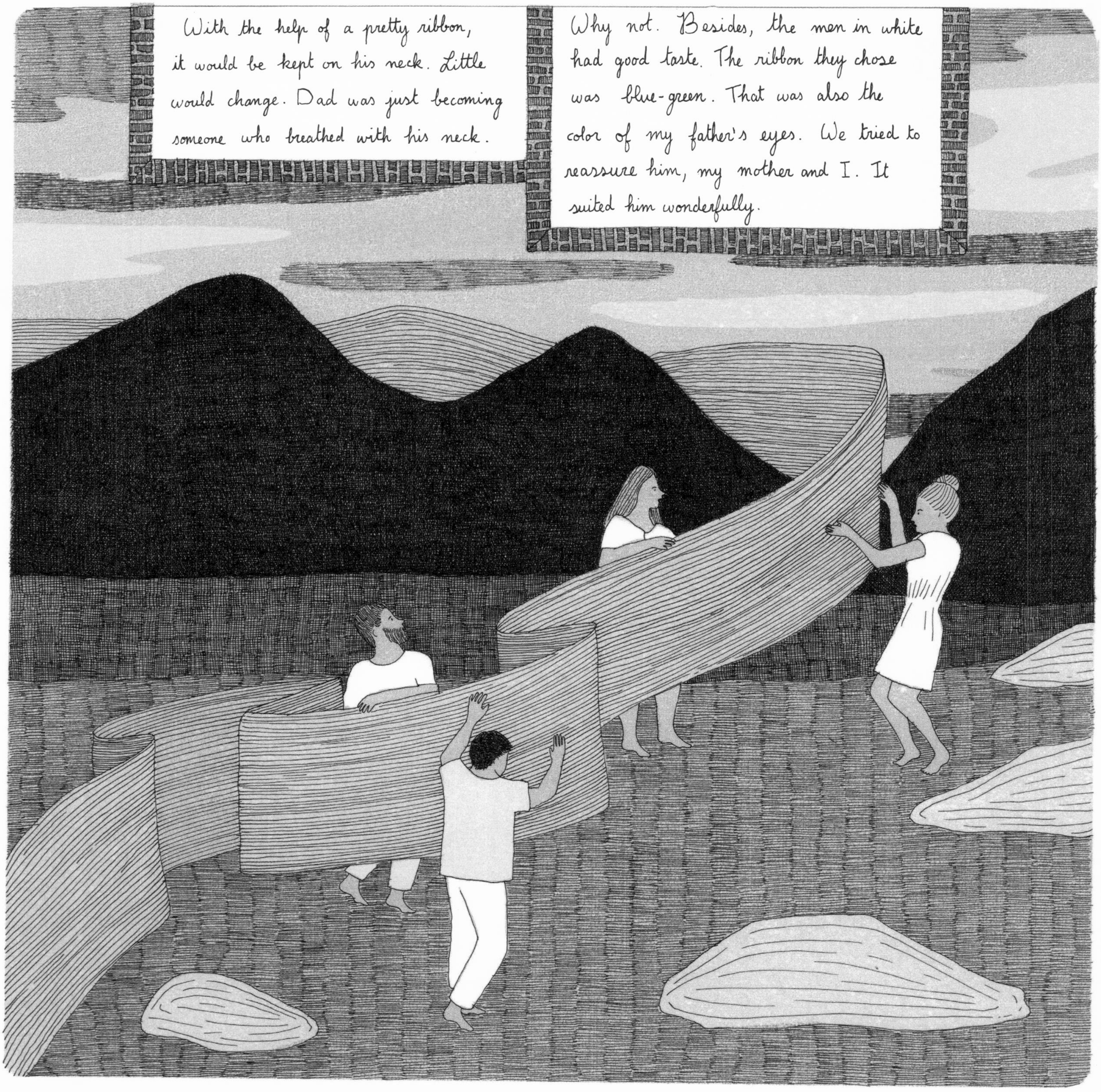
With the help of a pretty ribbon, it would be kept on his neck. Little would change. Dad was just becoming someone who breathed with his neck.
Why not. Besides, the men in white had good taste. The ribbon they chose was blue-green. That was also the color of my father's eyes. We tried to reassure him, my mother and I. It suited him wonderfully.

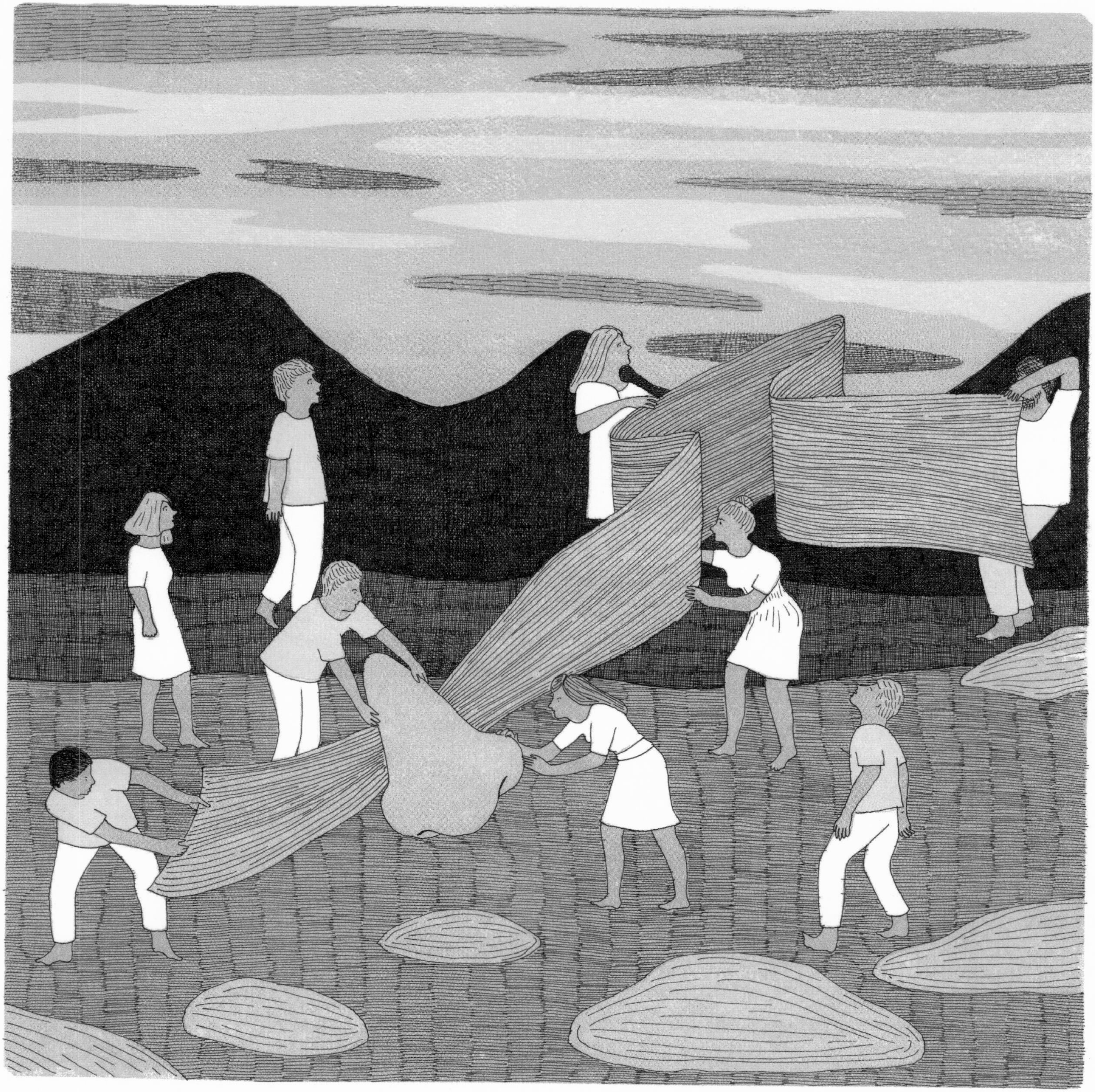

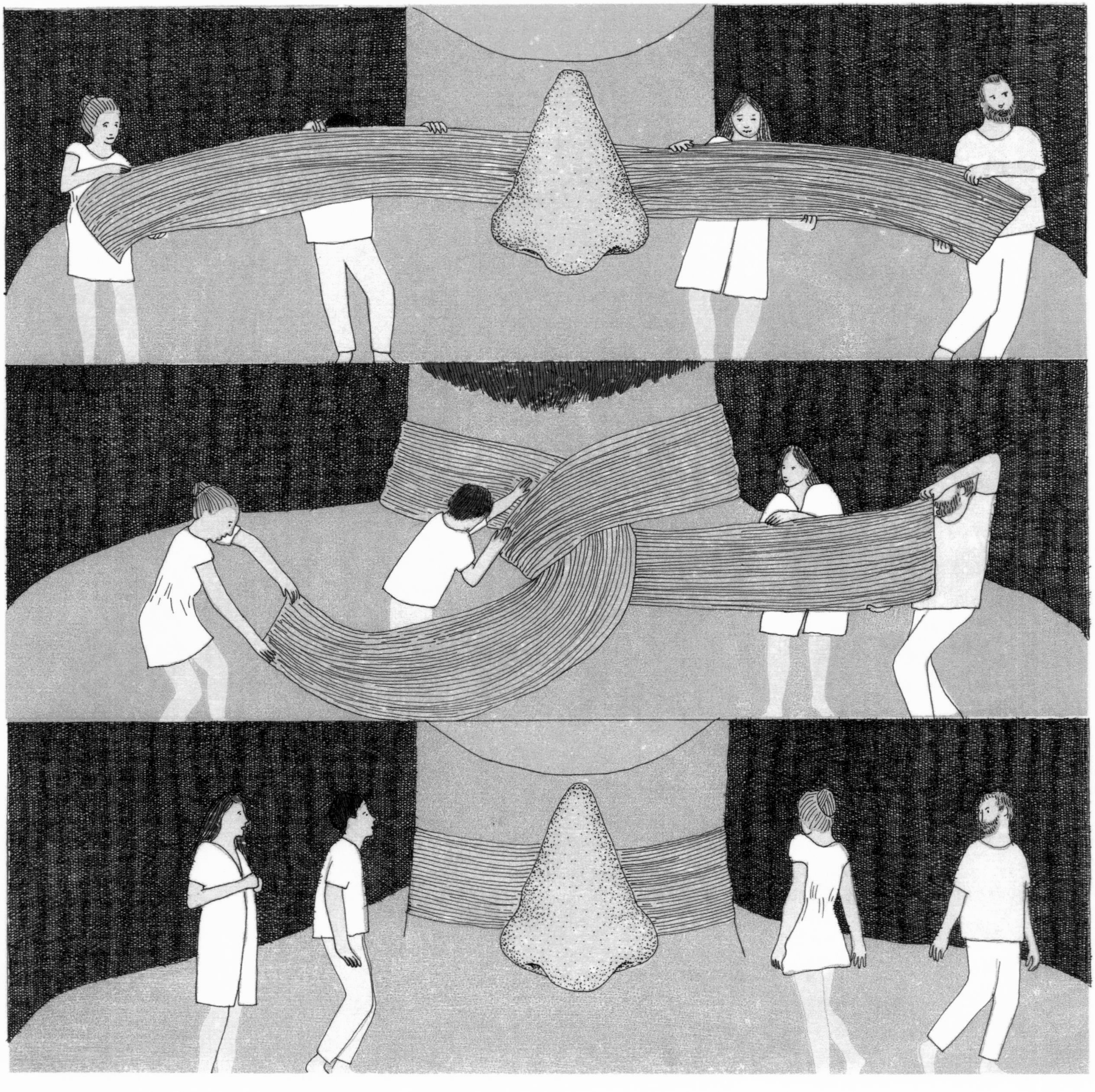

It drew attention to his gaze. Then we barely noticed it. Most people never get the chance to wear their nose as an ornament, like a rare pearl. It was original, and very classy. Having your nose in the middle of your face isn't so important, it turns out. What's more, his was quite large.

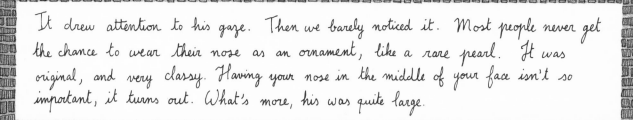

It had taken up a lot of space. His face was roomier now. His mouth was no longer in the shadow of that enormous nose, and his beard seemed shinier. His neck had been long and empty. With the new jewel, it was dressed. We should have thought of it before. The transformation was a success.

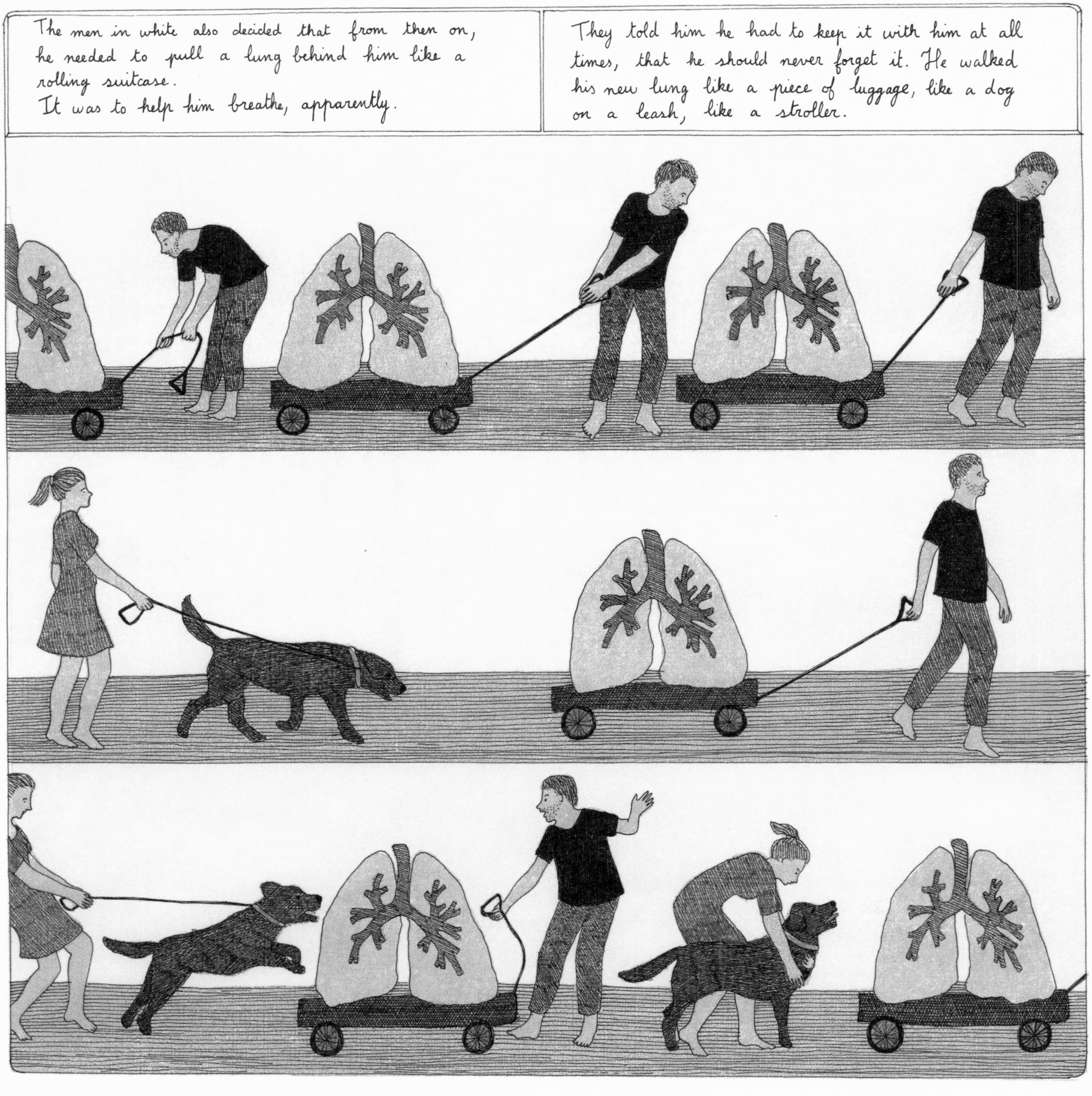
The men in white also decided that from then on, he needed to pull a lung behind him like a rolling suitcase.
It was to help him breathe, apparently.
They told him he had to keep it with him at all times, that he should never forget it. He walked his new lung like a piece of luggage, like a dog on a leash, like a stroller.

It got a bit heavy day after day, but my mother was right: it would have been even more tiring if he'd had to carry it on his back.

Dad's new companion had been well designed, and the wheels were a good idea. True, it was a little noisy. But you get used to noise.

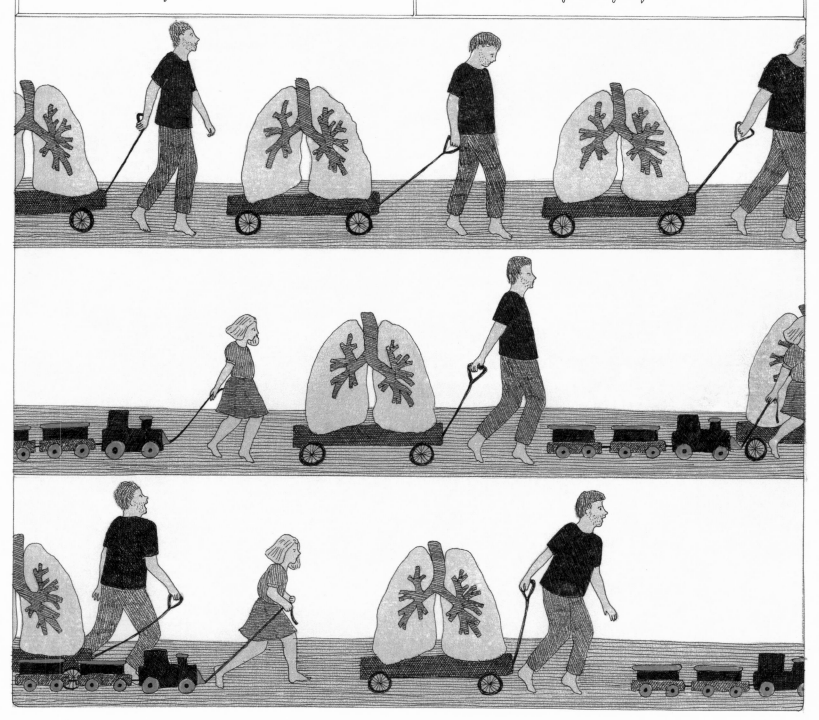

From then on, he always seemed to be setting out on a journey, always pulling a bit of his life along behind him. His luggage had an alarm inside, so he wouldn't forget it. No need for a name tag.

With such security measures, he couldn't forget his lung. Mom found the alert a bit too shrill. She would have liked to have been able to change the tune, the way you can on cell phones.

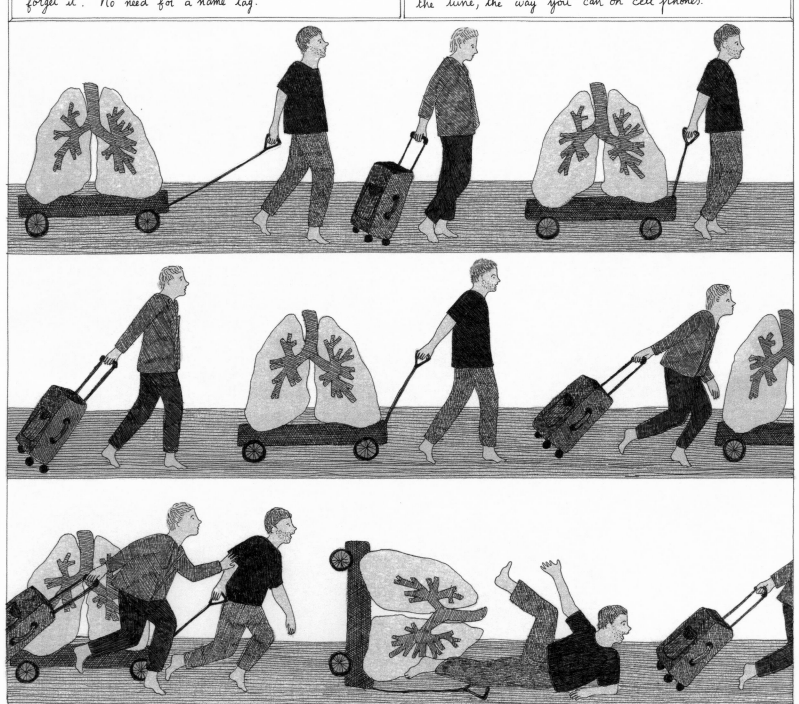

Bird sounds, that's what she would have liked. Dad didn't attach much importance to his lung's music. The signal helped him get attention.

All he had to do to make us come running with worry was let go of the handle for a few seconds. Birdsong would surely have been less effective.

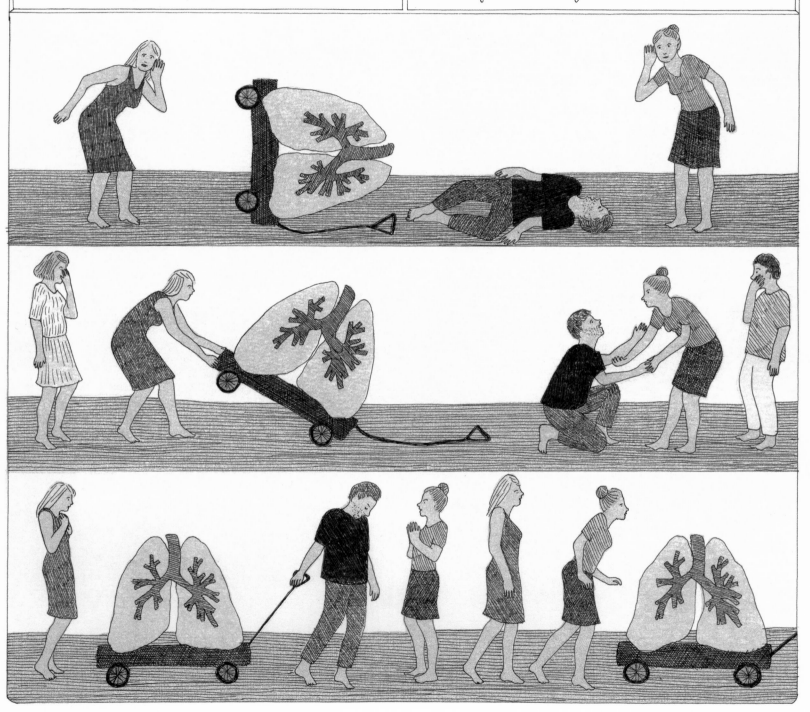

31

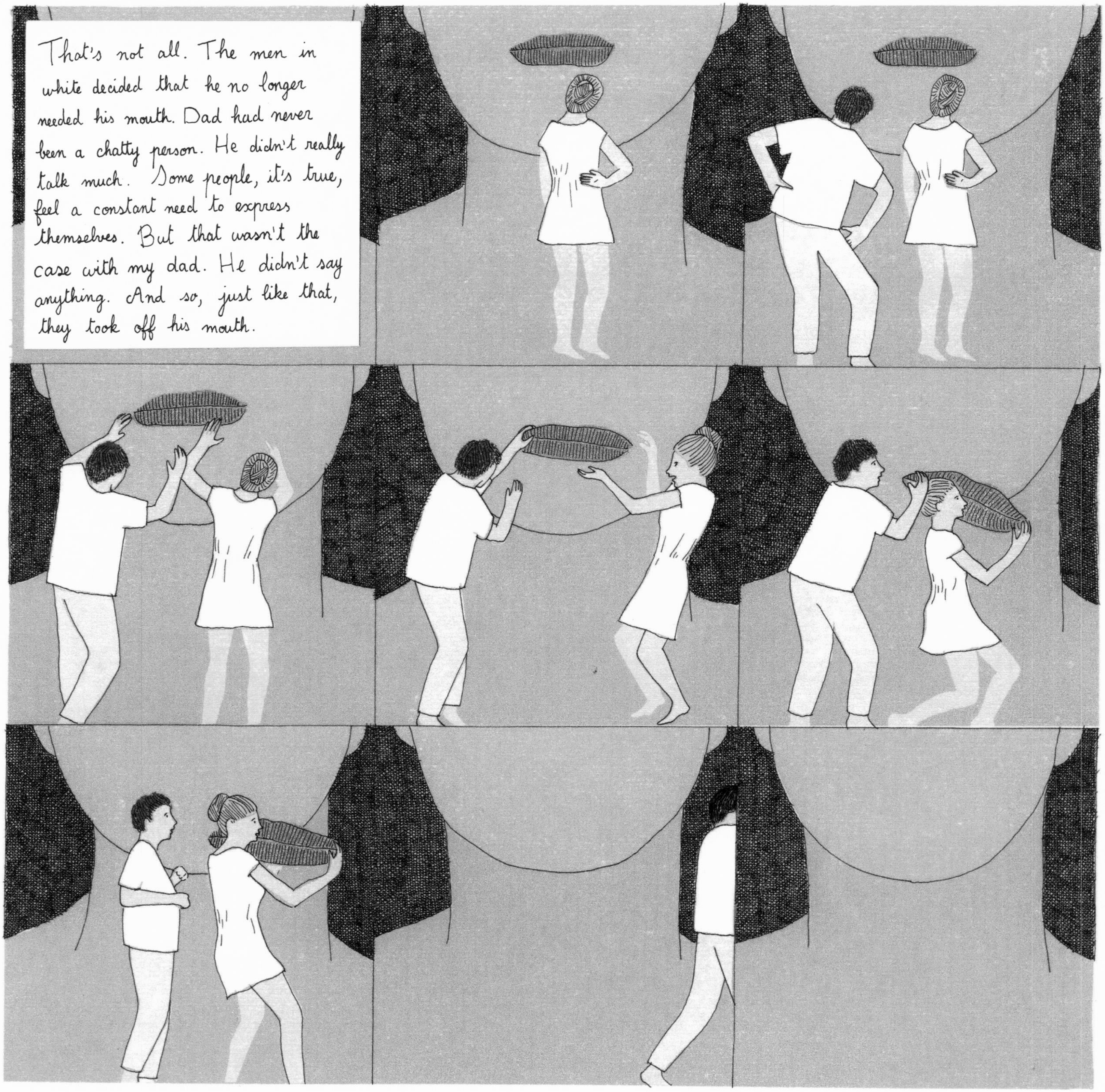
That's not all. The men in white decided that he no longer needed his mouth. Dad had never been a chatty person. He didn't really talk much. Some people, it's true, feel a constant need to express themselves. But that wasn't the case with my dad. He didn't say anything. And so, just like that, they took off his mouth.

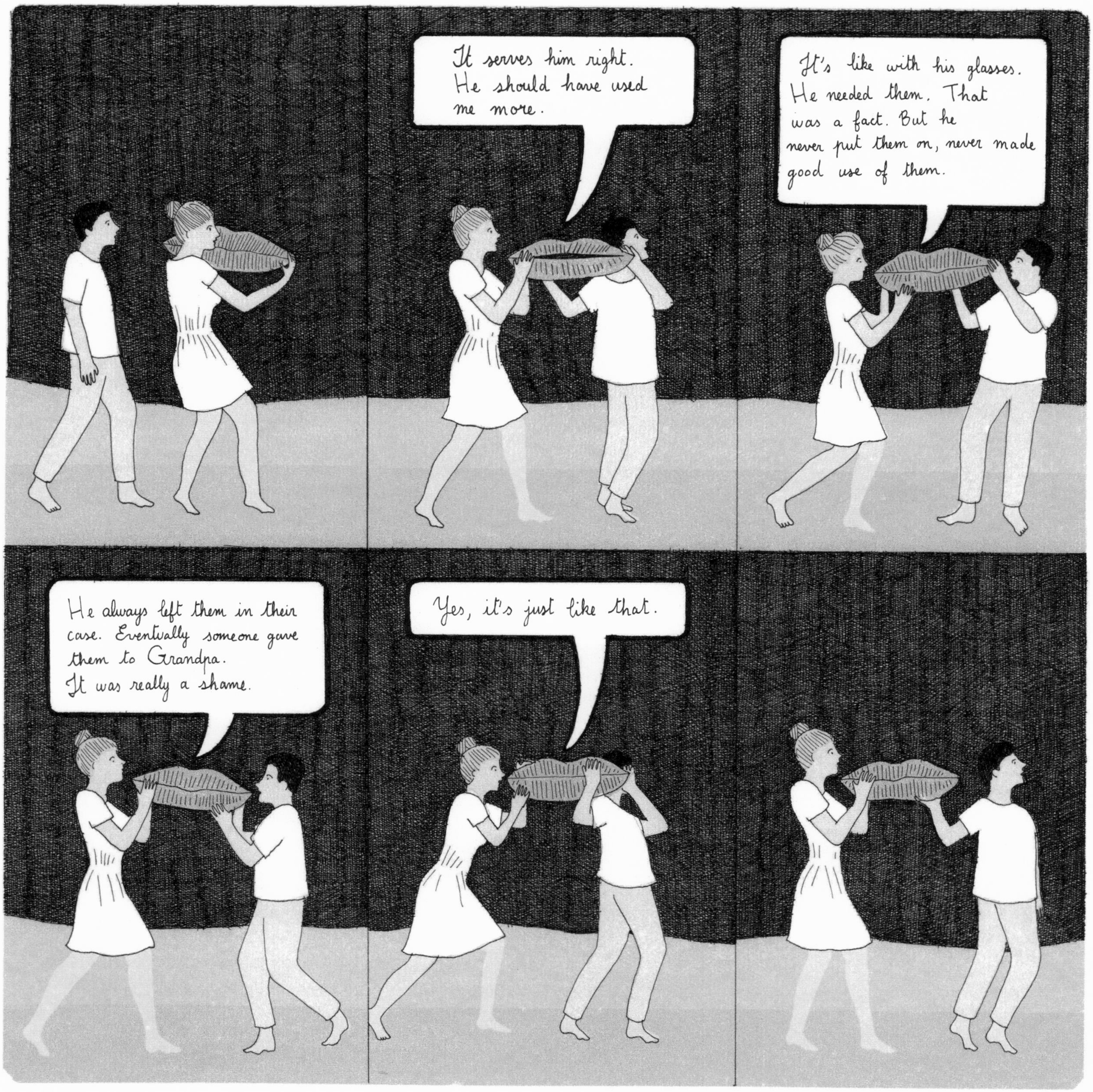
It serves him right.
He should have used me more.
It's like with his glasses. He needed them. That was a fact. But he never put them on, never made good use of them.
He always left them in their case. Eventually someone gave them to Grandpa.
It was really a shame.
Yes, it's just like that.

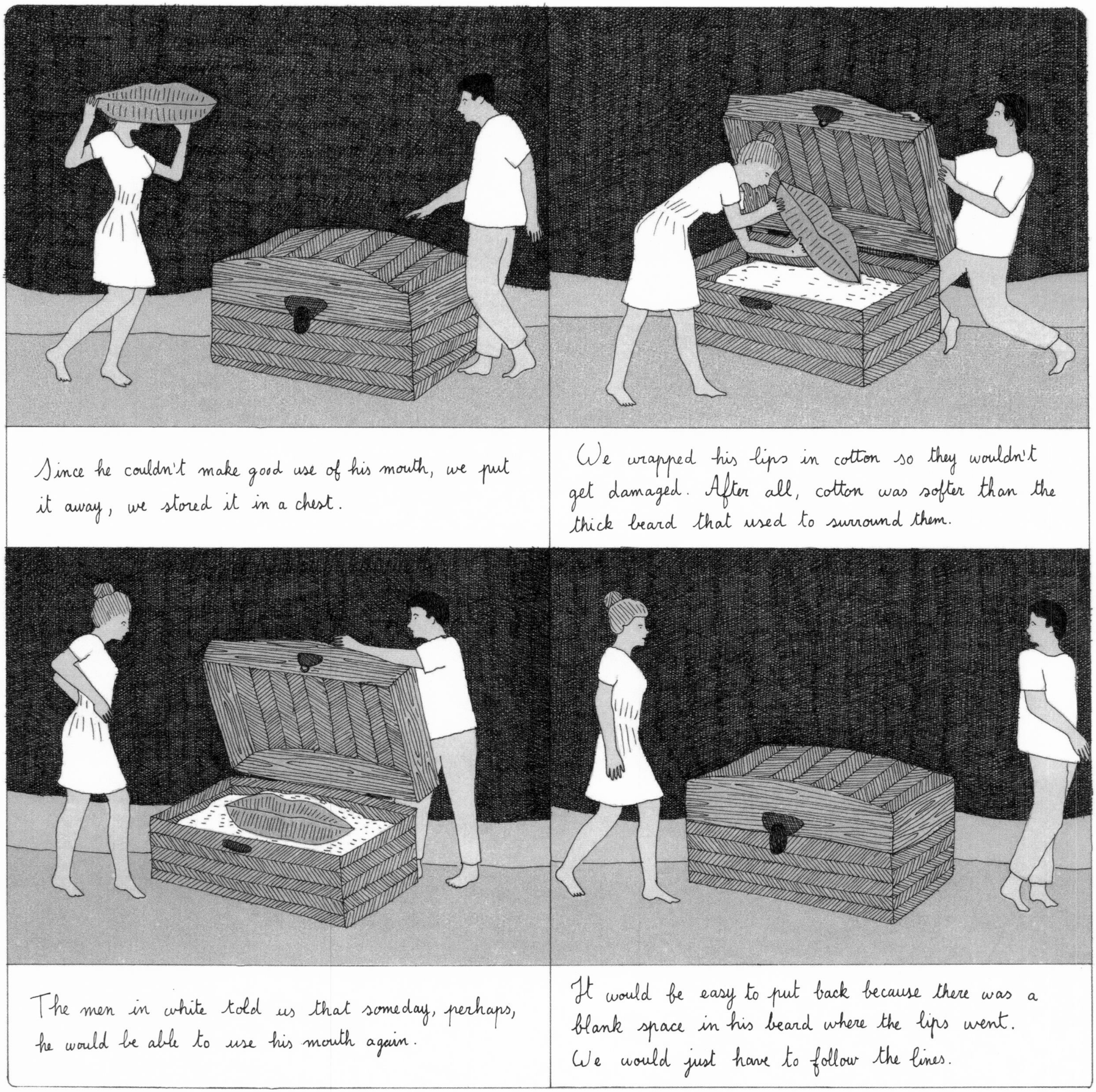
Since he couldn't make good use of his mouth, we put it away, we stored it in a chest.
We wrapped his lips in cotton so they wouldn't get damaged. After all, cotton was softer than the thick beard that used to surround them.
The men in white told us that someday, perhaps, he would be able to use his mouth again.
It would be easy to put back because there was a blank space in his beard where the lips went. We would just have to follow the lines.

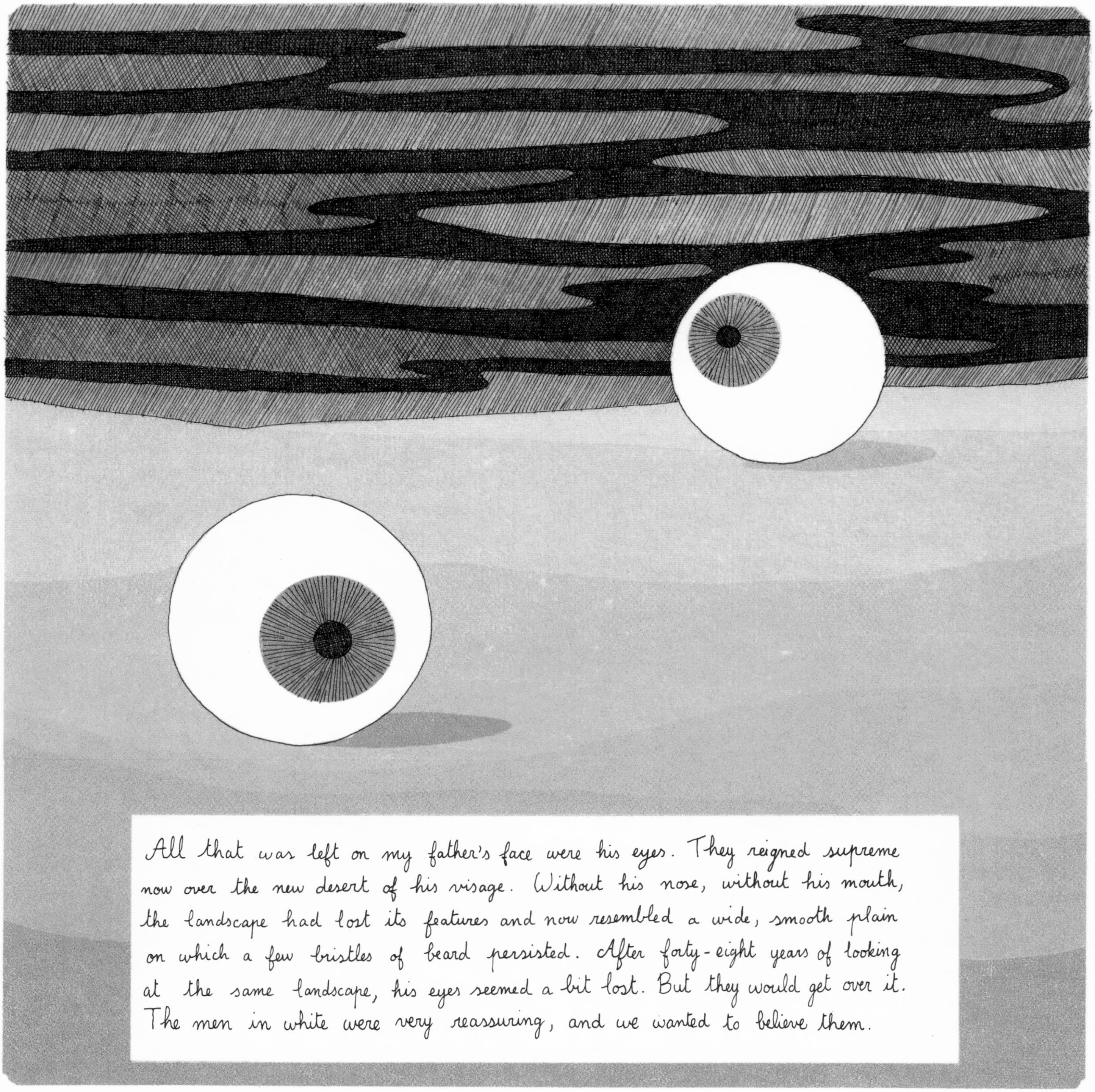
All that was left on my father's face were his eyes. They reigned supreme now over the new desert of his visage. Without his nose, without his mouth, the landscape had lost its features and now resembled a wide, smooth plain on which a few bristles of beard persisted. After forty-eight years of looking at the same landscape, his eyes seemed a bit lost. But they would get over it. The men in white were very reassuring, and we wanted to believe them.

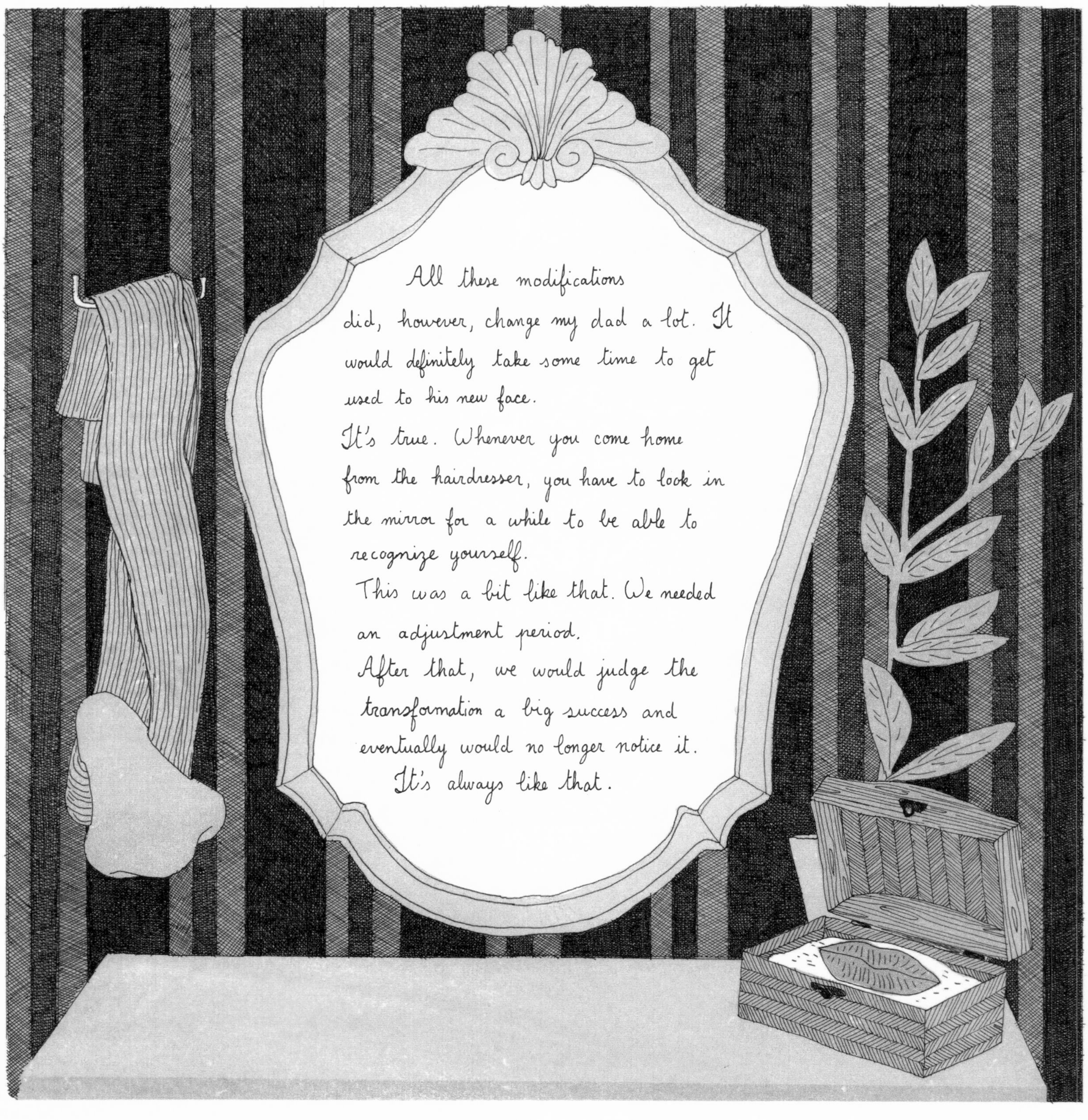
All these modifications
did, however, change my dad a lot. It
would definitely take some time to get
used to his new face.
It's true. Whenever you come home
from the hairdresser, you have to look in
the mirror for a while to be able to
recognize yourself.
This was a bit like that. We needed
an adjustment period.
After that, we would judge the
transformation a big success and
eventually would no longer notice it.
It's always like that.

II

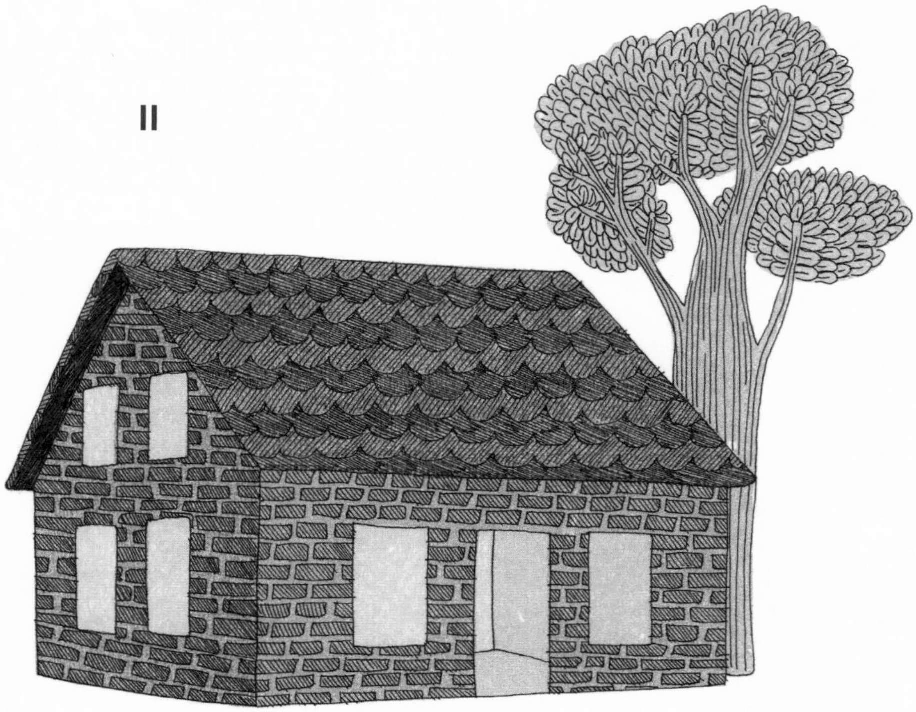

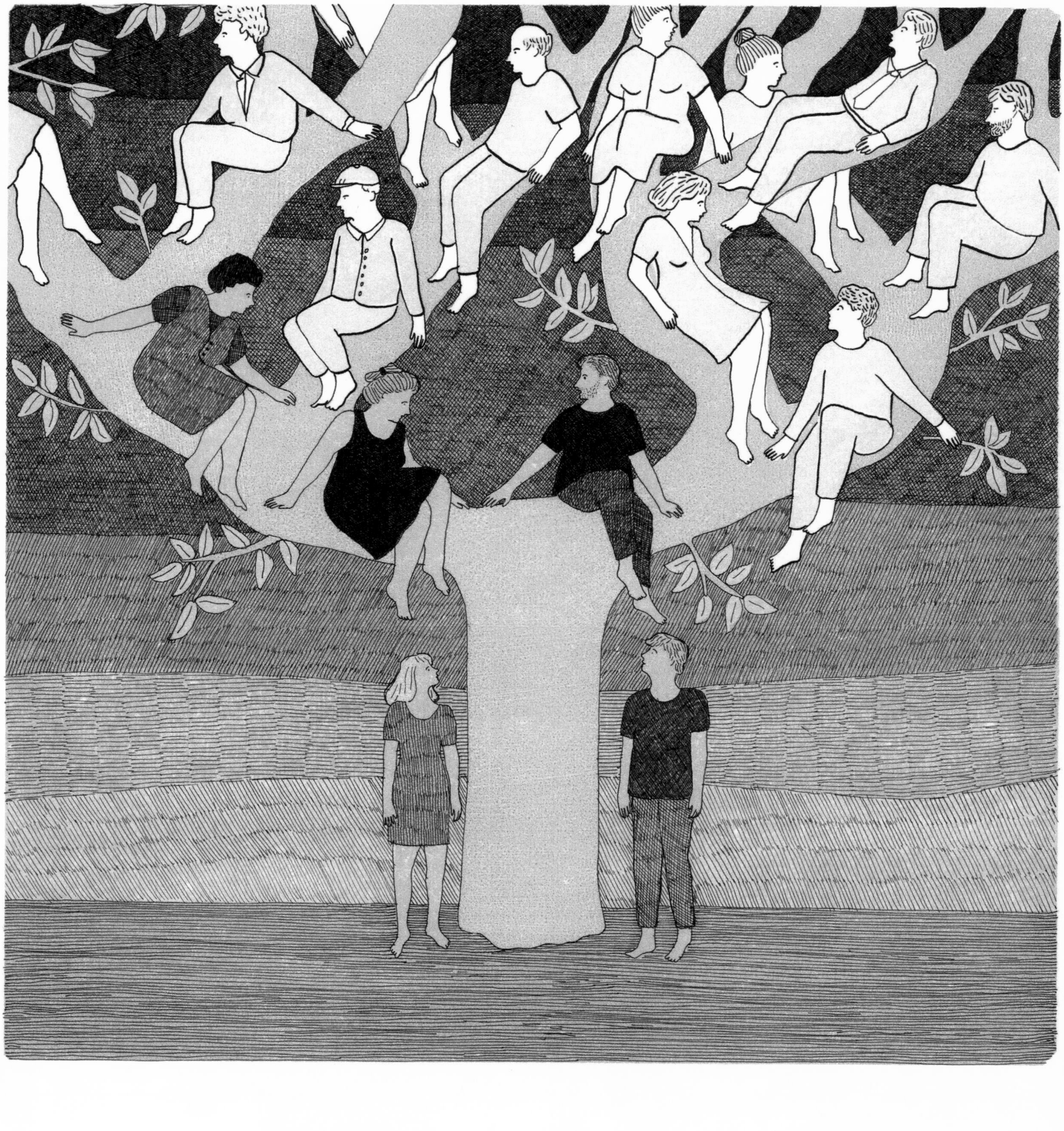

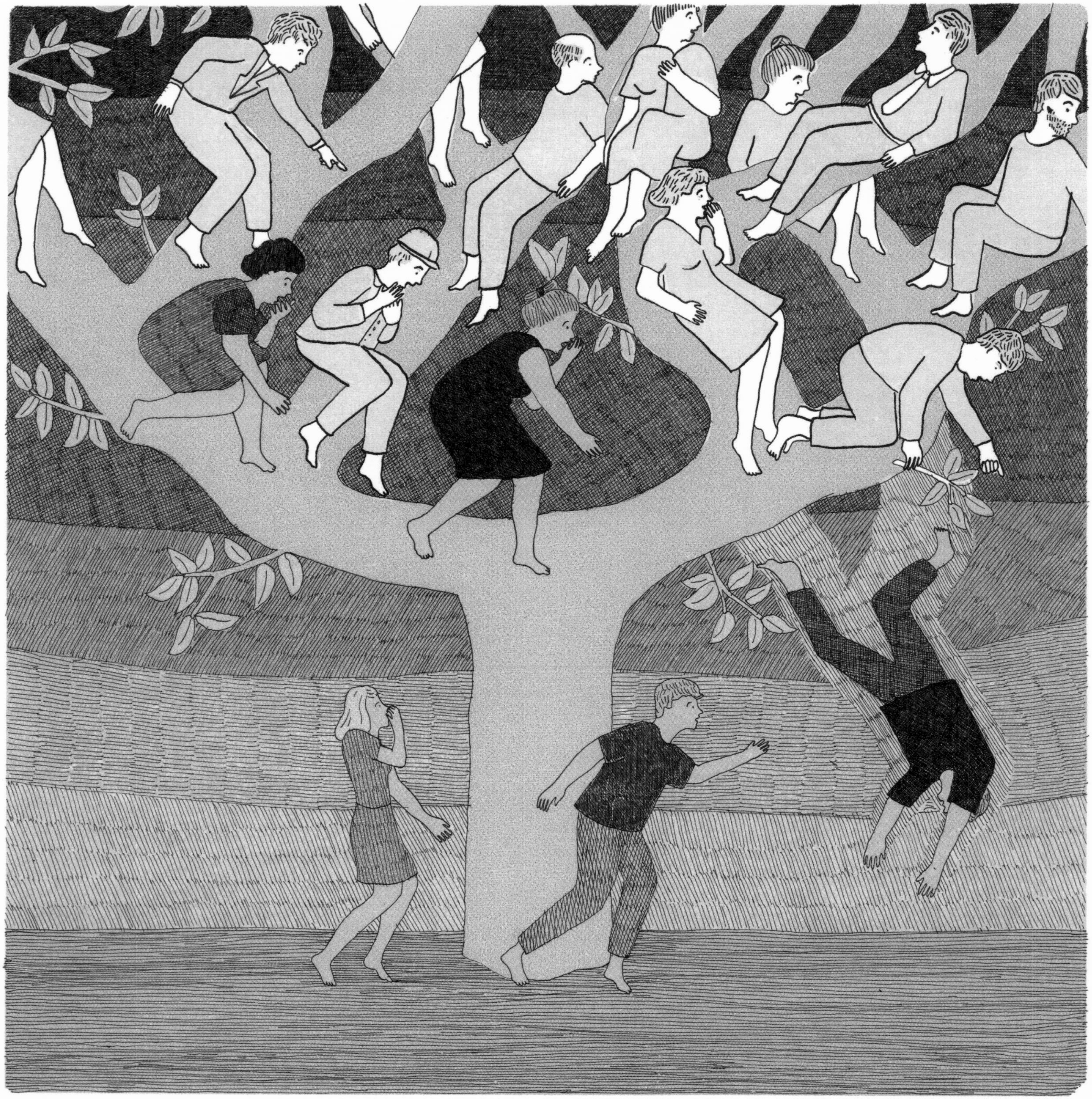

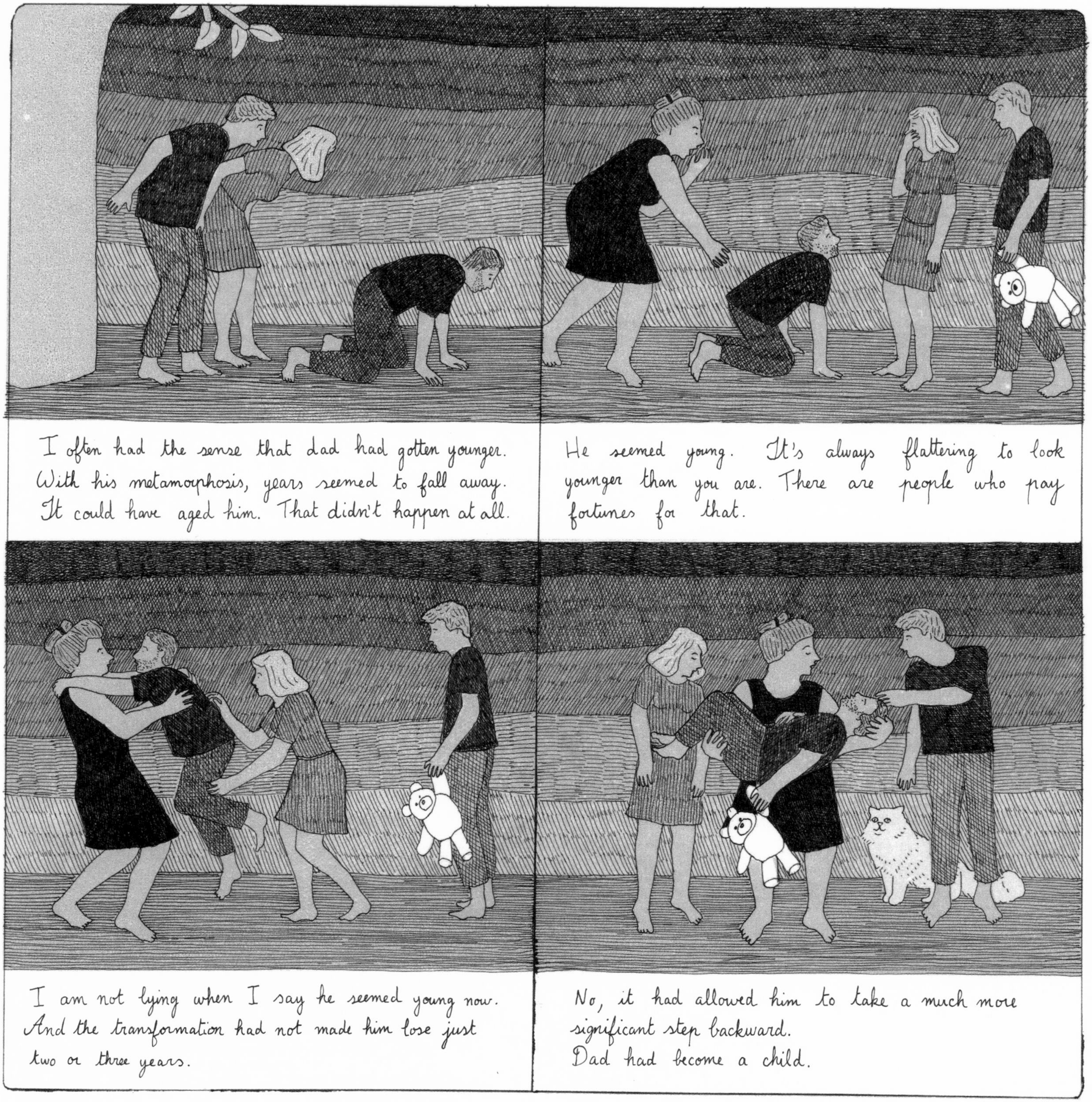
I often had the sense that dad had gotten younger. With his metamorphosis, years seemed to fall away. It could have aged him. That didn't happen at all.
He seemed young. It's always flattering to look younger than you are. There are people who pay fortunes for that.
I am not lying when I say he seemed young now. And the transformation had not made him lose just two or three years.
No, it had allowed him to take a much more significant step backward.
Dad had become a child.

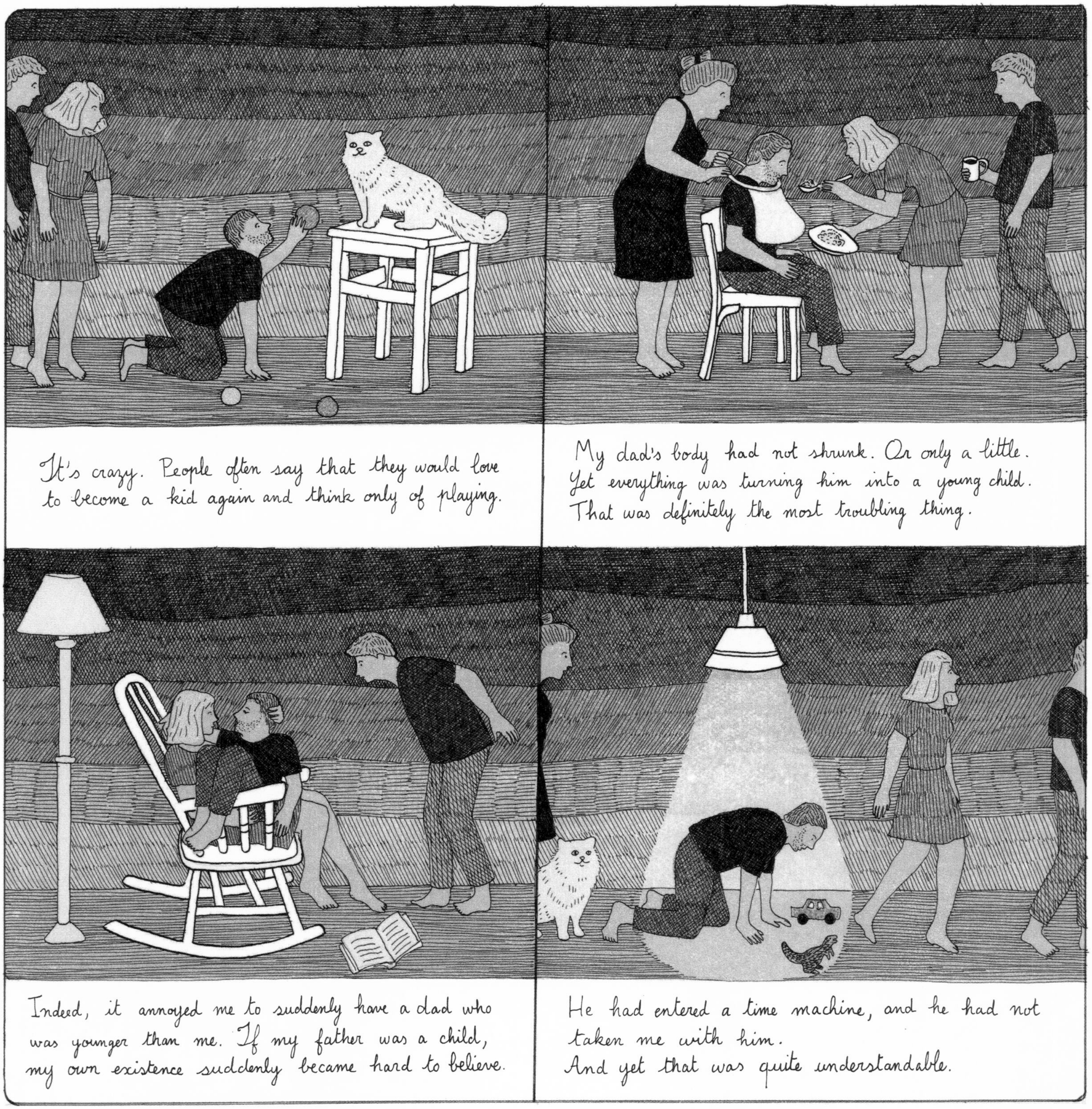
It's crazy. People often say that they would love to become a kid again and think only of playing.
My dad's body had not shrunk. Or only a little. Yet everything was turning him into a young child. That was definitely the most troubling thing.
Indeed, it annoyed me to suddenly have a dad who was younger than me. If my father was a child, my own existence suddenly became hard to believe.
He had entered a time machine, and he had not taken me with him. And yet that was quite understandable.

He could no longer walk. He had a very hard time finding his balance.

He no longer spoke. A few sounds came out of his mouth but that was all.

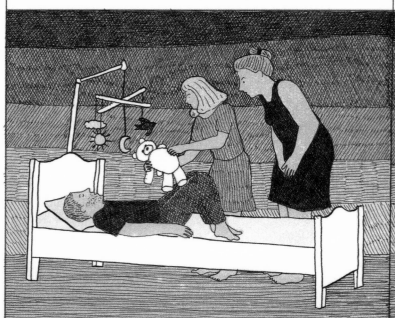

He got into the habit of taking a long nap every afternoon. It's ridiculous how much sleep children need.

My mother wasn't wrong: at least when he was sleeping, we could relax. The rest of the time we were constantly on call.

Someone had to help him walk, change his diapers, make sure nothing went wrong.
It's true, accidents can happen at any time.

He could have fallen out of bed, misplaced his lung, or hurt himself by losing his balance.
My little dad was very fragile.

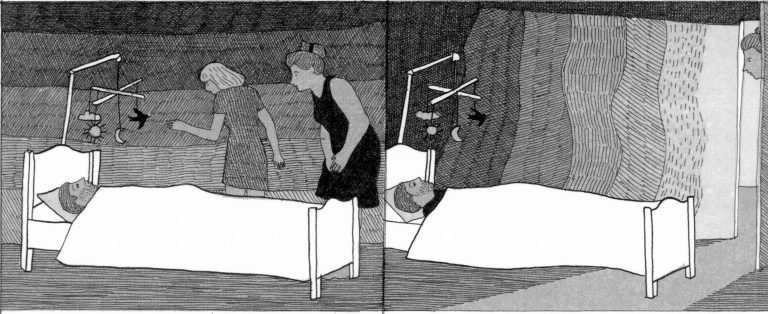

At night, he loved to pull his quilt up to his eyes. That way it hid his new face, with its missing nose and mouth.
As an adult, he hadn't been very affectionate.

Now, he always wanted a kiss on the forehead before going to sleep. Then he wanted us to leave the door slightly ajar. That way, he would be safe and my mother could keep an eye on him.

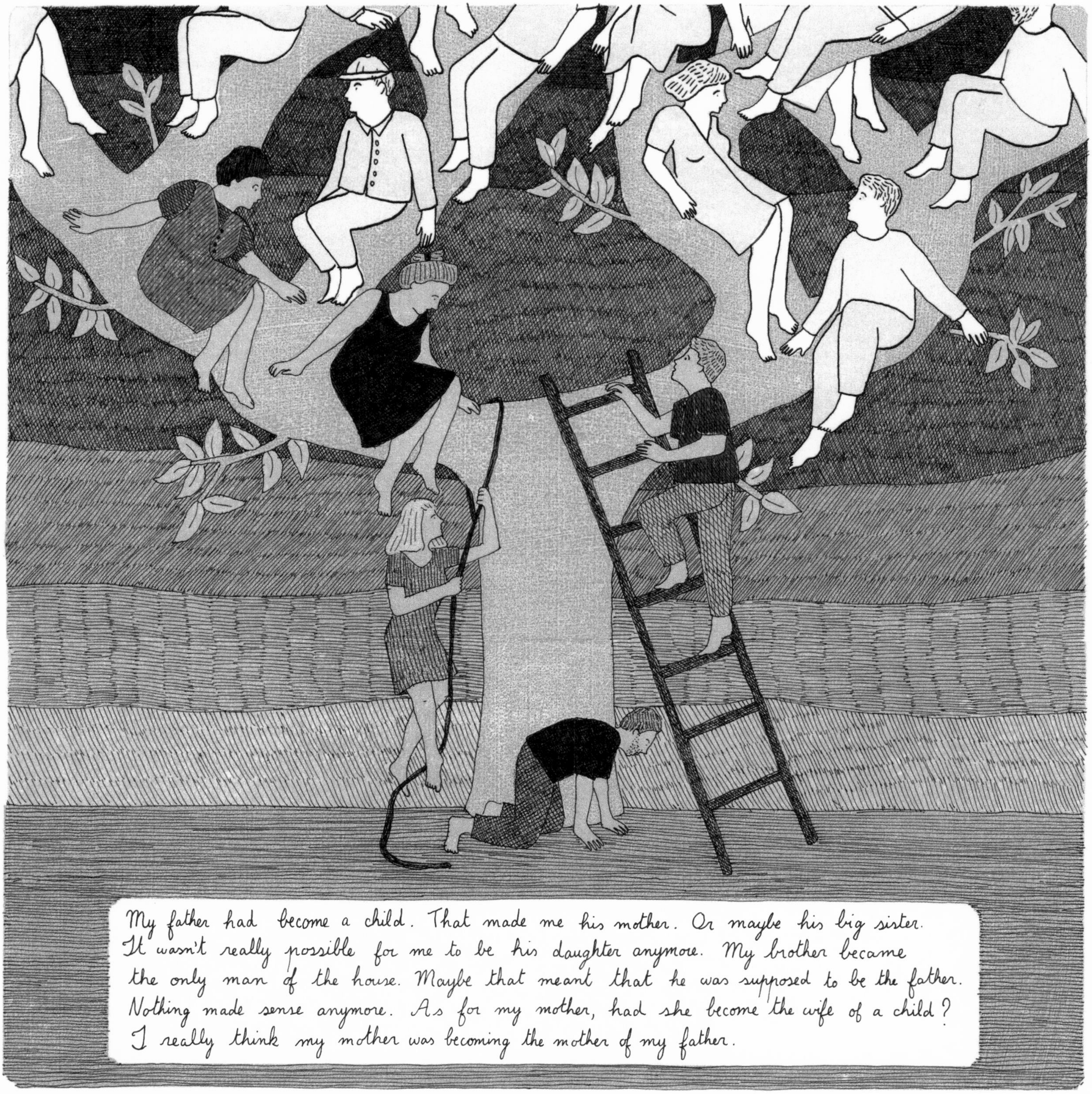
My father had become a child. That made me his mother. Or maybe his big sister. It wasn't really possible for me to be his daughter anymore. My brother became the only man of the house. Maybe that meant that he was supposed to be the father. Nothing made sense anymore. As for my mother, had she become the wife of a child? I really think my mother was becoming the mother of my father.

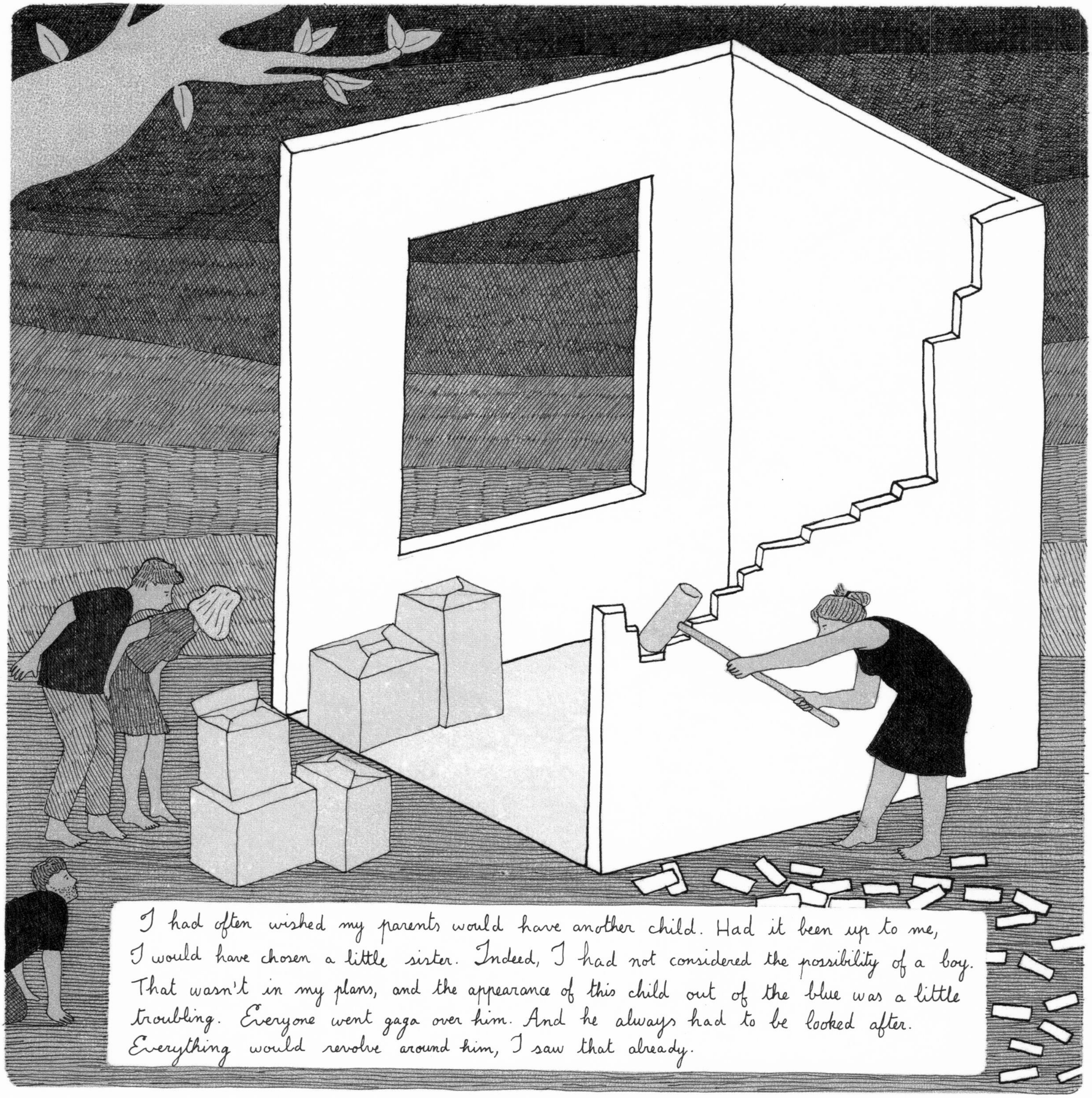
I had often wished my parents would have another child. Had it been up to me, I would have chosen a little sister. Indeed, I had not considered the possibility of a boy. That wasn't in my plans, and the appearance of this child out of the blue was a little troubling. Everyone went gaga over him. And he always had to be looked after. Everything would revolve around him, I saw that already.

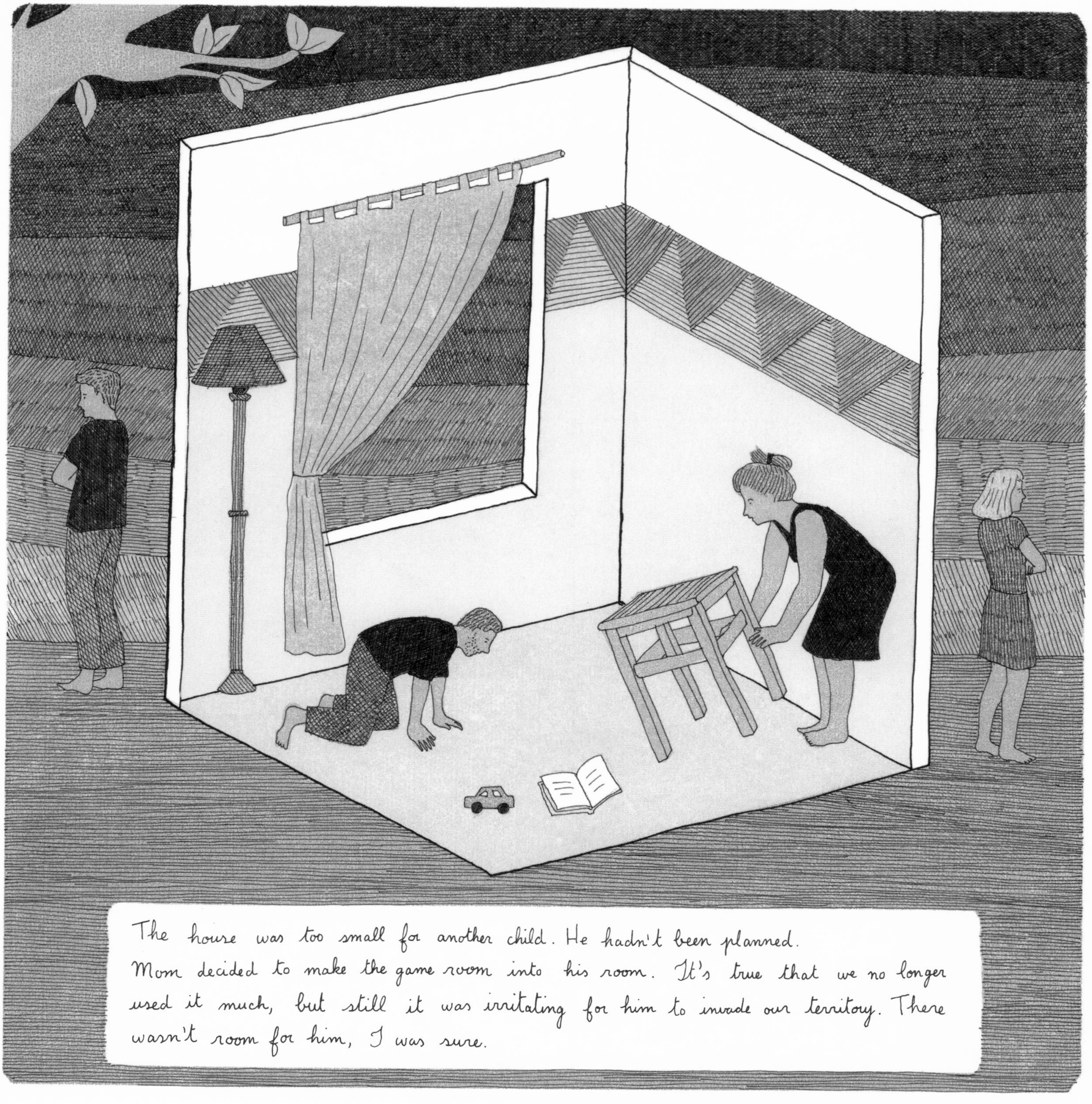
The house was too small for another child. He hadn't been planned.
Mom decided to make the game room into his room. It's true that we no longer used it much, but still it was irritating for him to invade our territory. There wasn't room for him, I was sure.

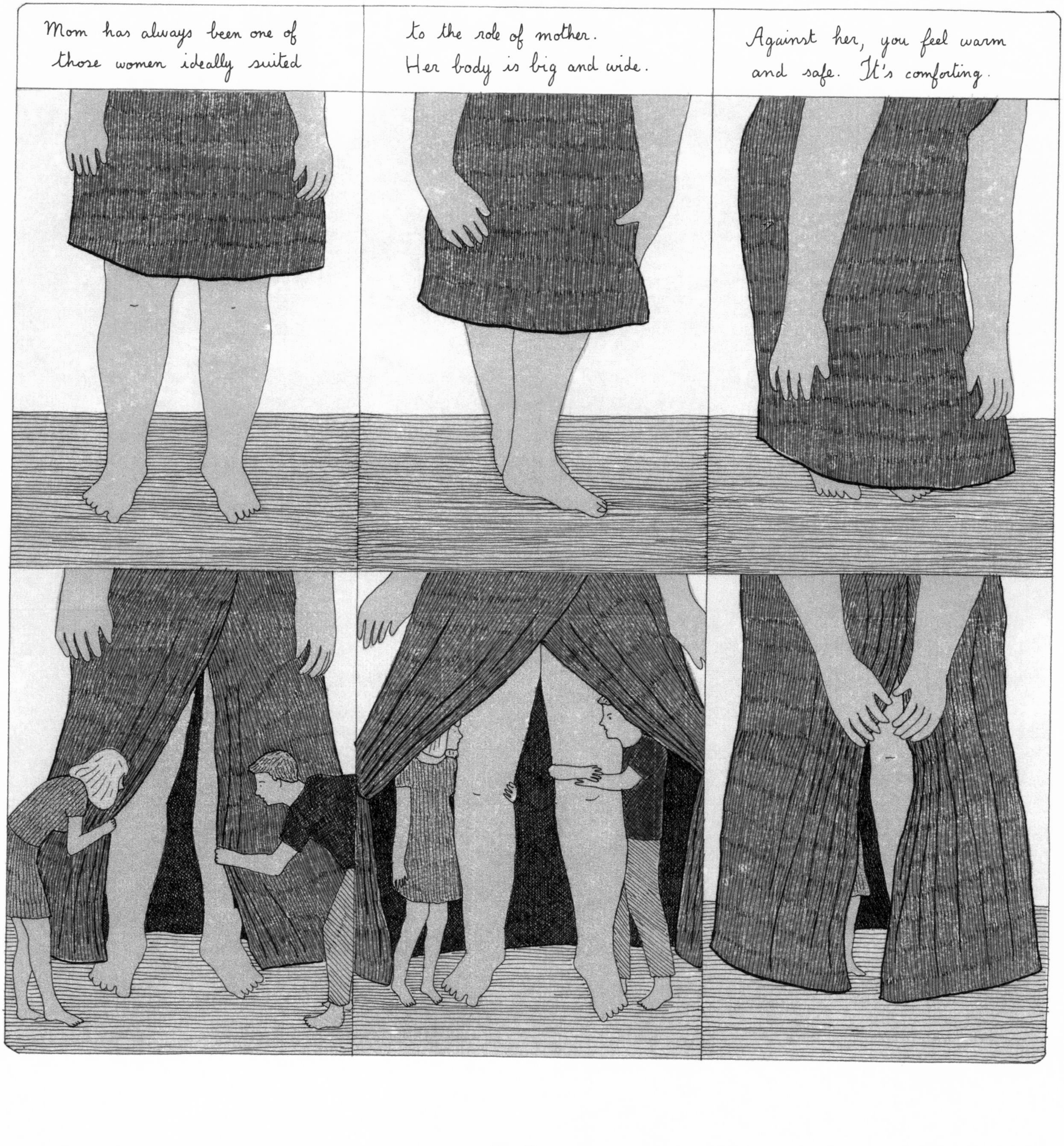
Mom has always been one of those women ideally suited
to the role of mother. Her body is big and wide.
Against her, you feel warm and safe. It's comforting.

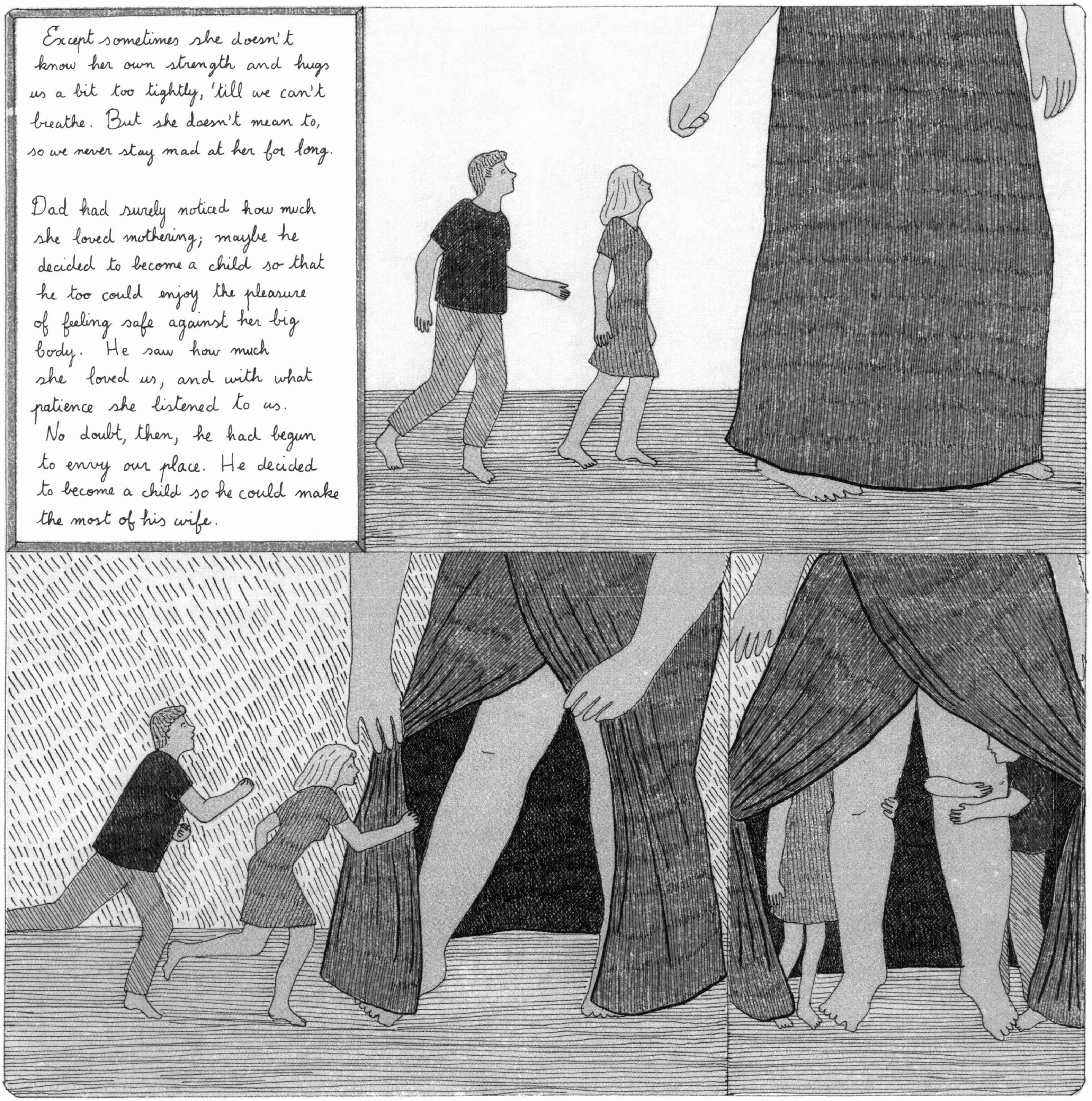
Except sometimes she doesn't know her own strength and hugs us a bit too tightly, 'till we can't breathe. But she doesn't mean to, so we never stay mad at her for long.
Dad had surely noticed how much she loved mothering; maybe he decided to become a child so that he too could enjoy the pleasure of feeling safe against her big body. He saw how much she loved us, and with what patience she listened to us. No doubt, then, he had begun to envy our place. He decided to become a child so he could make the most of his wife.

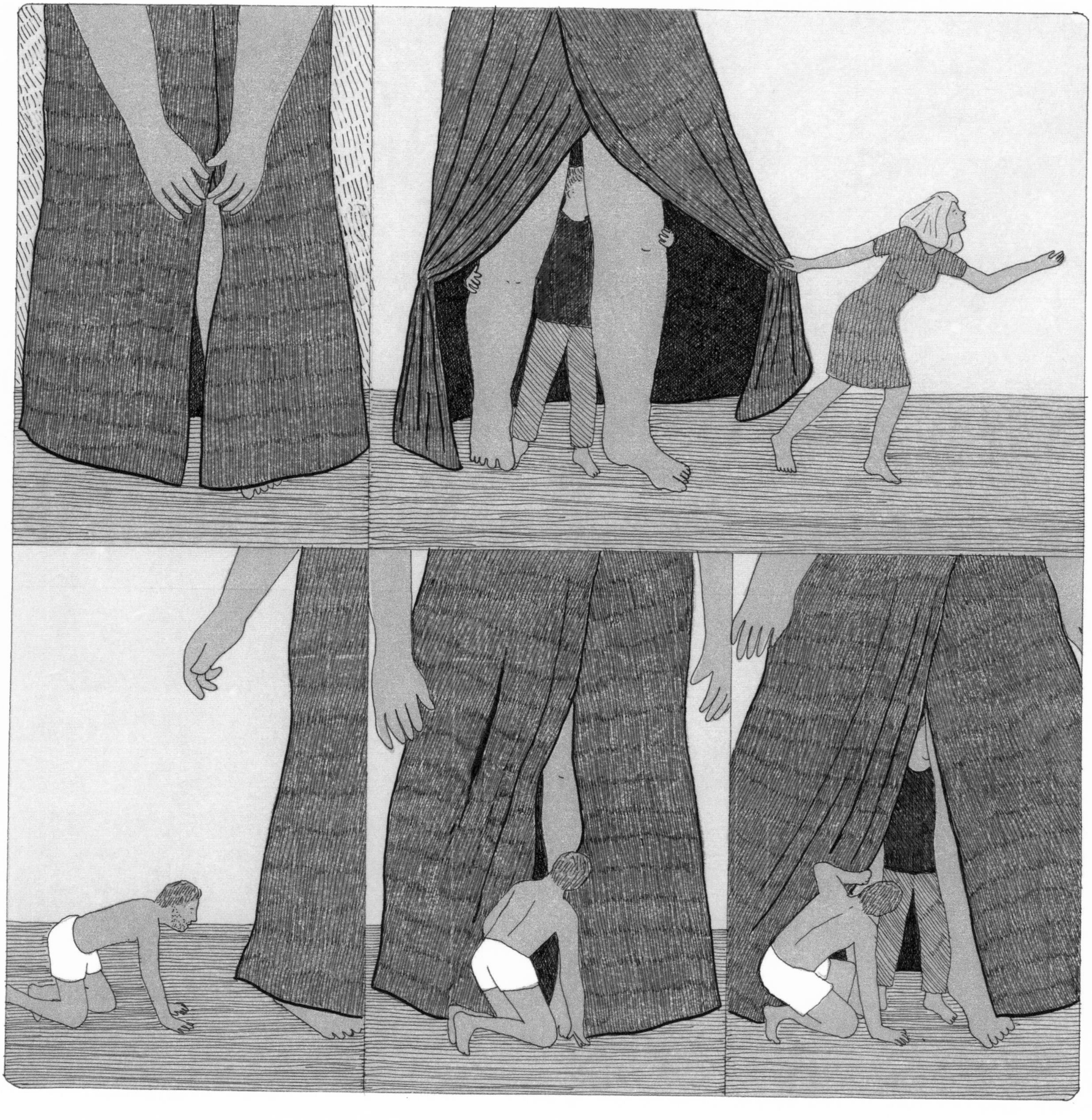

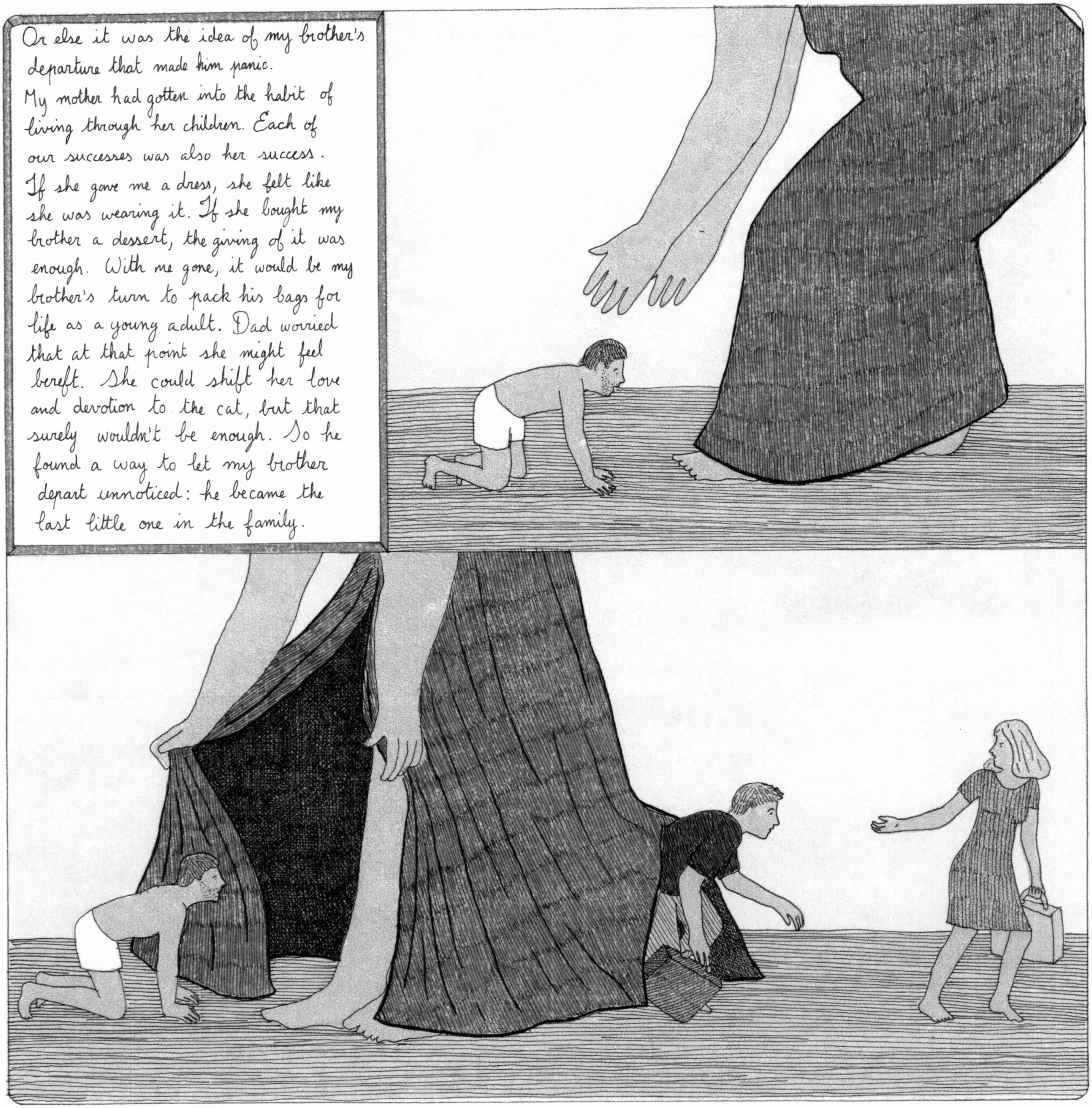
Or else it was the idea of my brother's departure that made him panic.
My mother had gotten into the habit of living through her children. Each of our successes was also her success. If she gave me a dress, she felt like she was wearing it. If she bought my brother a dessert, the giving of it was enough. With me gone, it would be my brother's turn to pack his bags for life as a young adult. Dad worried that at that point she might feel bereft. She could shift her love and devotion to the cat, but that surely wouldn't be enough. So he found a way to let my brother depart unnoticed: he became the last little one in the family.

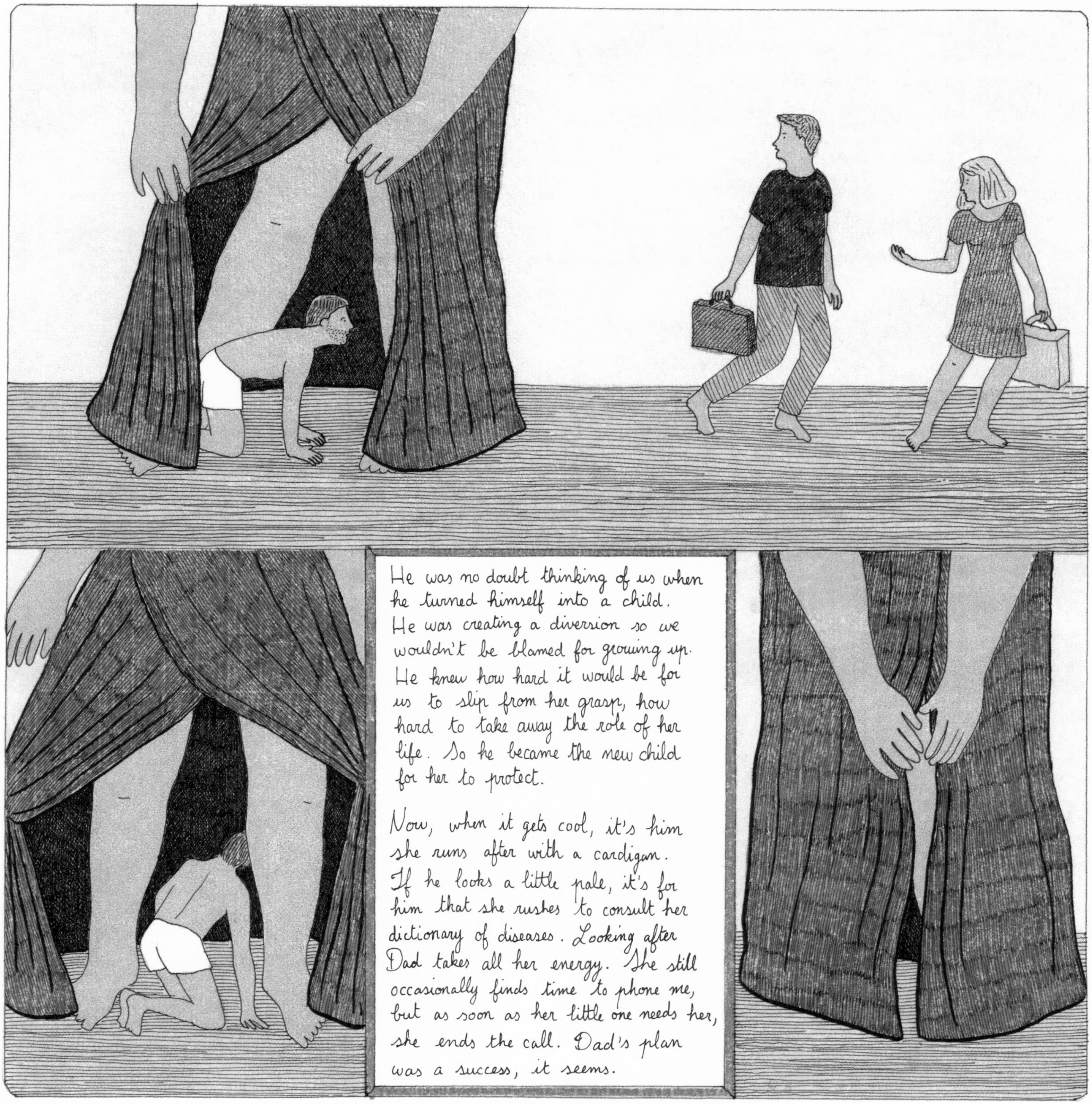
He was no doubt thinking of us when he turned himself into a child. He was creating a diversion so we wouldn't be blamed for growing up. He knew how hard it would be for us to slip from her grasp, how hard to take away the role of her life. So he became the new child for her to protect.
Now, when it gets cool, it's him she runs after with a cardigan. If he looks a little pale, it's for him that she rushes to consult her dictionary of diseases. Looking after Dad takes all her energy. She still occasionally finds time to phone me, but as soon as her little one needs her, she ends the call. Dad's plan was a success, it seems.

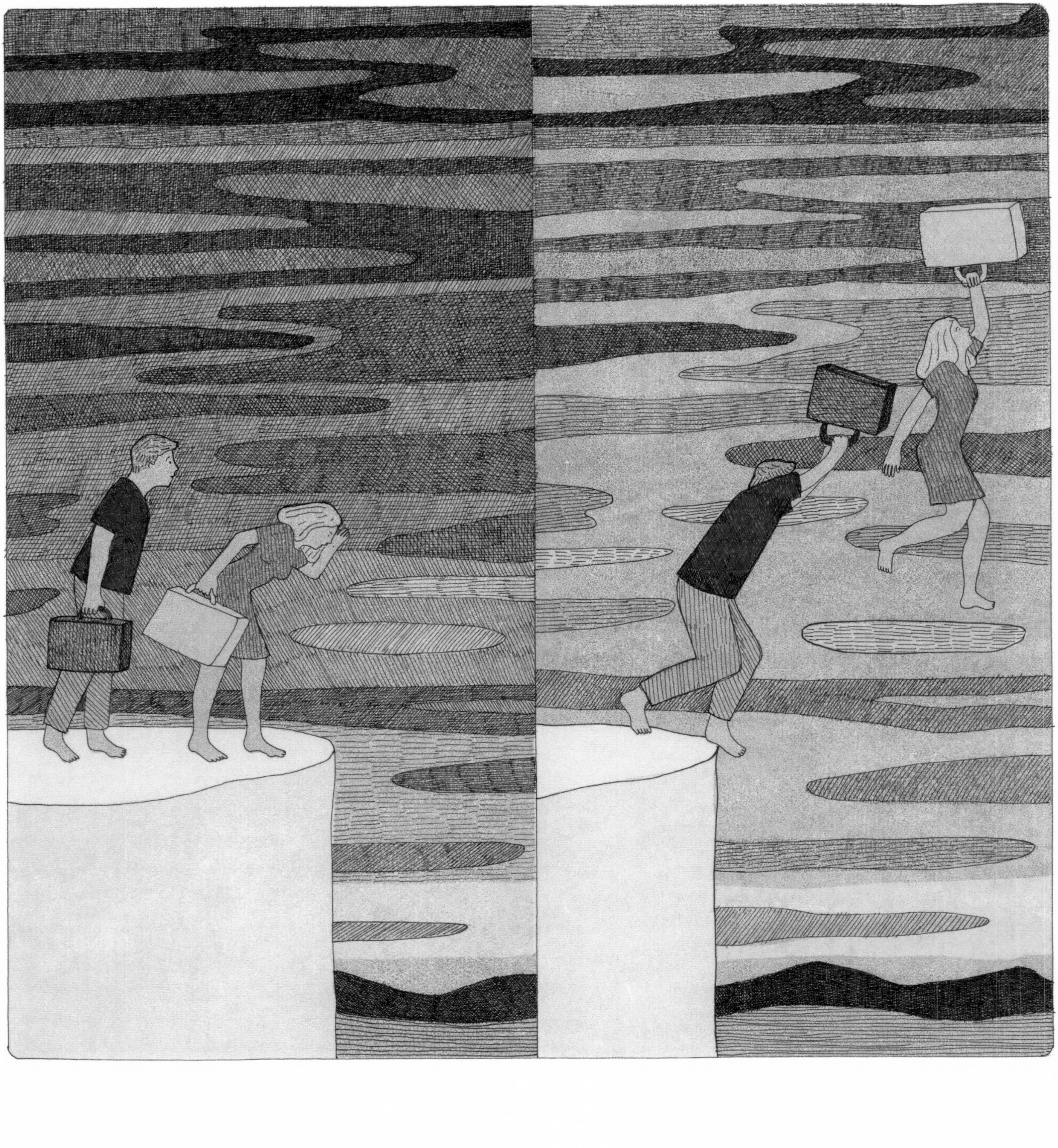

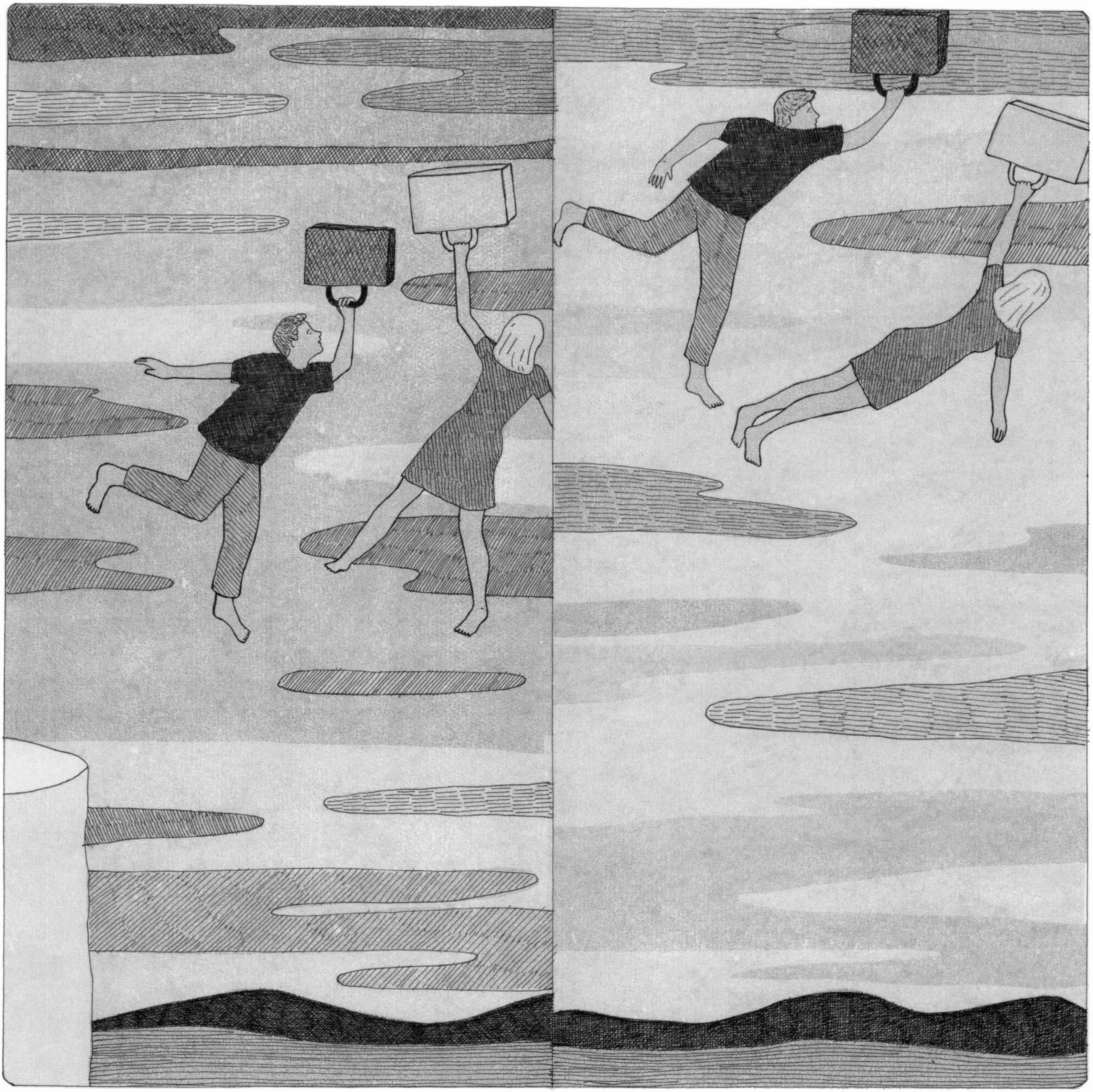

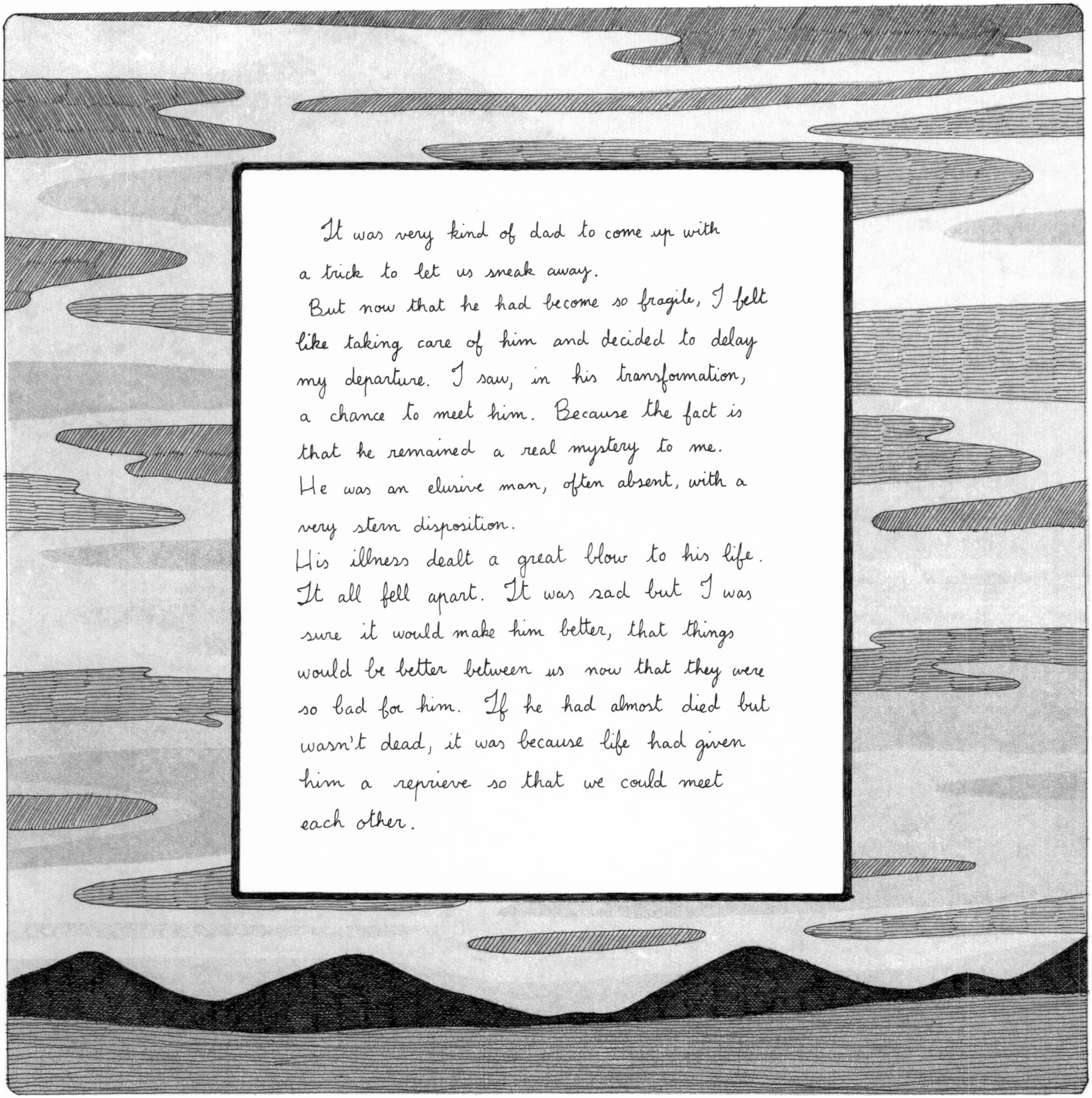
It was very kind of dad to come up with a trick to let us sneak away.
But now that he had become so fragile, I felt like taking care of him and decided to delay my departure. I saw, in his transformation, a chance to meet him. Because the fact is that he remained a real mystery to me. He was an elusive man, often absent, with a very stern disposition.
His illness dealt a great blow to his life. It all fell apart. It was sad but I was sure it would make him better, that things would be better between us now that they were so bad for him. If he had almost died but wasn't dead, it was because life had given him a reprieve so that we could meet each other.

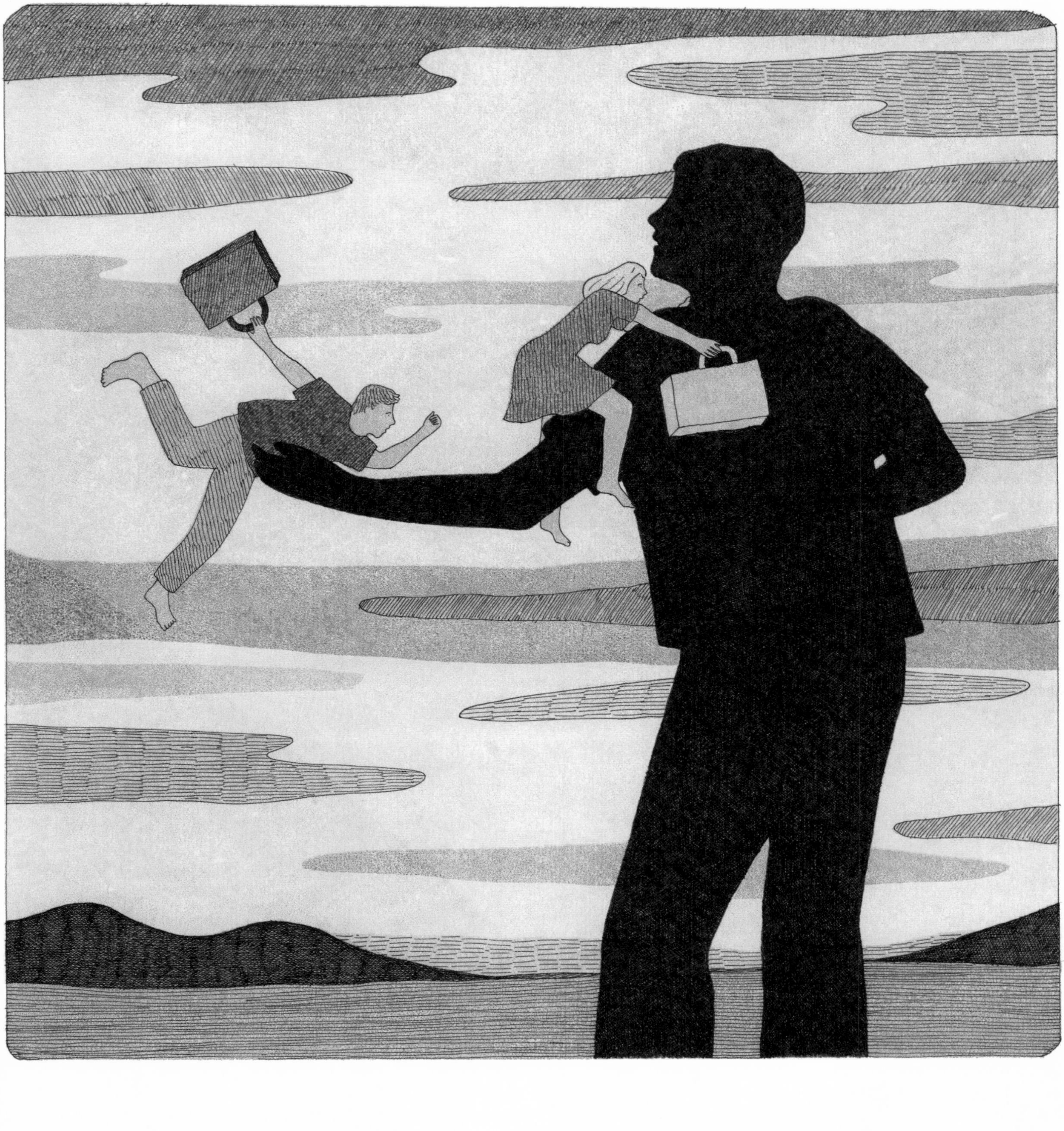

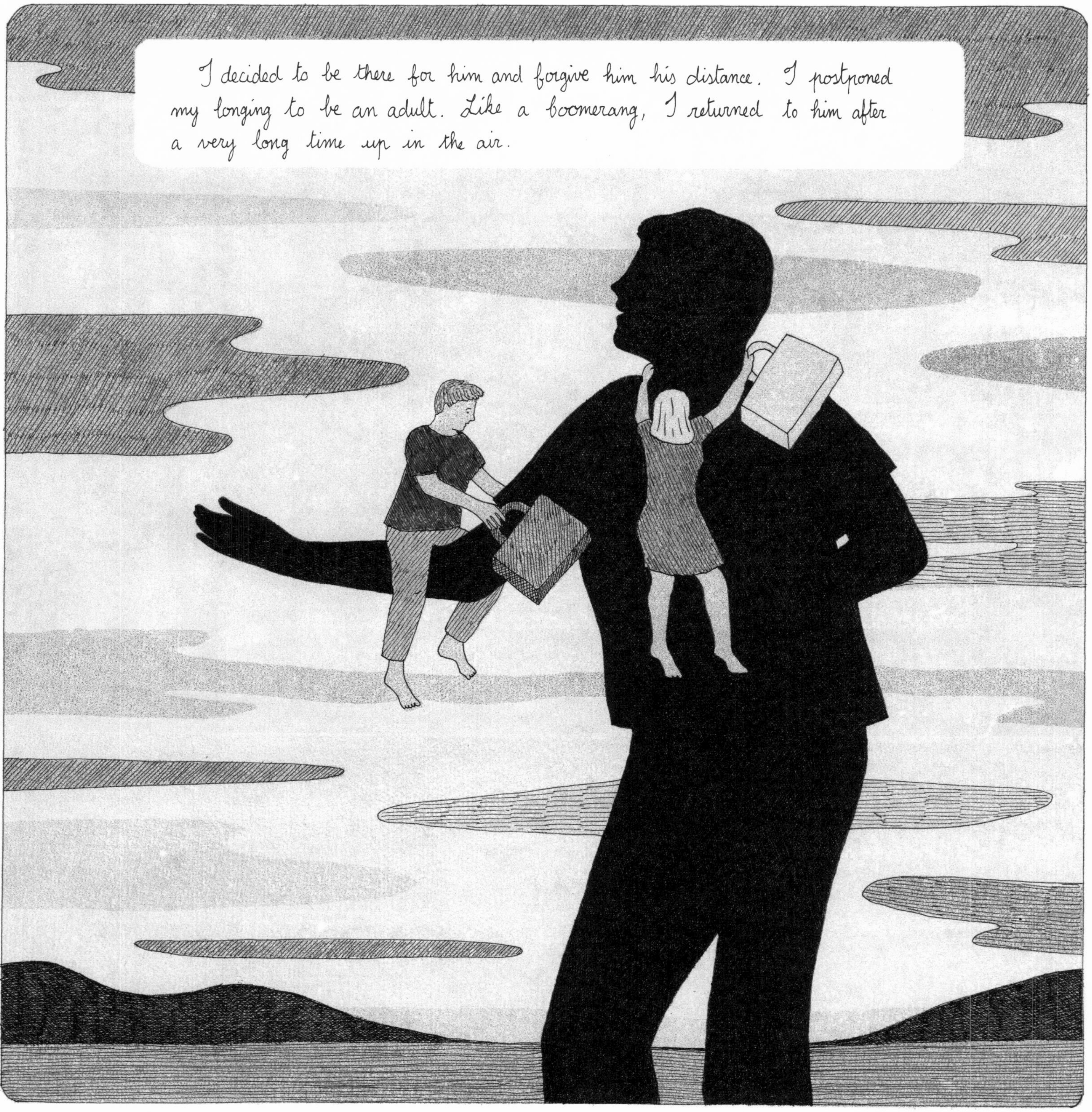
I decided to be there for him and forgive him his distance. I postponed my longing to be an adult. Like a boomerang, I returned to him after a very long time up in the air.

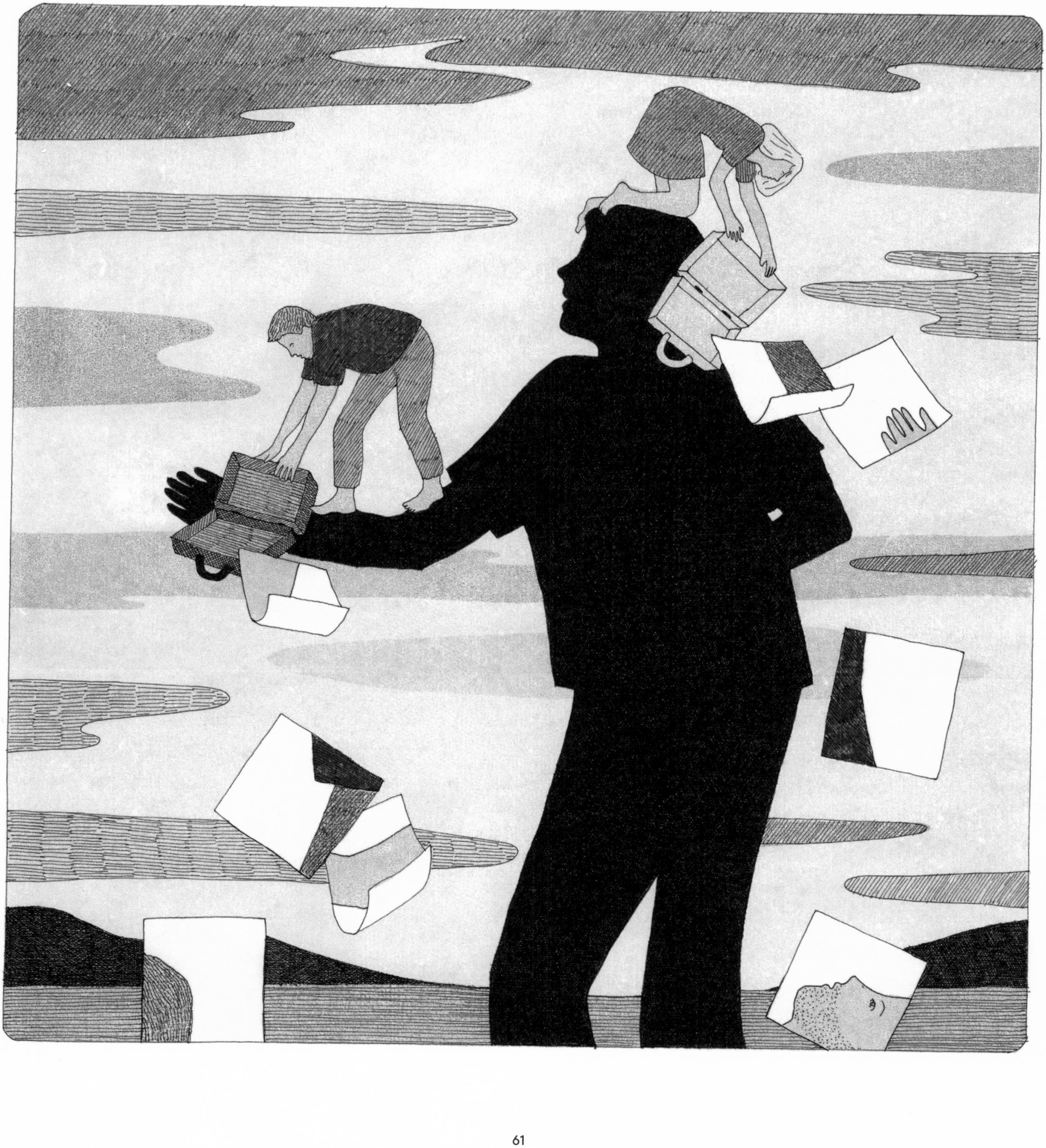

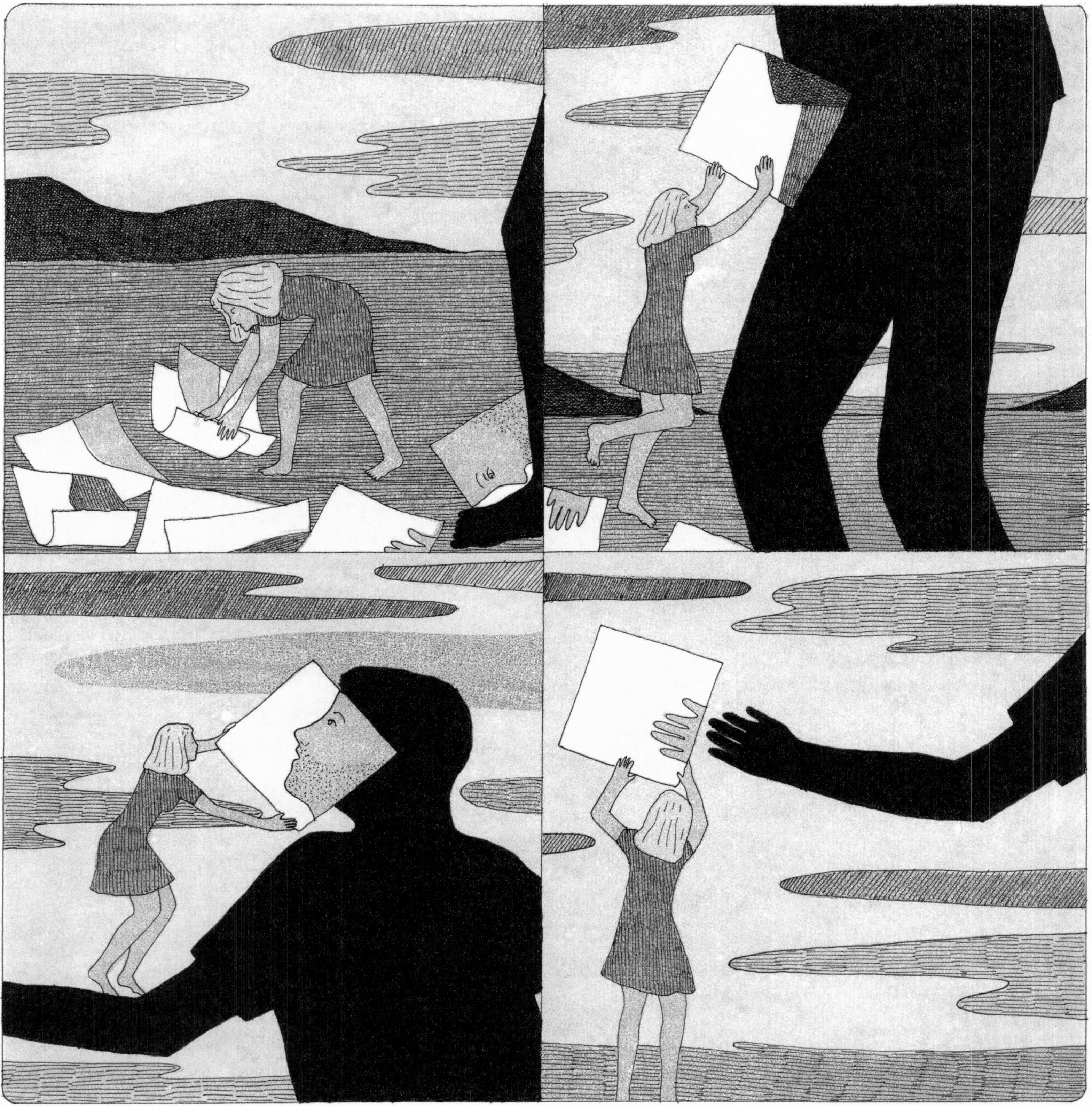

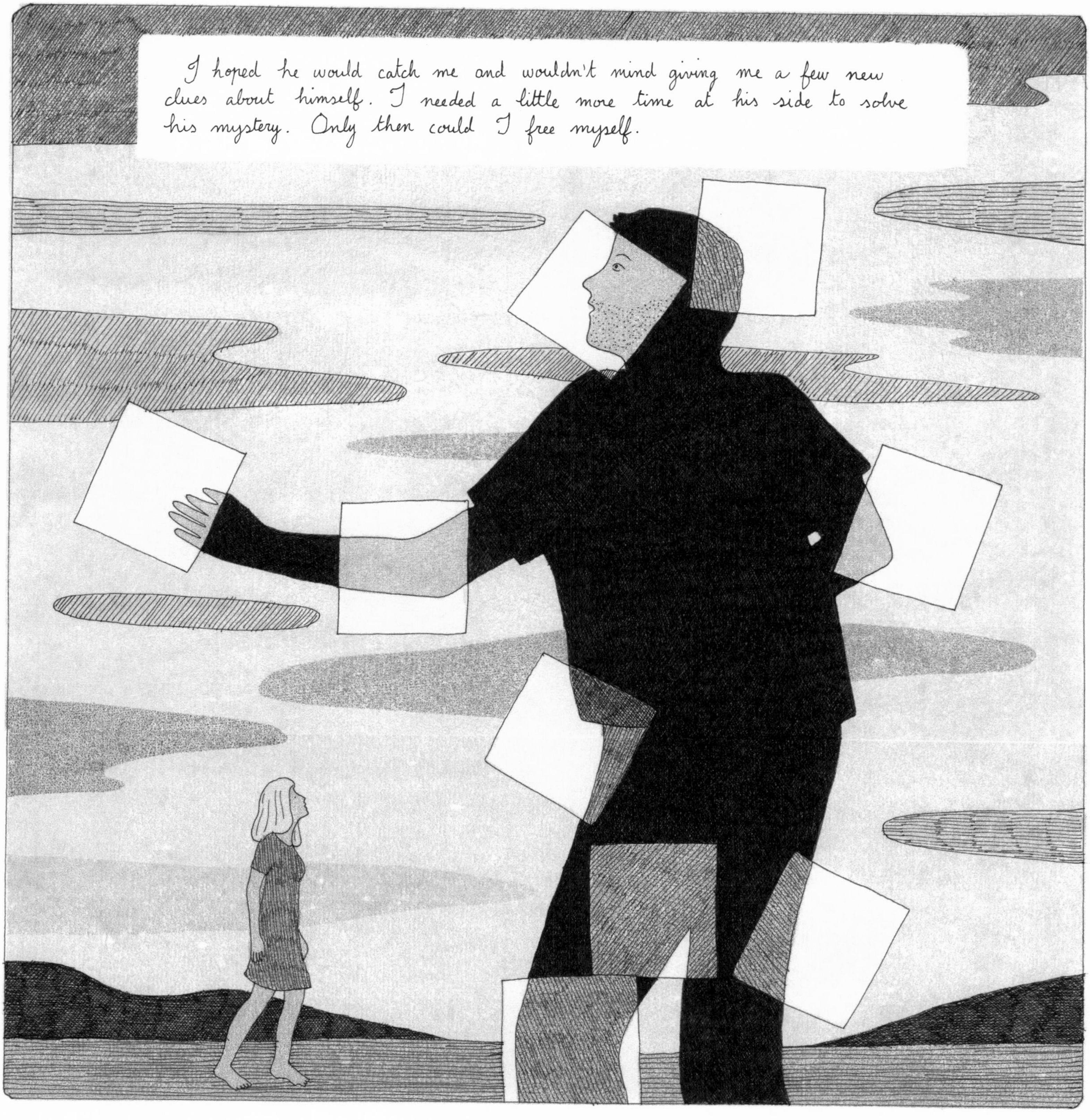
I hoped he would catch me and wouldn't mind giving me a few new clues about himself. I needed a little more time at his side to solve his mystery. Only then could I free myself.

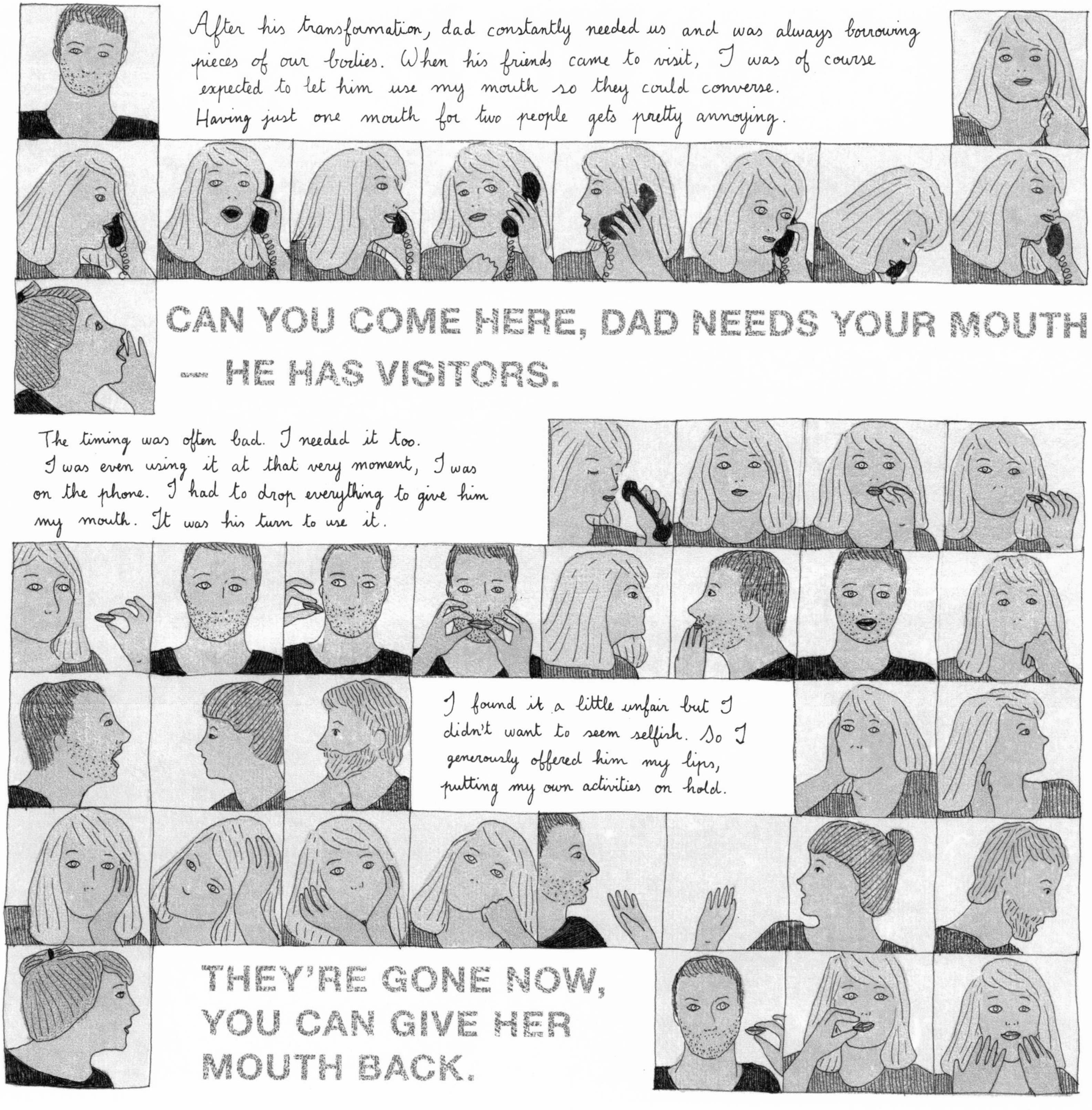
After his transformation, dad constantly needed us and was always borrowing pieces of our bodies. When his friends came to visit, I was of course expected to let him use my mouth so they could converse.
Having just one mouth for two people gets pretty annoying.
CAN YOU COME HERE, DAD NEEDS YOUR MOUTH – HE HAS VISITORS.
The timing was often bad. I needed it too. I was even using it at that very moment, I was on the phone. I had to drop everything to give him my mouth. It was his turn to use it.
I found it a little unfair but I didn't want to seem selfish. So I generously offered him my lips, putting my own activities on hold.
THEY'RE GONE NOW, YOU CAN GIVE HER MOUTH BACK.

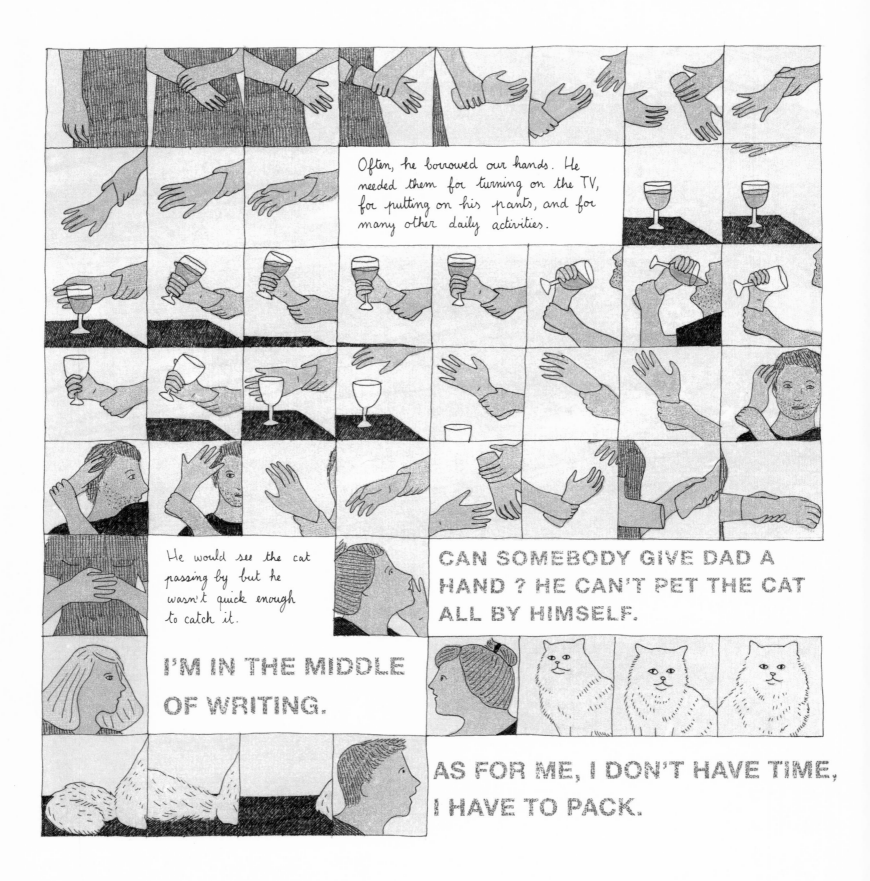

Often, he borrowed our hands. He needed them for turning on the TV, for putting on his pants, and for many other daily activities.

He would see the cat passing by but he wasn't quick enough to catch it.

CAN SOMEBODY GIVE DAD A HAND ? HE CAN'T PET THE CAT ALL BY HIMSELF.

I'M IN THE MIDDLE OF WRITING.

AS FOR ME, I DON'T HAVE TIME, I HAVE TO PACK.

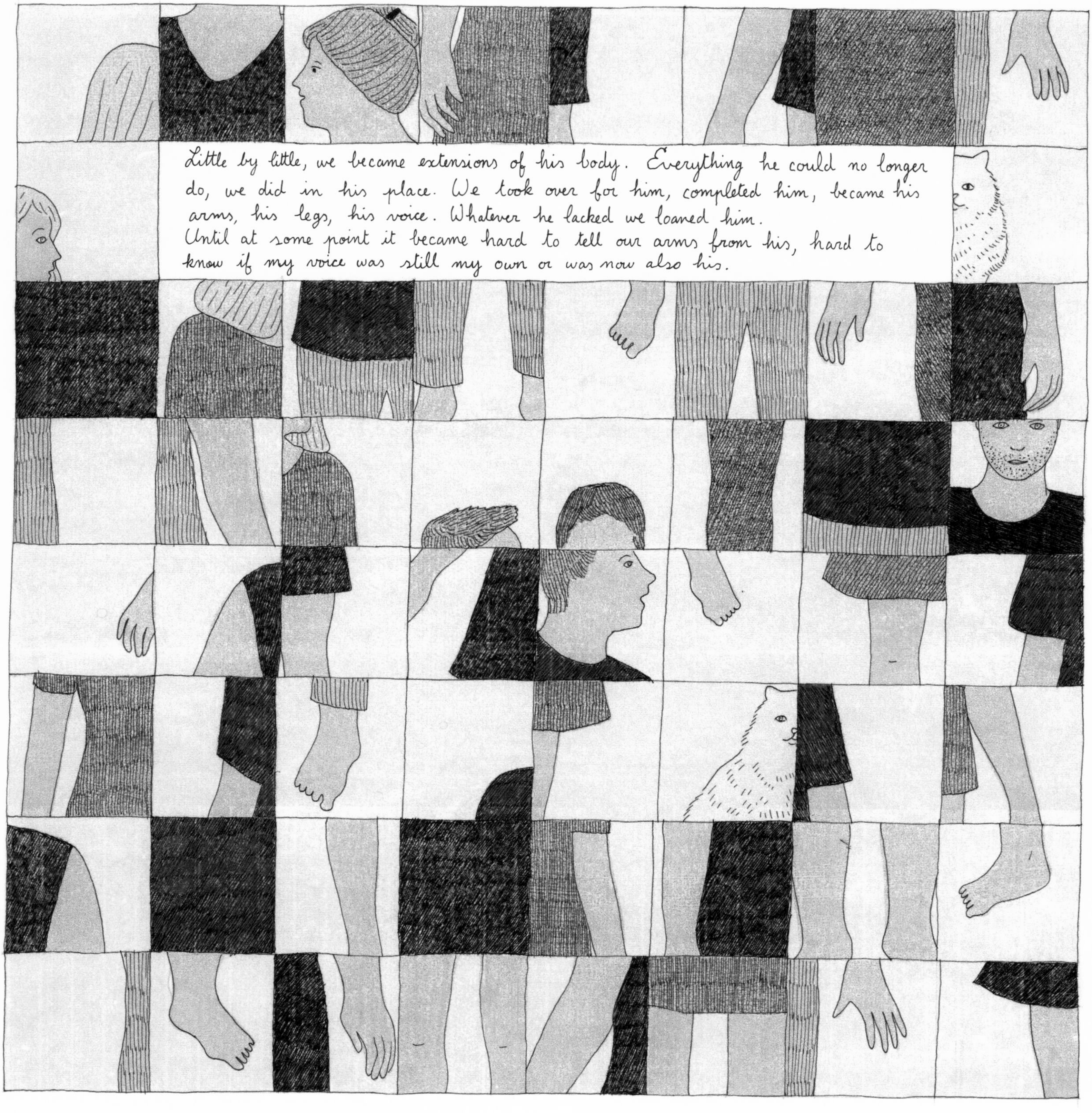
Little by little, we became extensions of his body. Everything he could no longer do, we did in his place. We took over for him, completed him, became his arms, his legs, his voice. Whatever he lacked we loaned him.
Until at some point it became hard to tell our arms from his, hard to know if my voice was still my own or was now also his.

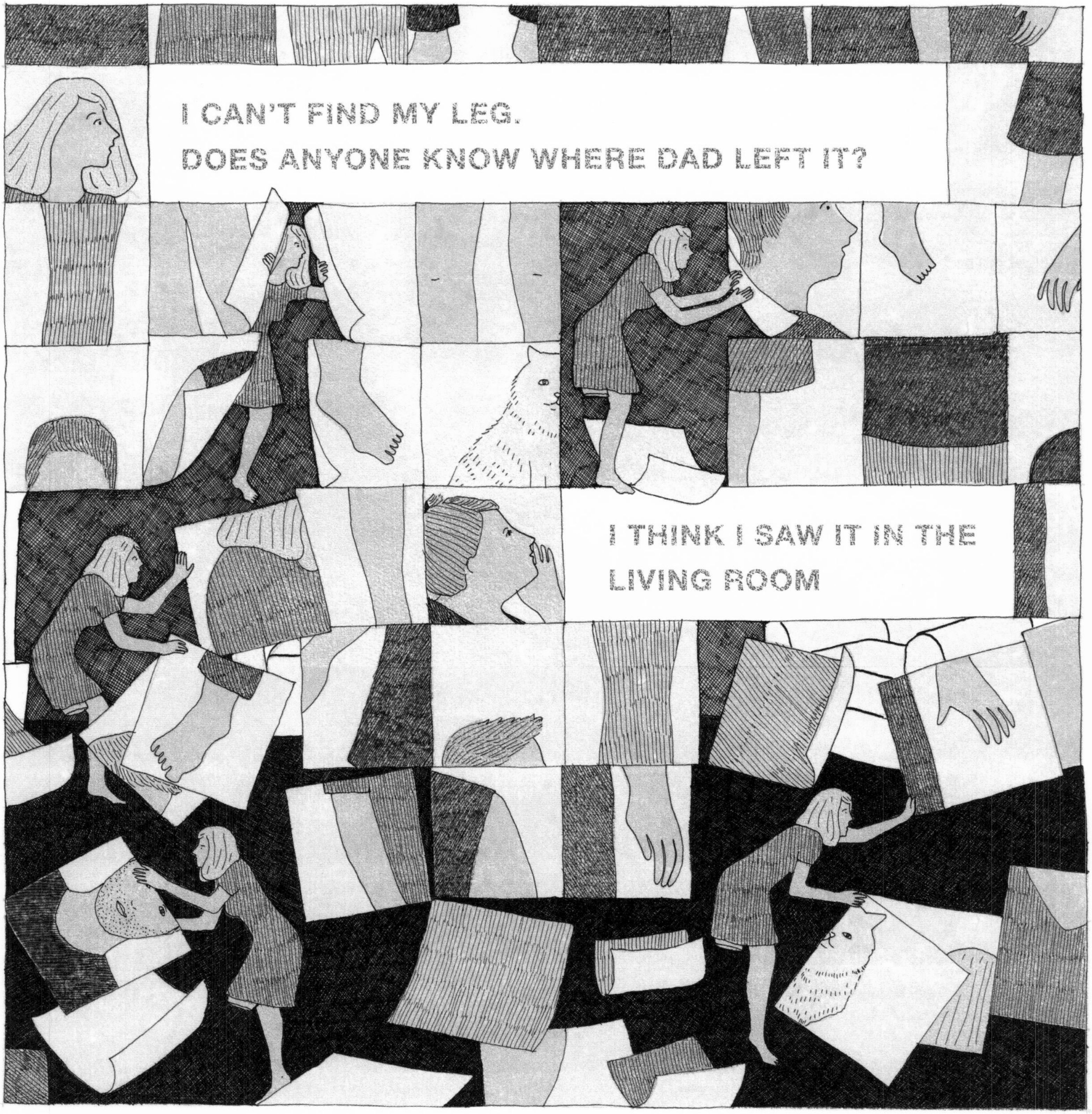
I CAN'T FIND MY LEG.
DOES ANYONE KNOW WHERE DAD LEFT IT?
I THINK I SAW IT IN THE LIVING ROOM

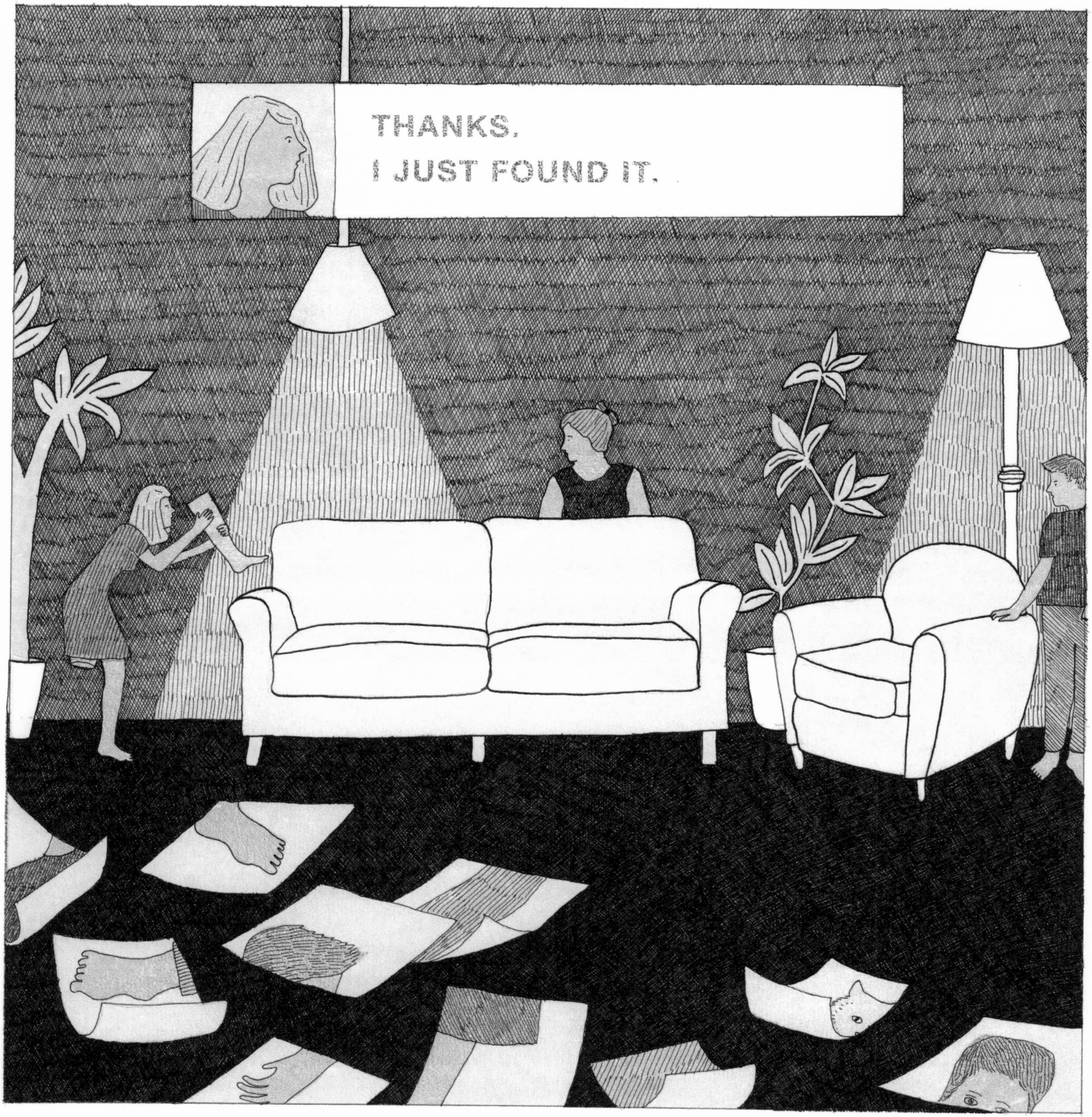
THANKS.
I JUST FOUND IT.

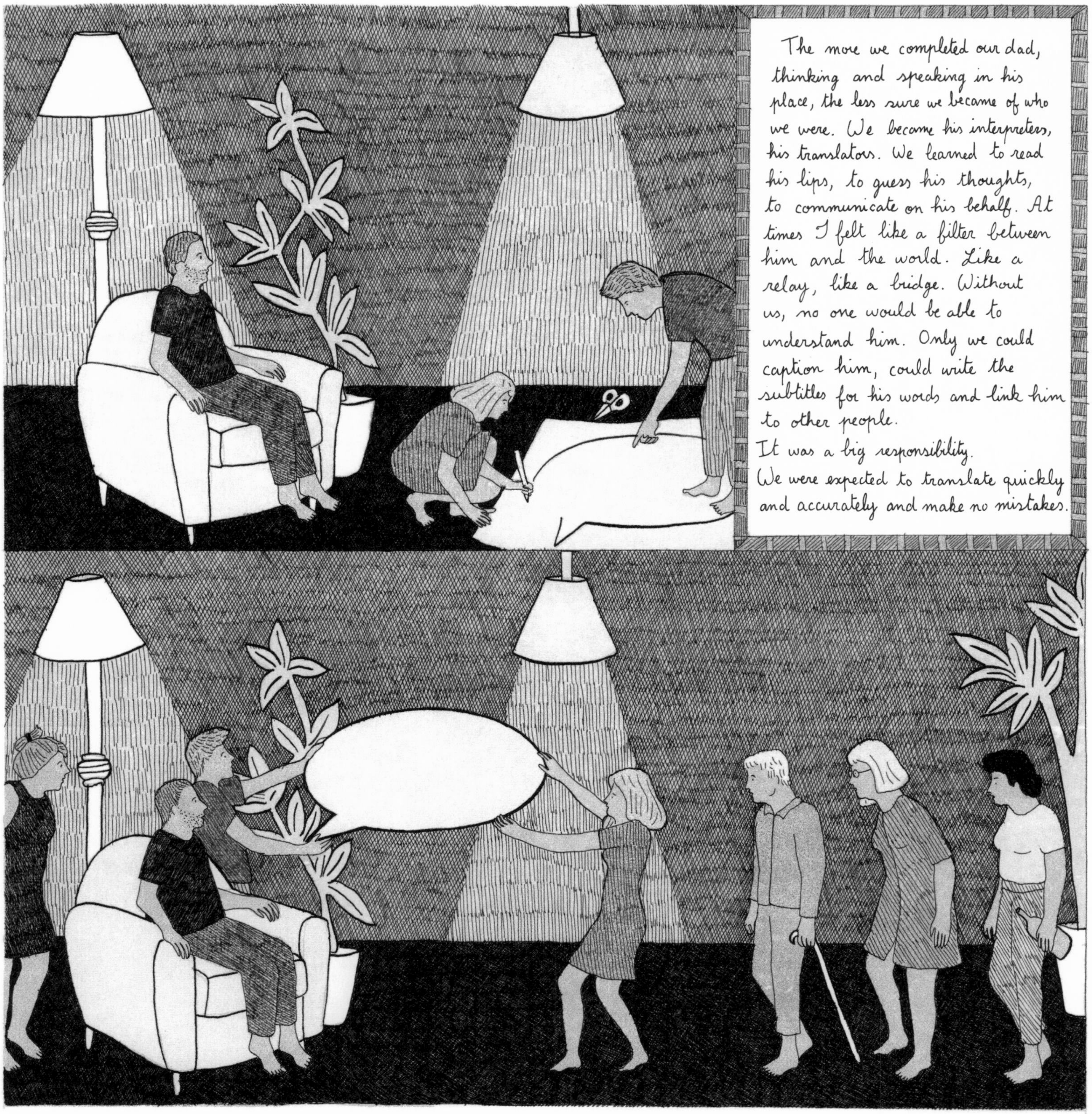
The more we completed our dad, thinking and speaking in his place, the less sure we became of who we were. We became his interpreters, his translators. We learned to read his lips, to guess his thoughts, to communicate on his behalf. At times I felt like a filter between him and the world. Like a relay, like a bridge. Without us, no one would be able to understand him. Only we could caption him, could write the subtitles for his words and link him to other people.
It was a big responsibility.
We were expected to translate quickly and accurately and make no mistakes.

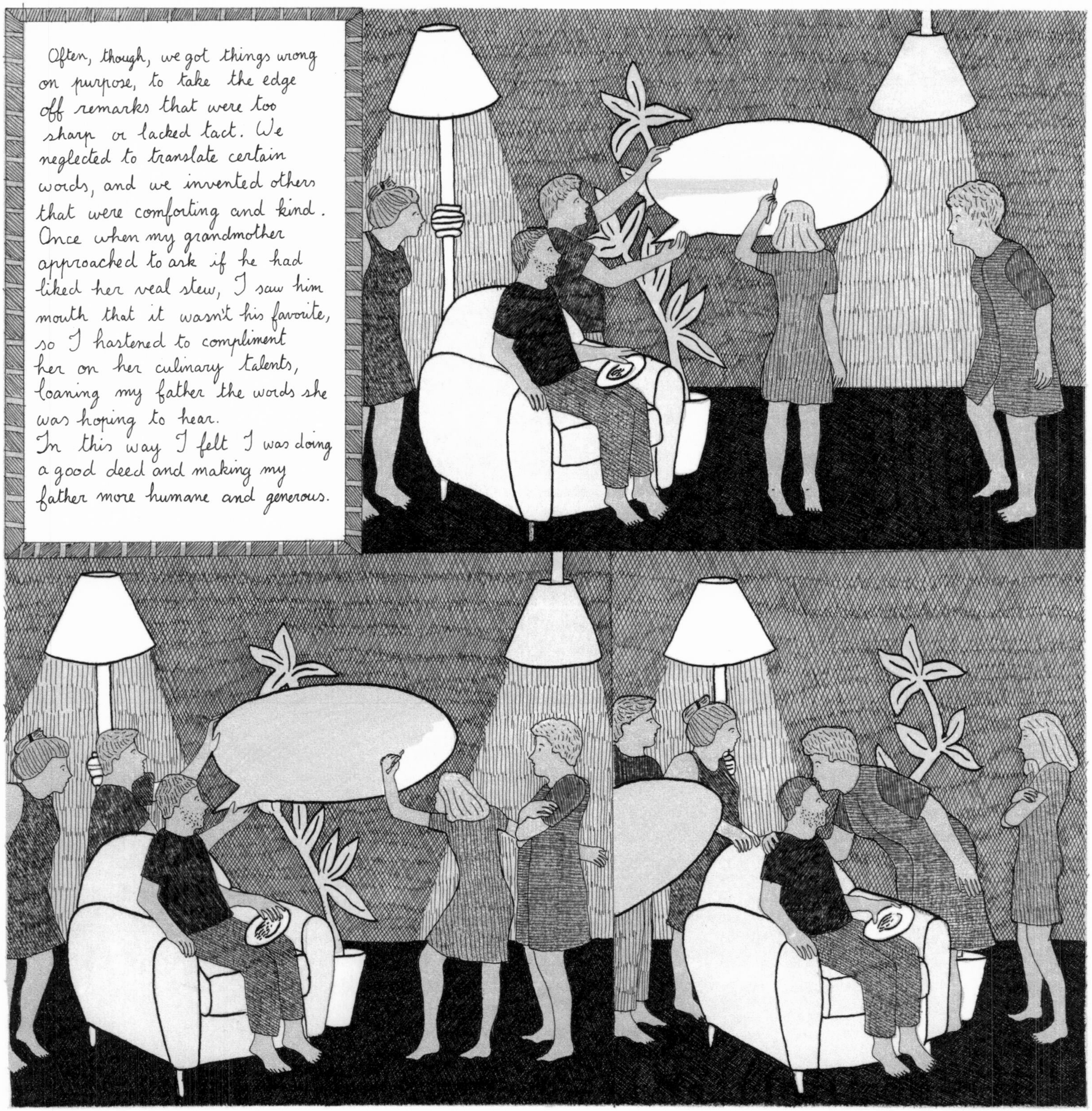
Often, though, we got things wrong on purpose, to take the edge off remarks that were too sharp or lacked tact. We neglected to translate certain words, and we invented others that were comforting and kind. Once when my grandmother approached to ask if he had liked her veal stew, I saw him mouth that it wasn't his favorite, so I hastened to compliment her on her culinary talents, loaning my father the words she was hoping to hear.
In this way I felt I was doing a good deed and making my father more humane and generous.

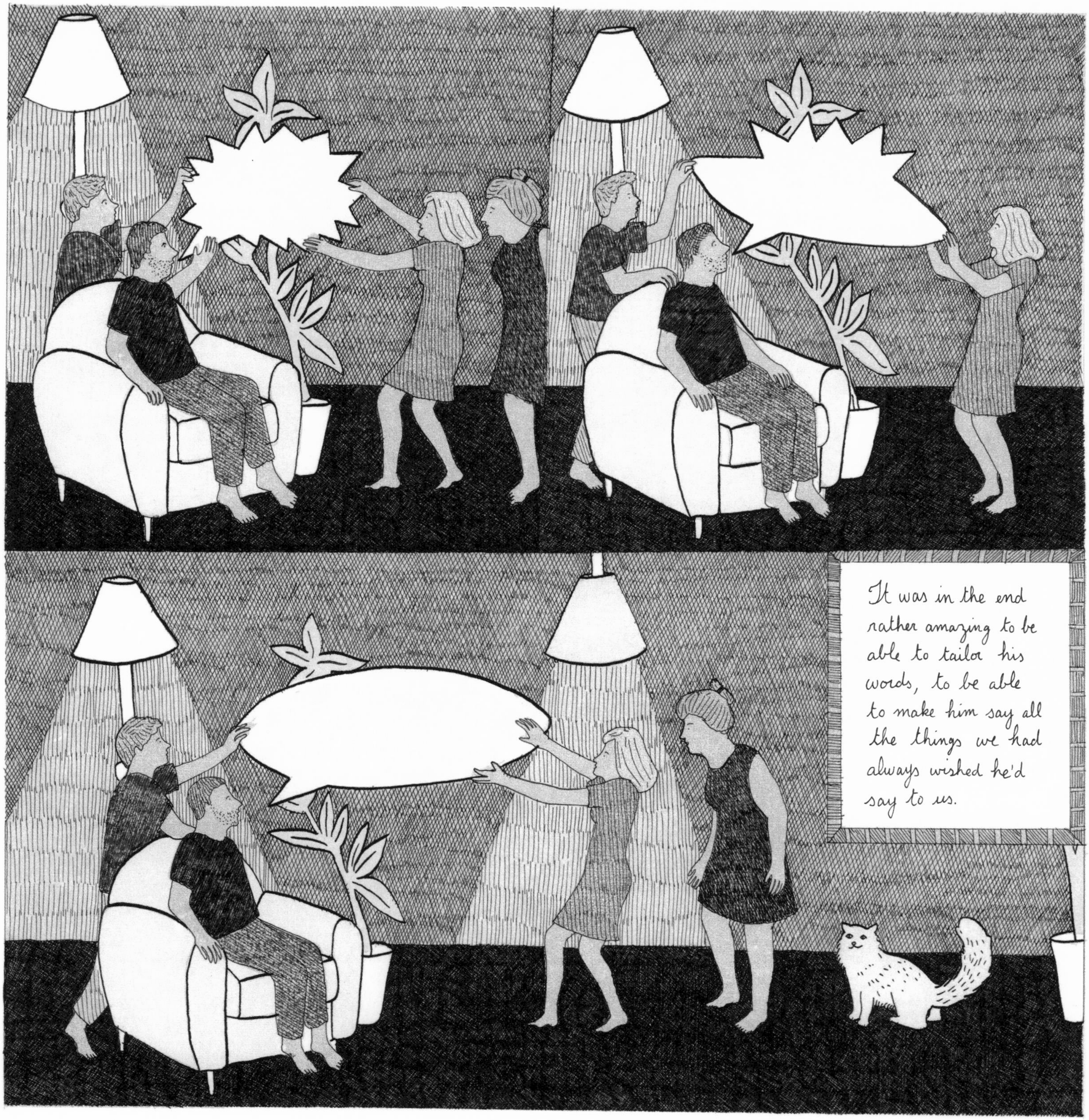
It was in the end rather amazing to be able to tailor his words, to be able to make him say all the things we had always wished he'd say to us.

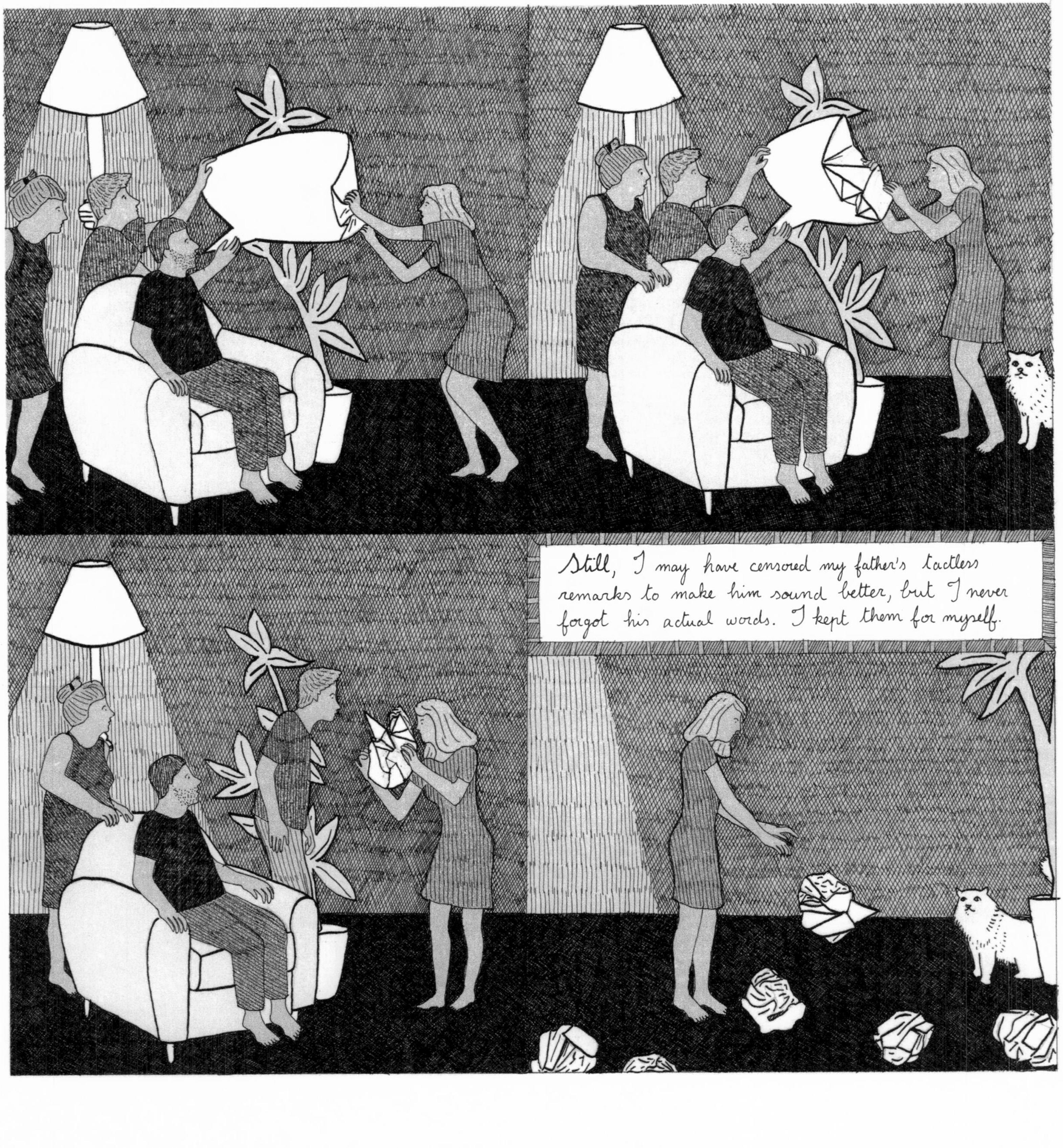
Still, I may have censored my father's tactless remarks to make him sound better, but I never forgot his actual words. I kept them for myself.

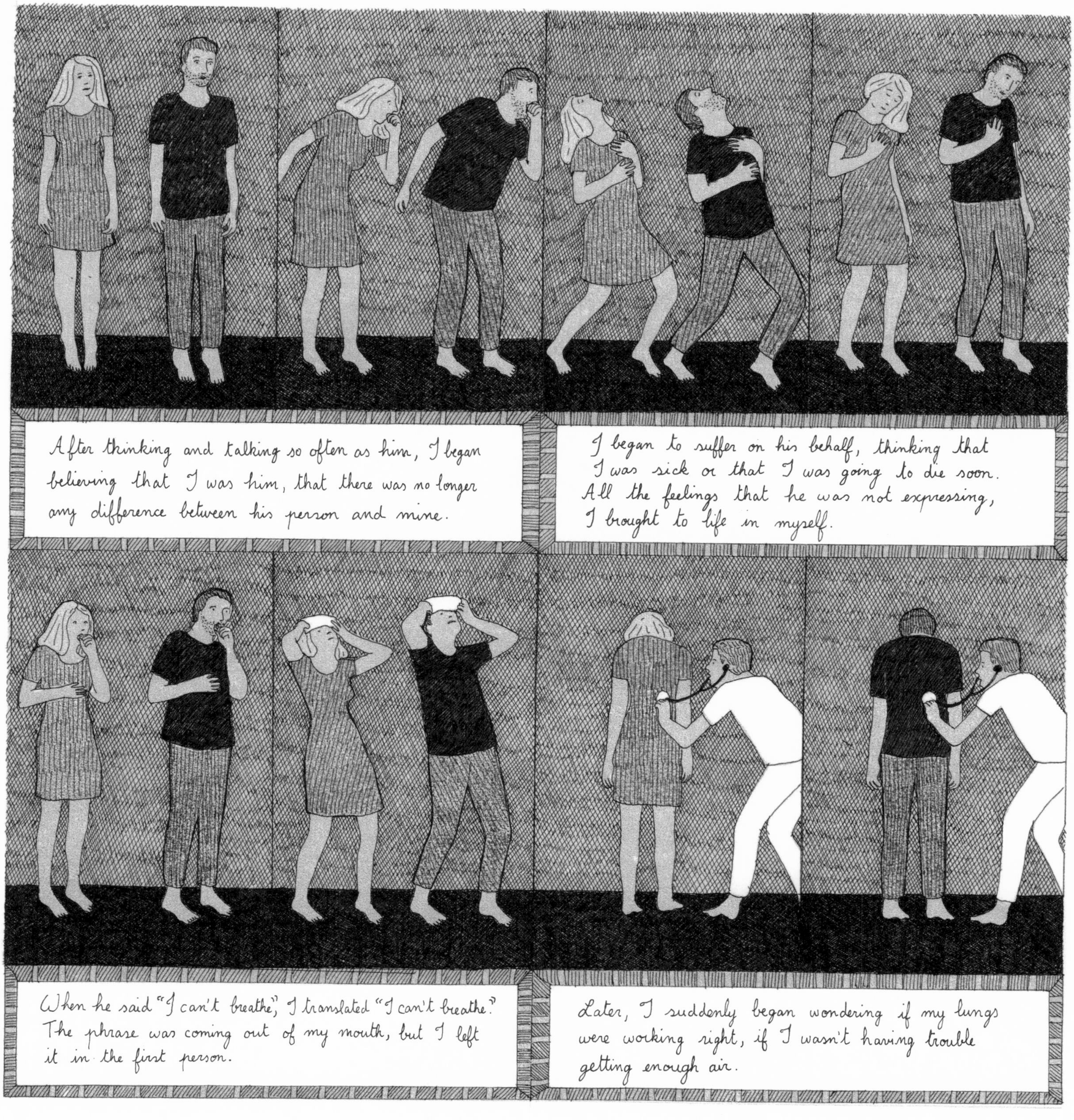
After thinking and talking so often as him, I began believing that I was him, that there was no longer any difference between his person and mine.
I began to suffer on his behalf, thinking that I was sick or that I was going to die soon. All the feelings that he was not expressing, I brought to life in myself.
When he said "I can't breathe," I translated "I can't breathe." The phrase was coming out of my mouth, but I left it in the first person.
Later, I suddenly began wondering if my lungs were working right, if I wasn't having trouble getting enough air.

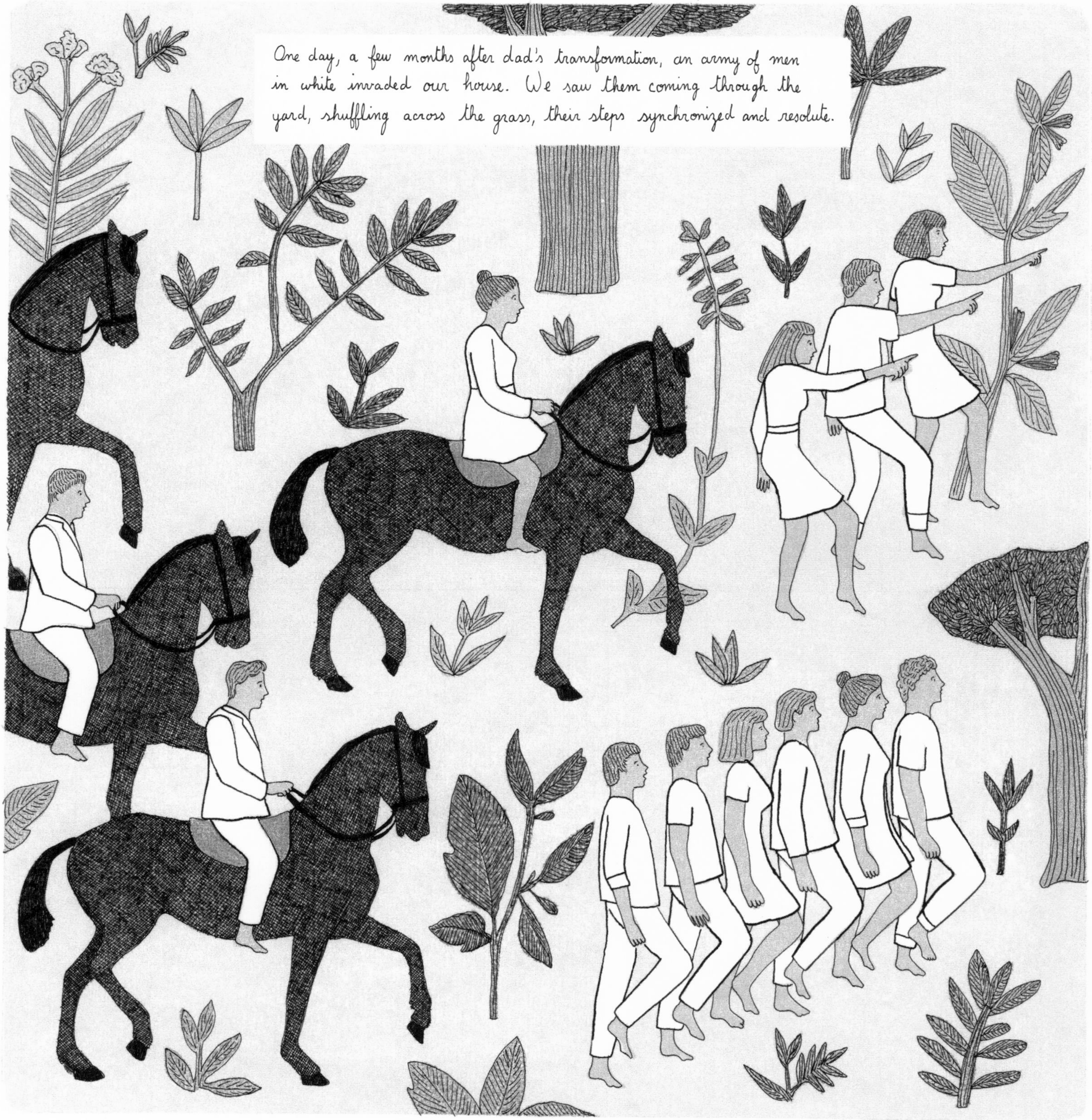
One day, a few months after dad's transformation, an army of men in white invaded our house. We saw them coming through the yard, shuffling across the grass, their steps synchronized and resolute.

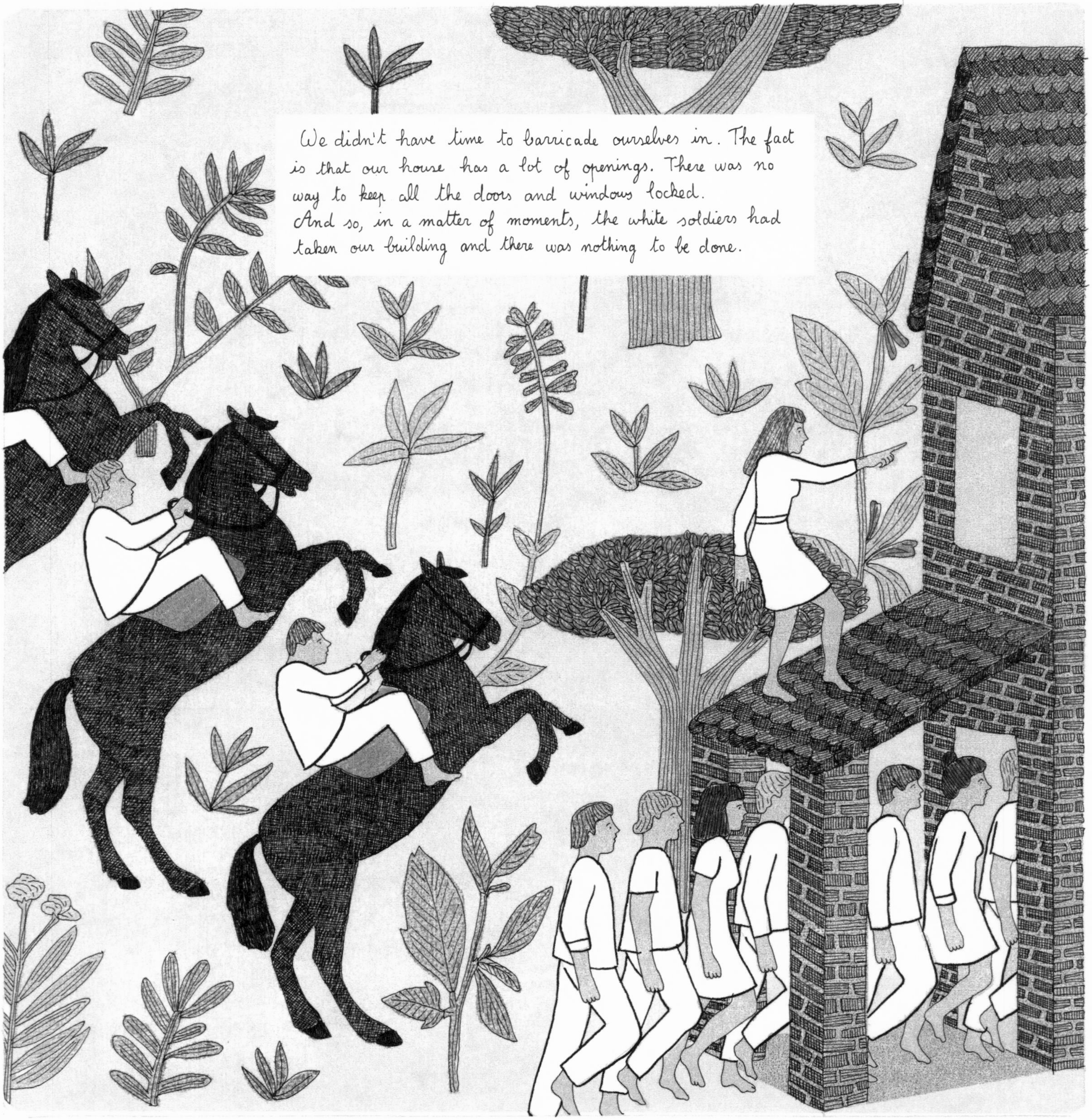
We didn't have time to barricade ourselves in. The fact is that our house has a lot of openings. There was no way to keep all the doors and windows locked.
And so, in a matter of moments, the white soldiers had taken our building and there was nothing to be done.

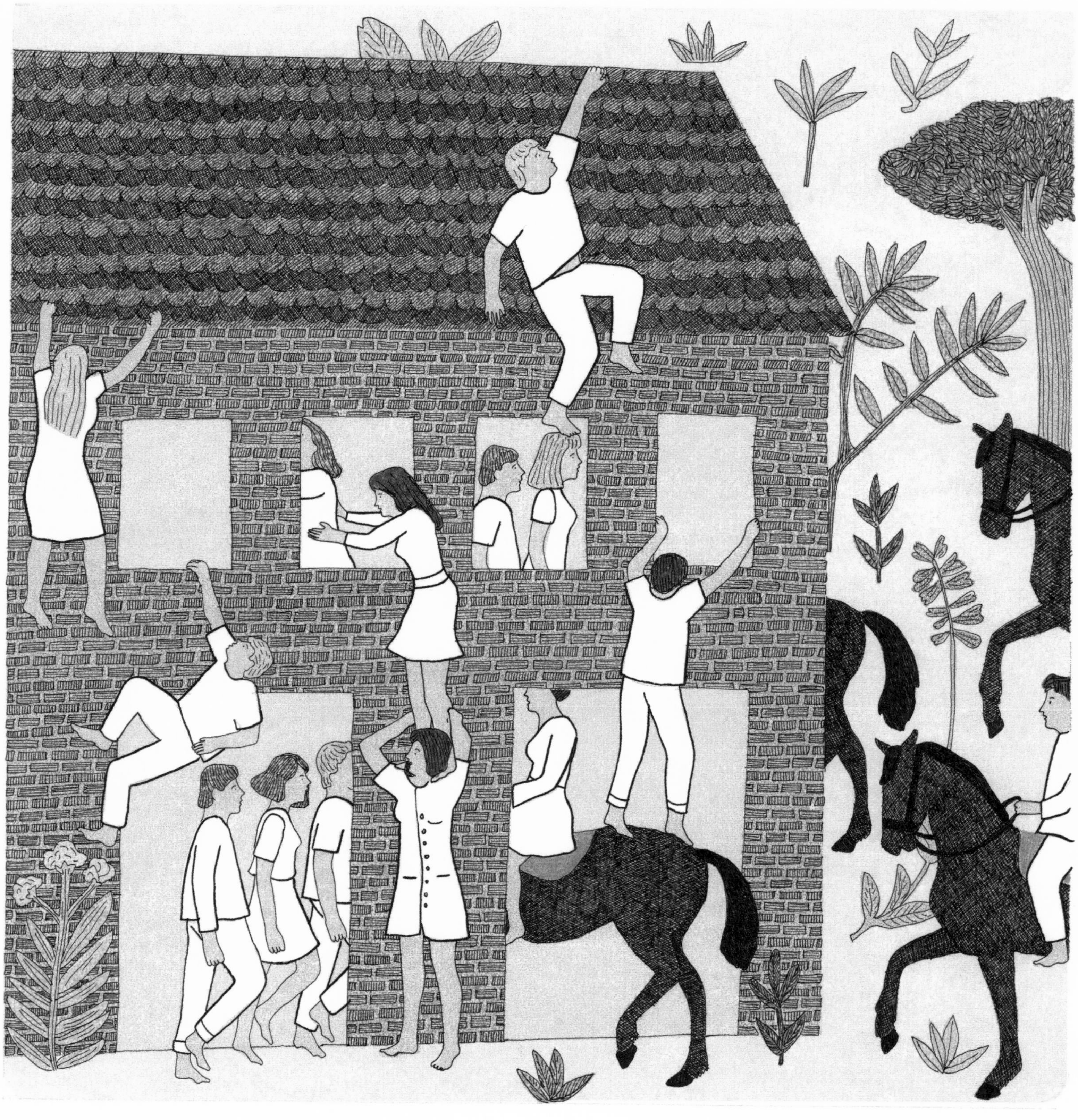

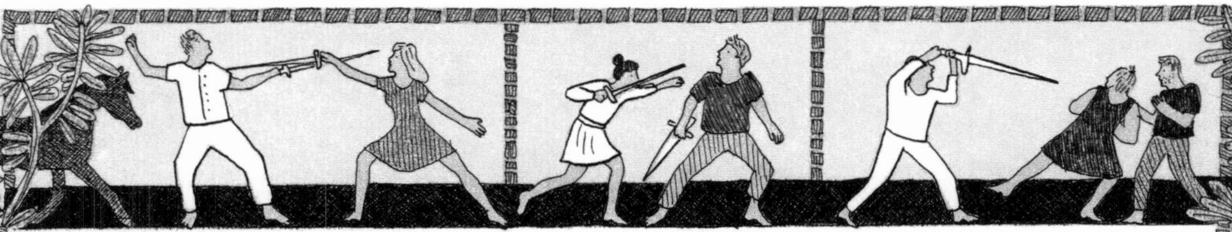

Every room now had a guard, sort of like in museums.
We were being watched.
We were afraid to move, worried we might be judged or simply knock something over. We didn't dare sleep late in the mornings for fear they would think us lazy.
Mom began to eat balanced meals so she wouldn't have to endure hurtful remarks. For that matter we all tried to make a good impression.
That's normal.

We felt as if we were always being filmed, and in the beginning we found it impossible to forget the camera. We paid attention to the clothes we wore and whether they matched, we sat up straight at the table, we remained calm, and above all, we tried to pass for a family that was close-knit and almost too perfect.
No doubt we thought that the white soldiers would eventually leave if we were beyond reproach.
Watching our lives was no more interesting than watching a bad TV show. I couldn't understand how they managed not to fall asleep.
Of course, they worked in shifts. The reveille brigade woke my father in the morning. Fresh troops in the afternoon for his physical therapy. More cavalry in the evening to escort him to bed.

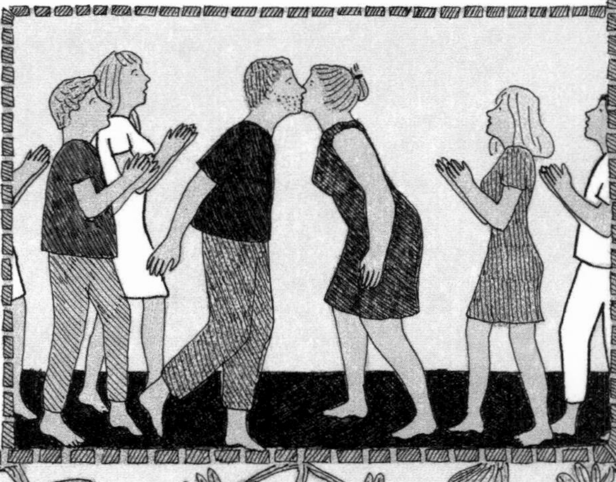

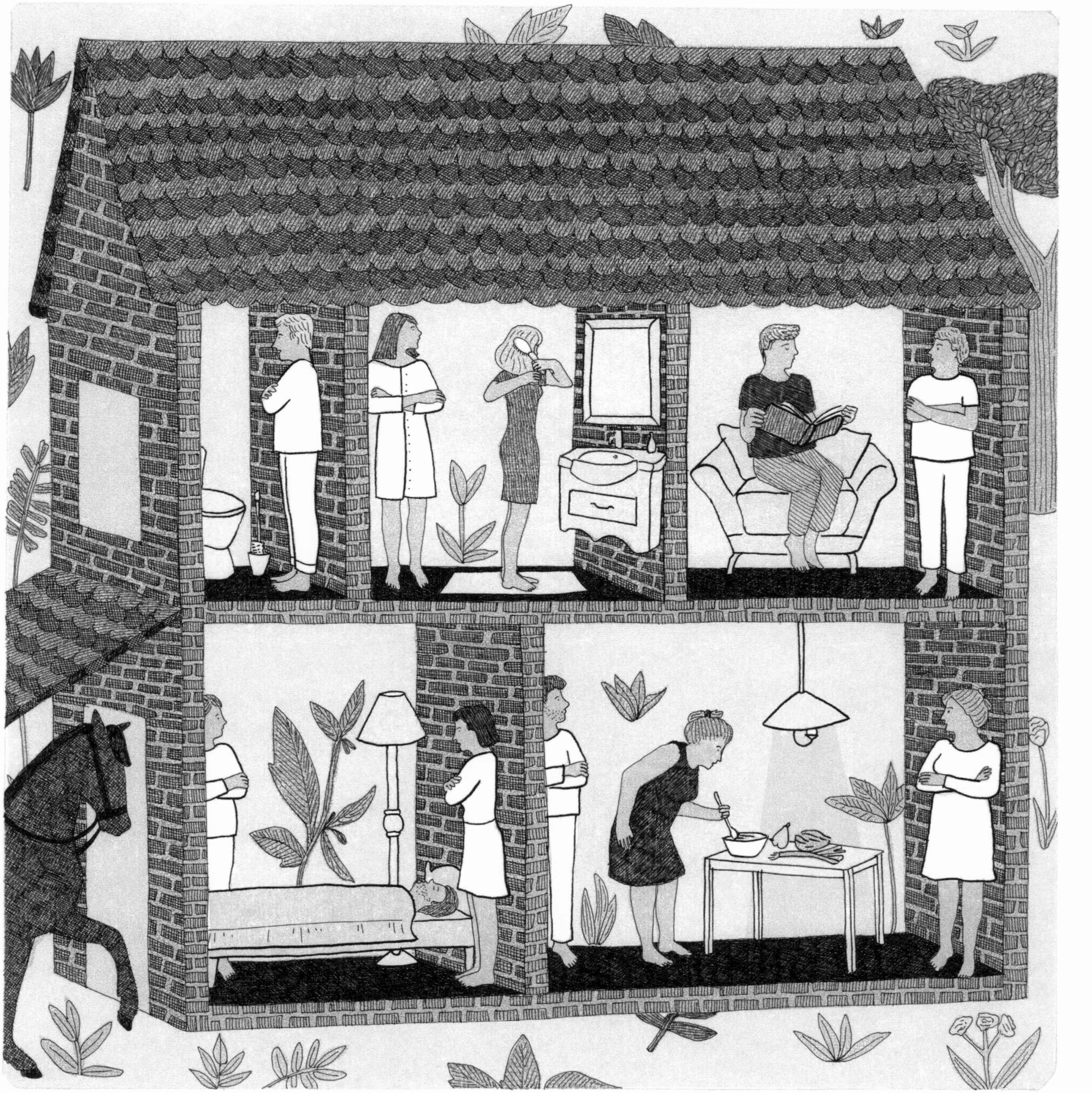

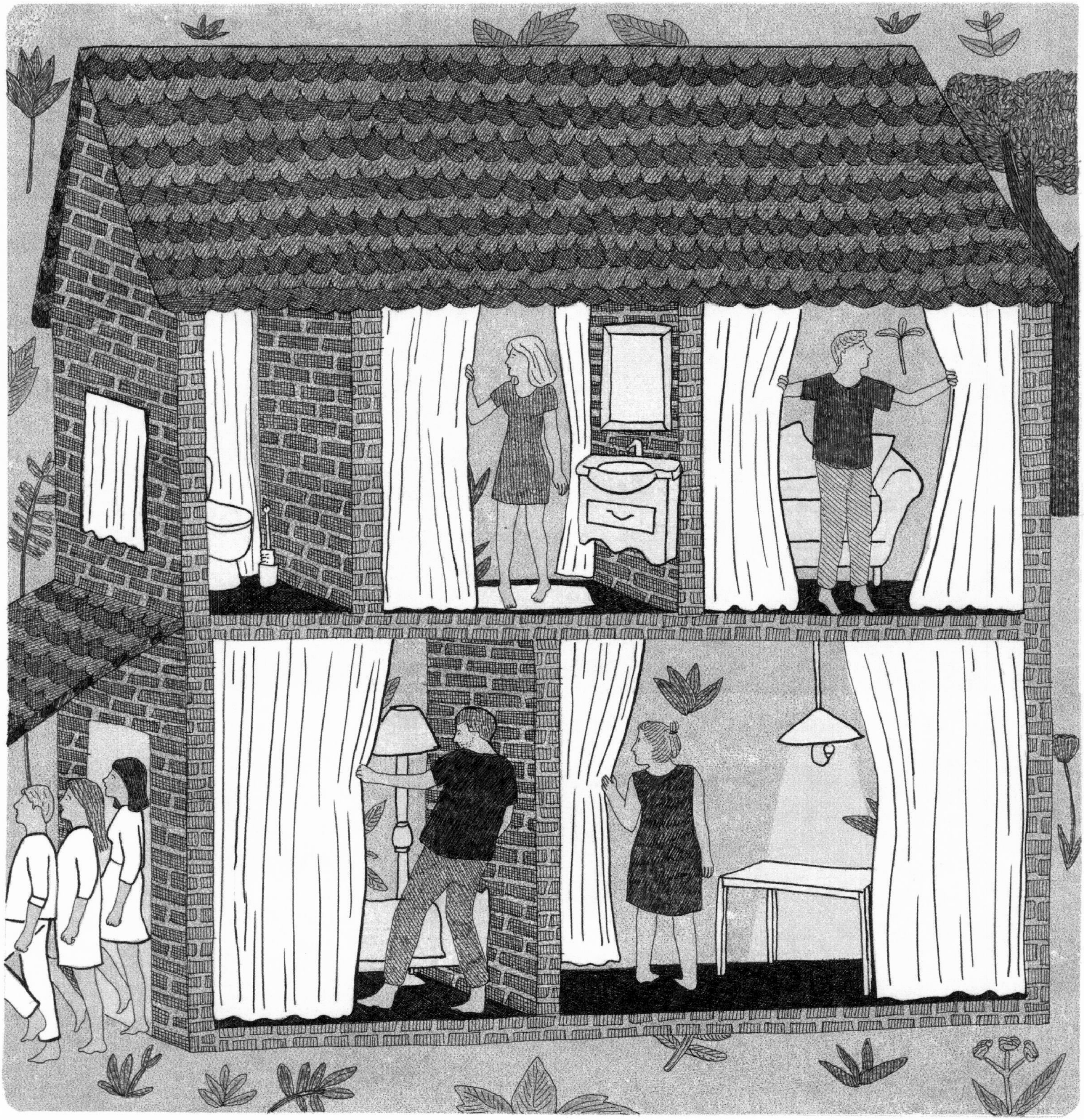

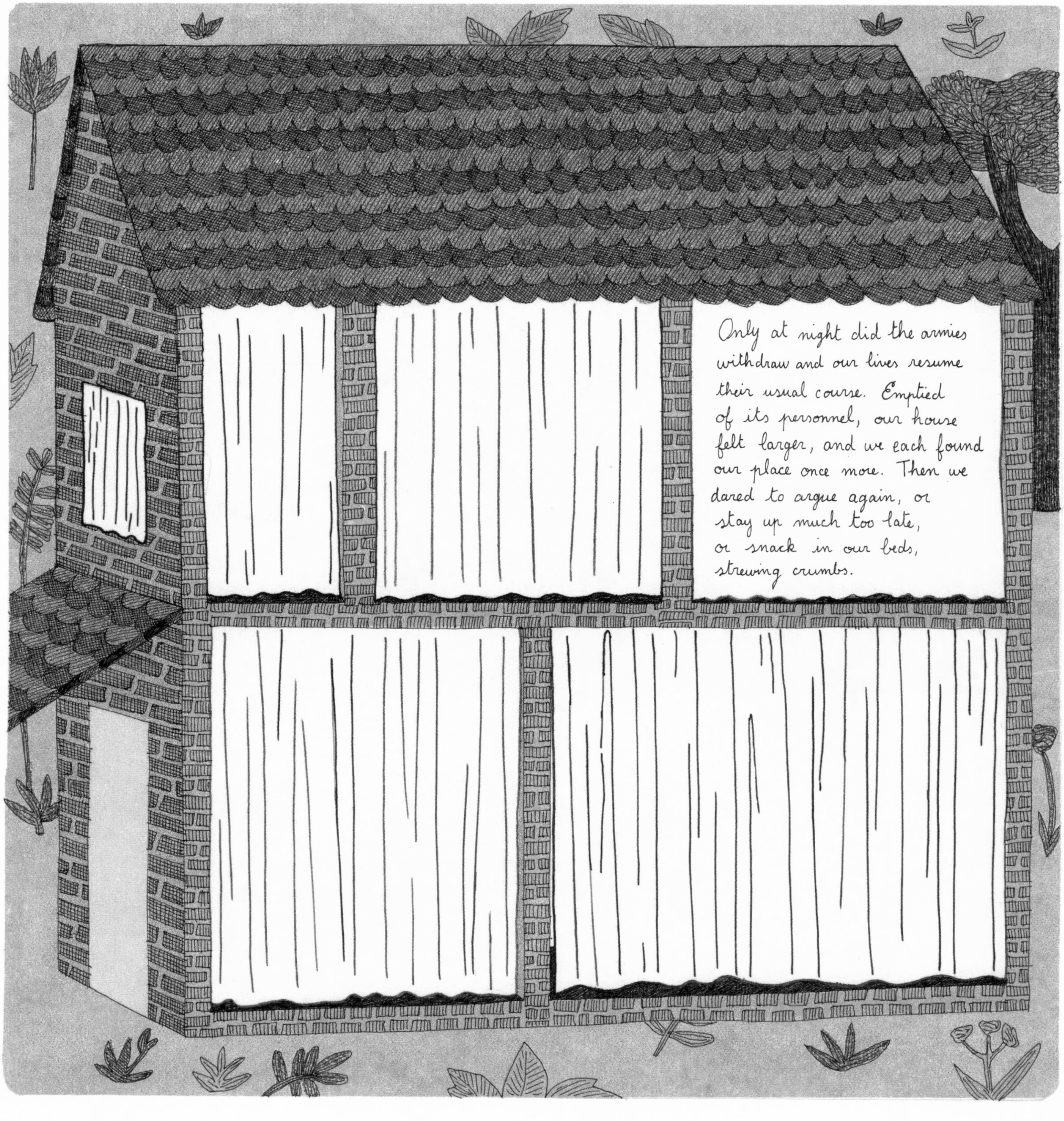
Only at night did the armies withdraw and our lives resume their usual course. Emptied of its personnel, our house felt larger, and we each found our place once more. Then we dared to argue again, or stay up much too late, or snack in our beds, strewing crumbs.

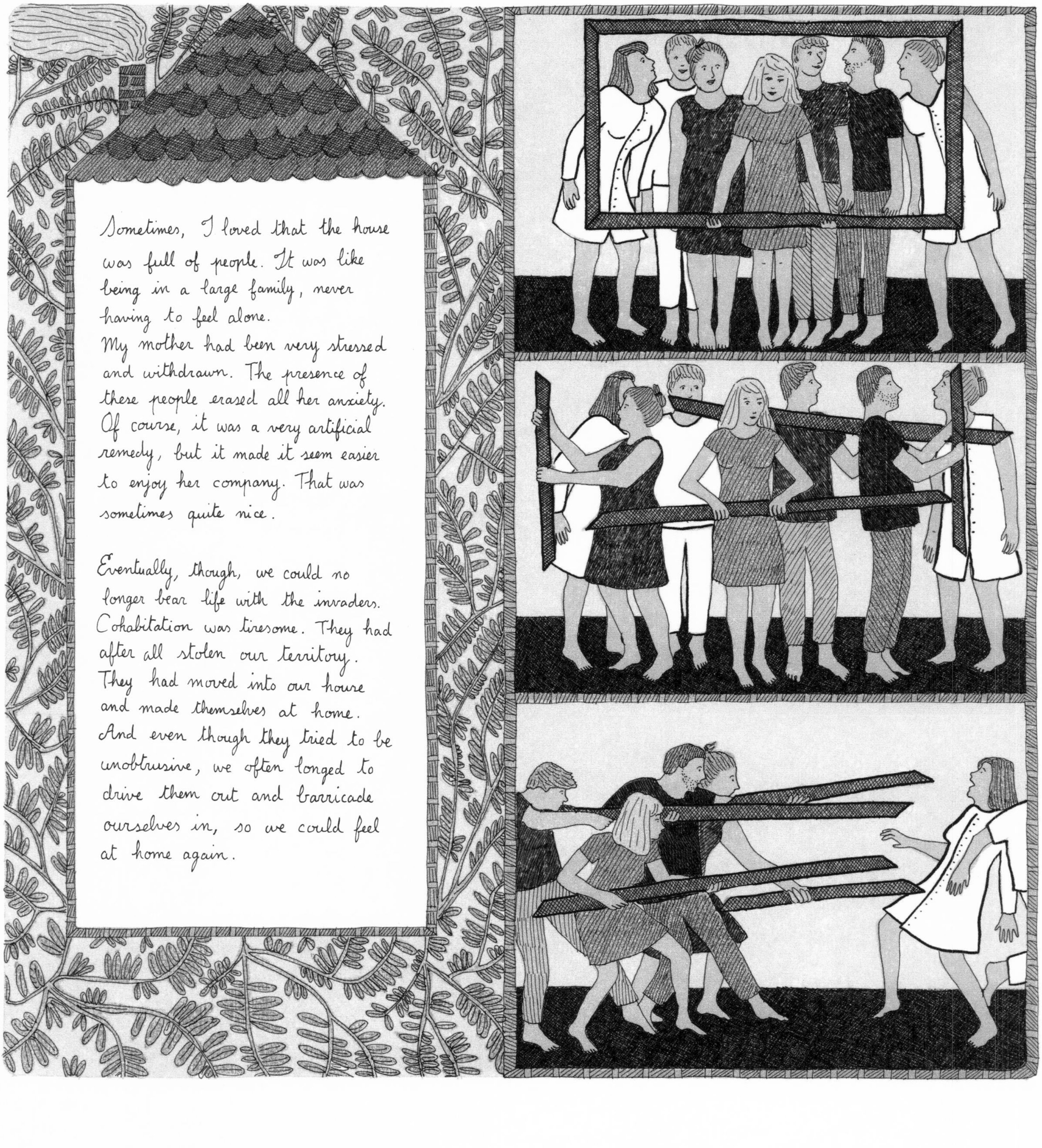
Sometimes, I loved that the house was full of people. It was like being in a large family, never having to feel alone.
My mother had been very stressed and withdrawn. The presence of these people erased all her anxiety. Of course, it was a very artificial remedy, but it made it seem easier to enjoy her company. That was sometimes quite nice.
Eventually, though, we could no longer bear life with the invaders. Cohabitation was tiresome. They had after all stolen our territory. They had moved into our house and made themselves at home. And even though they tried to be unobtrusive, we often longed to drive them out and barricade ourselves in, so we could feel at home again.

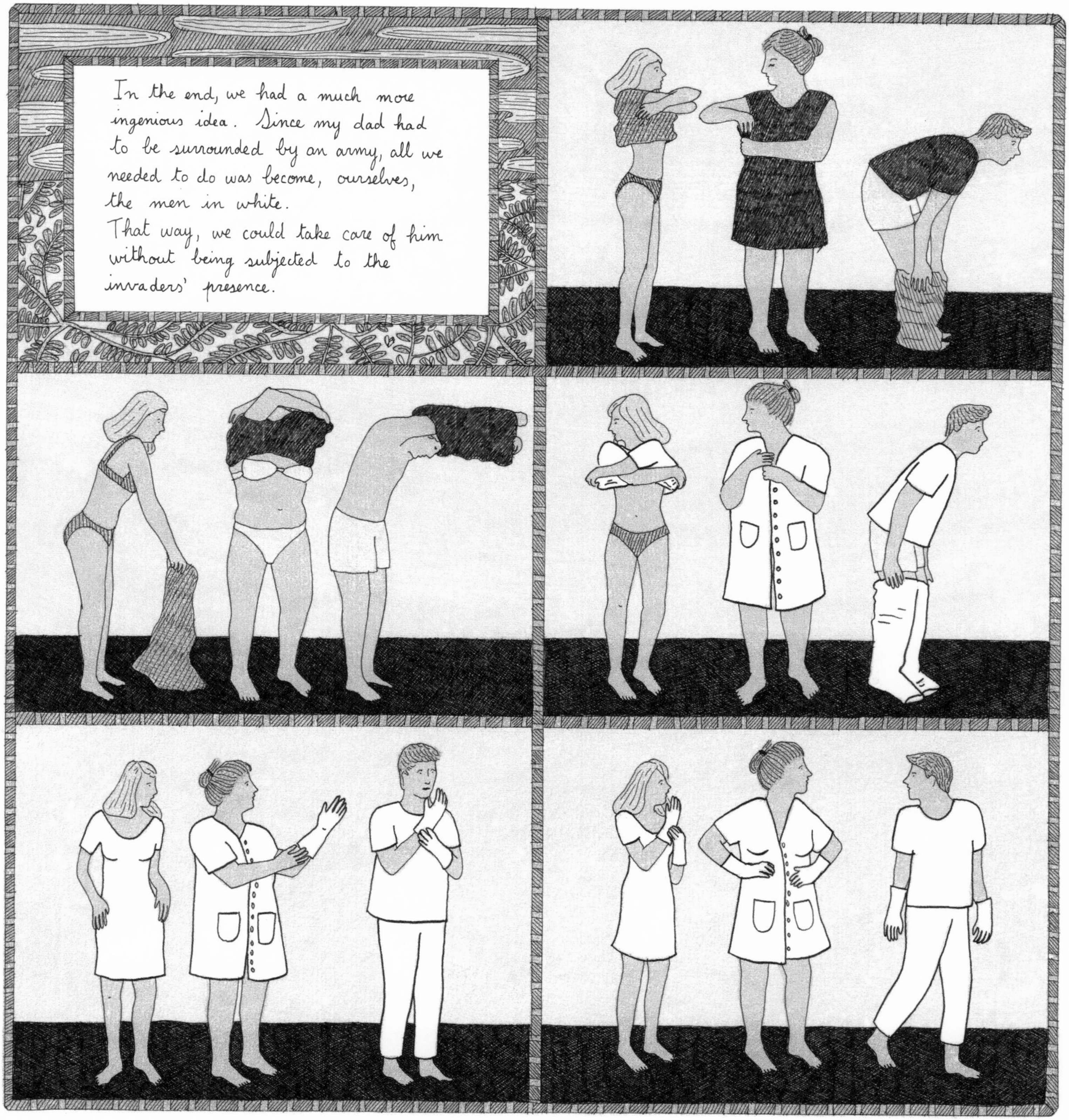
In the end, we had a much more ingenious idea. Since my dad had to be surrounded by an army, all we needed to do was become, ourselves, the men in white.
That way, we could take care of him without being subjected to the invaders' presence.

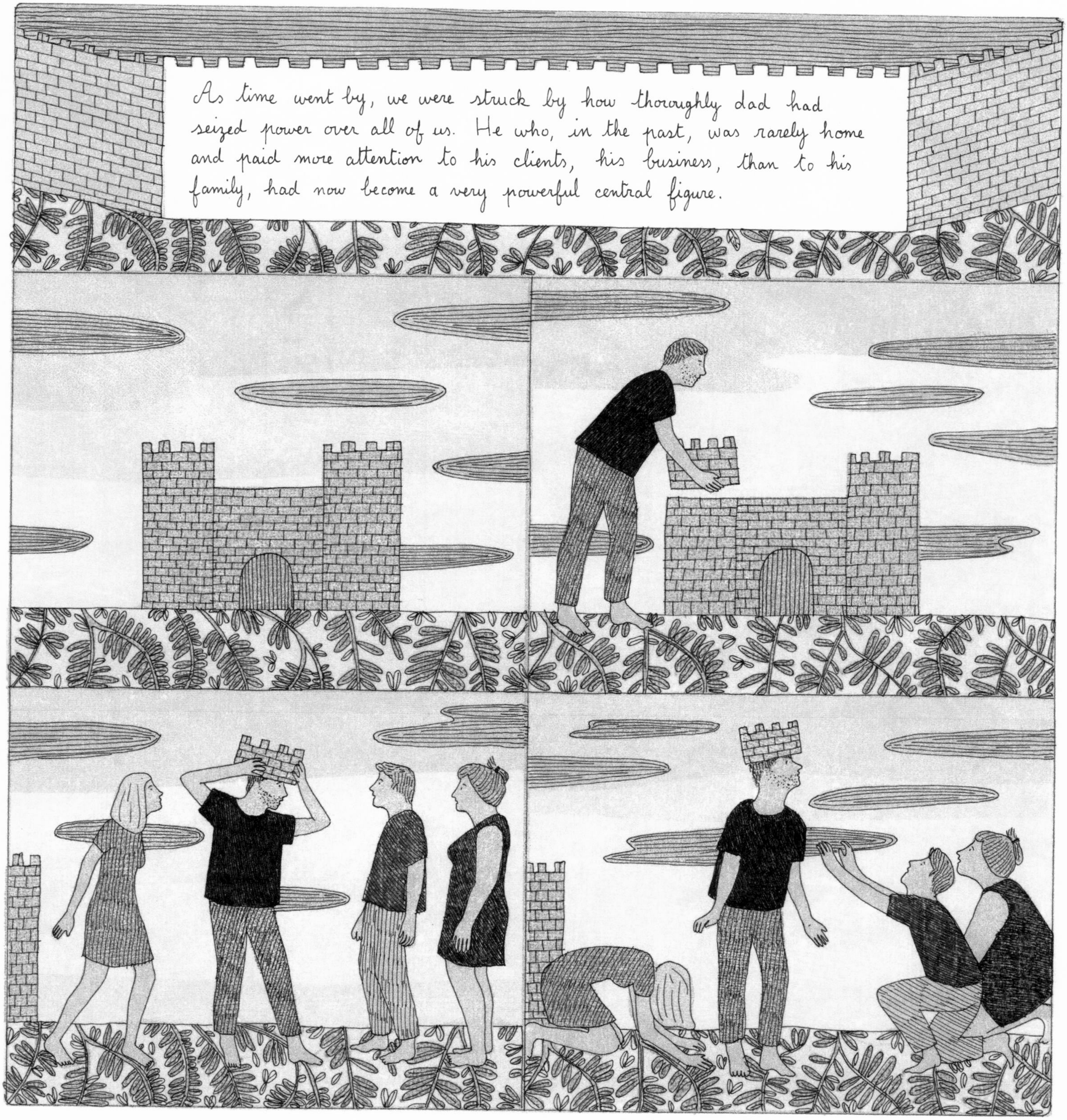
As time went by, we were struck by how thoroughly dad had seized power over all of us. He who, in the past, was rarely home and paid more attention to his clients, his business, than to his family, had now become a very powerful central figure.

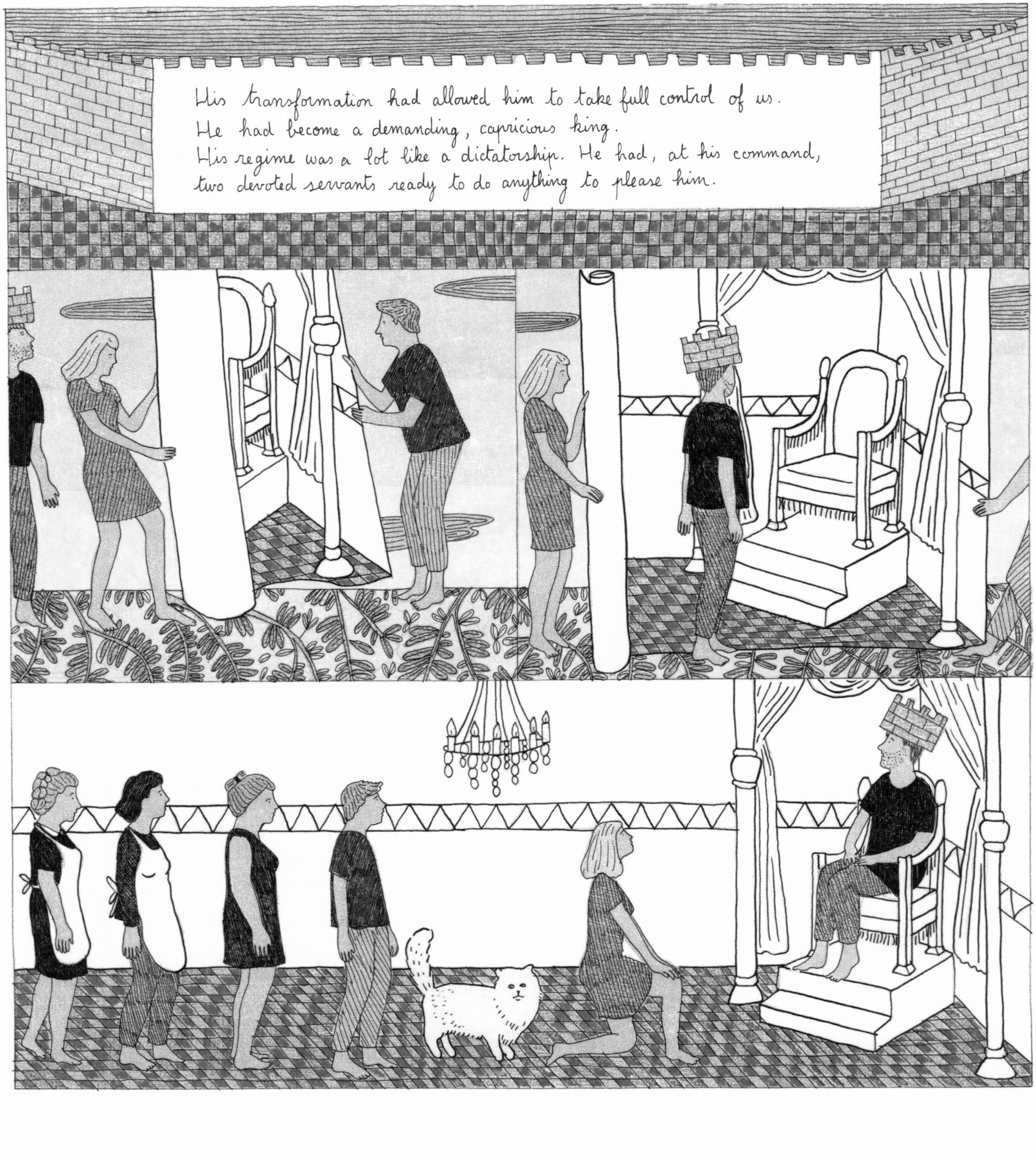
His transformation had allowed him to take full control of us.
He had become a demanding, capricious king.
His regime was a lot like a dictatorship. He had, at his command,
two devoted servants ready to do anything to please him.

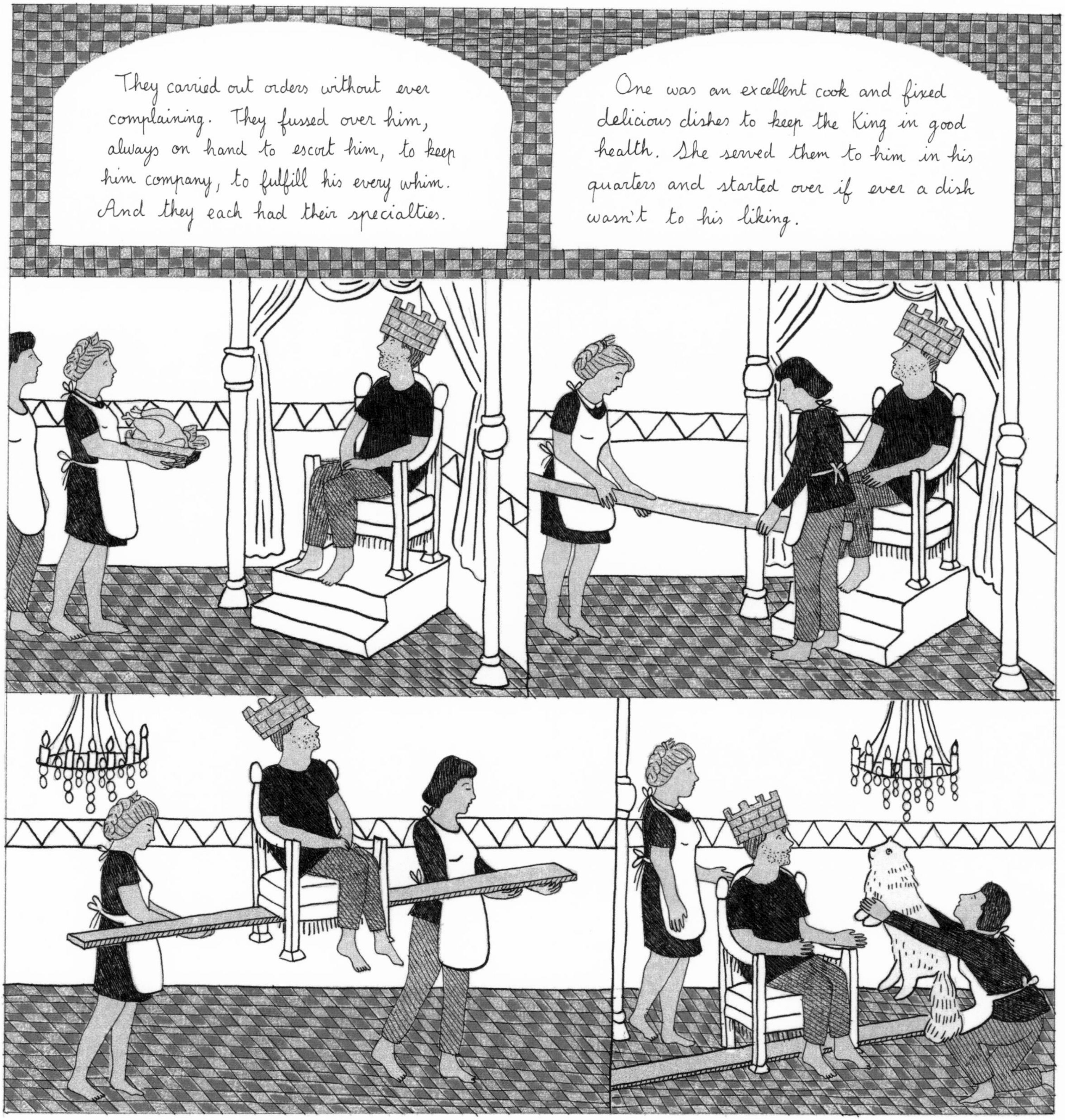
They carried out orders without ever complaining. They fussed over him, always on hand to escort him, to keep him company, to fulfill his every whim. And they each had their specialties.
One was an excellent cook and fixed delicious dishes to keep the King in good health. She served them to him in his quarters and started over if ever a dish wasn't to his liking.

The other was both the gardener and delightful company. She maintained the grounds around our house according to my father's instructions and kept him informed about the goings-on in town. The King loved to hear about his friends.

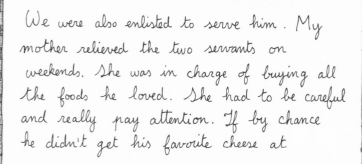

We were also enlisted to serve him. My mother relieved the two servants on weekends. She was in charge of buying all the foods he loved. She had to be careful and really pay attention. If by chance he didn't get his favorite cheese at dinner, he'd fly into a rage. It was also my mother who watched over the King while we slept. His bed wasn't far from hers and she was used to being awoken in the night to take care of His Majesty. He had no qualms about disturbing her.

My brother was the coffee expert. Several times each day he waited on the King: he required one and a half sugars, and his schedule had to be strictly followed. My brother understood and was happy to do it.

As for me, I was entrusted with tasks related to the King's appearance. It was of course an honor to be his designated stylist and to be in charge of his toilette. He liked his hair very short on the sides, a little longer on top. I worked hard at it because I knew what a privilege it was. After handing him the mirror, I'd wait, trembling, for his verdict. Mostly, he would be pleased, apart from a few details. Then I would do a bit more around the ears, prune his eyebrows, shave his face with a faux professionalism, until he thought it was perfect.

The King's days were regular as clockwork. If anyone tried to make a slight change in his schedule, he got furious. That's how it often is. People with too much power get temperamental and capricious. You can't get mad at them for it — they don't realize, they lose touch.

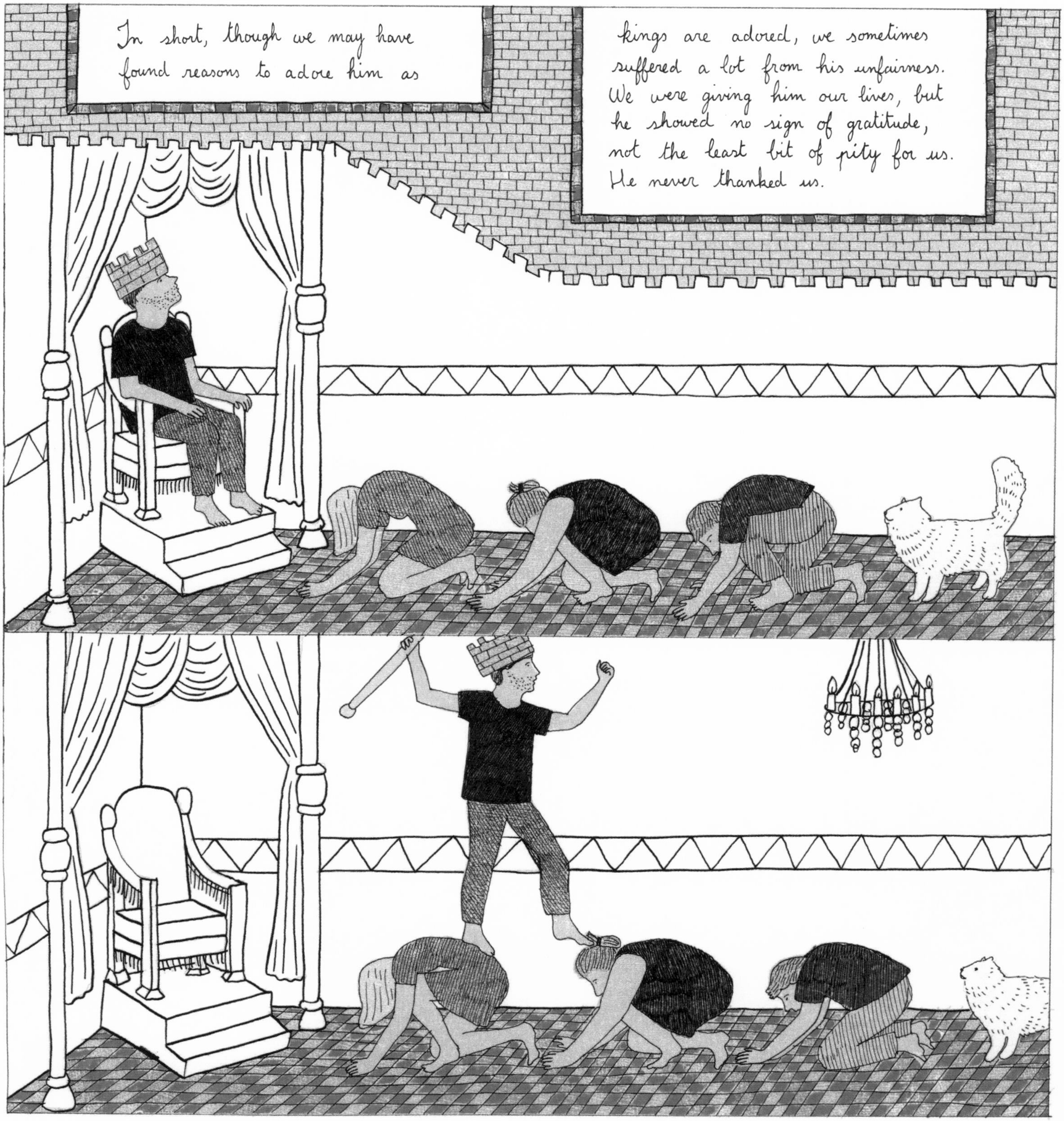
In short, though we may have found reasons to adore him as
kings are adored, we sometimes suffered a lot from his unfairness. We were giving him our lives, but he showed no sign of gratitude, not the least bit of pity for us. He never thanked us.

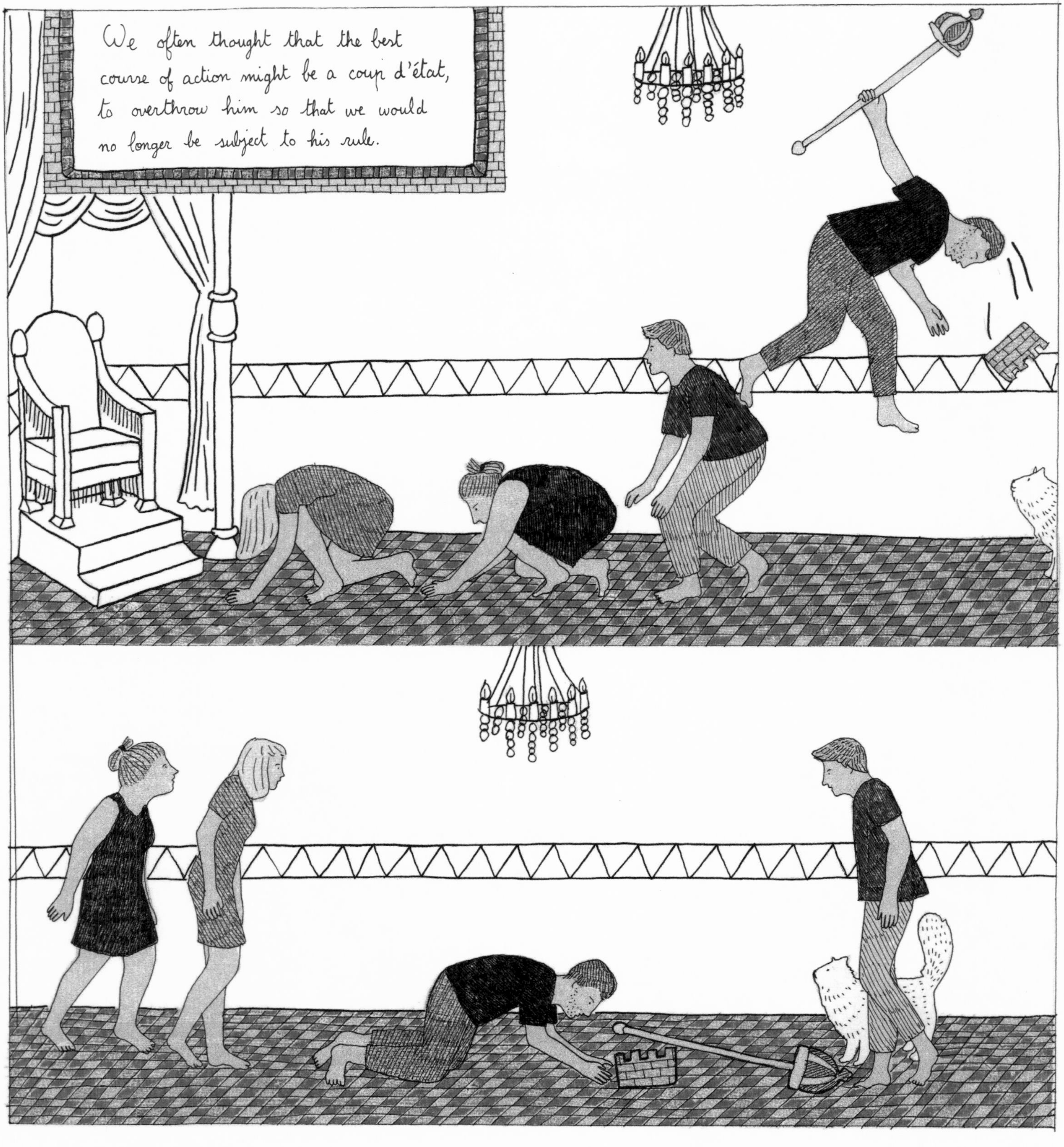
We often thought that the best course of action might be a coup d'état, to overthrow him so that we would no longer be subject to his rule.

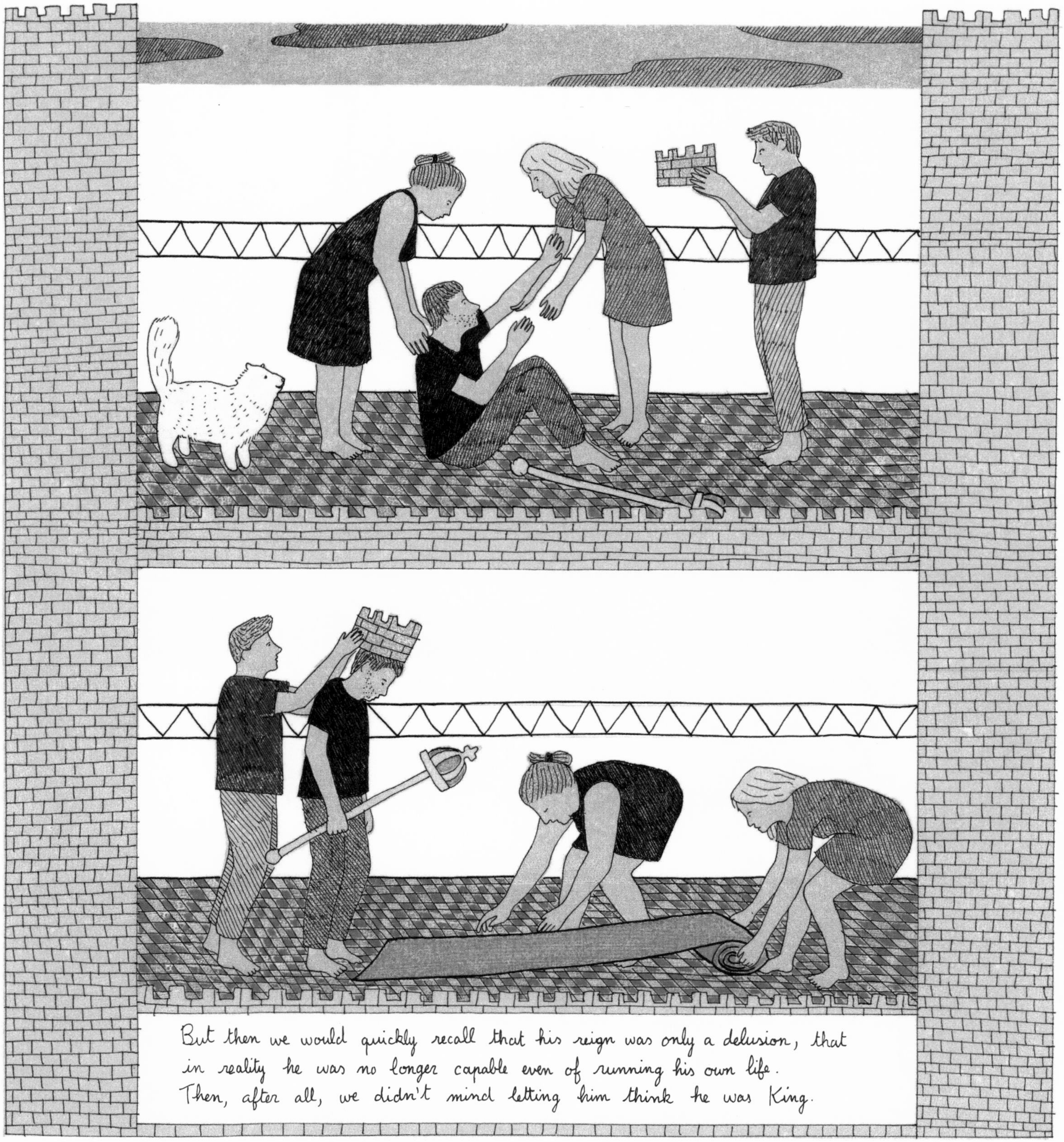
But then we would quickly recall that his reign was only a delusion, that in reality he was no longer capable even of running his own life.
Then, after all, we didn't mind letting him think he was King.

III

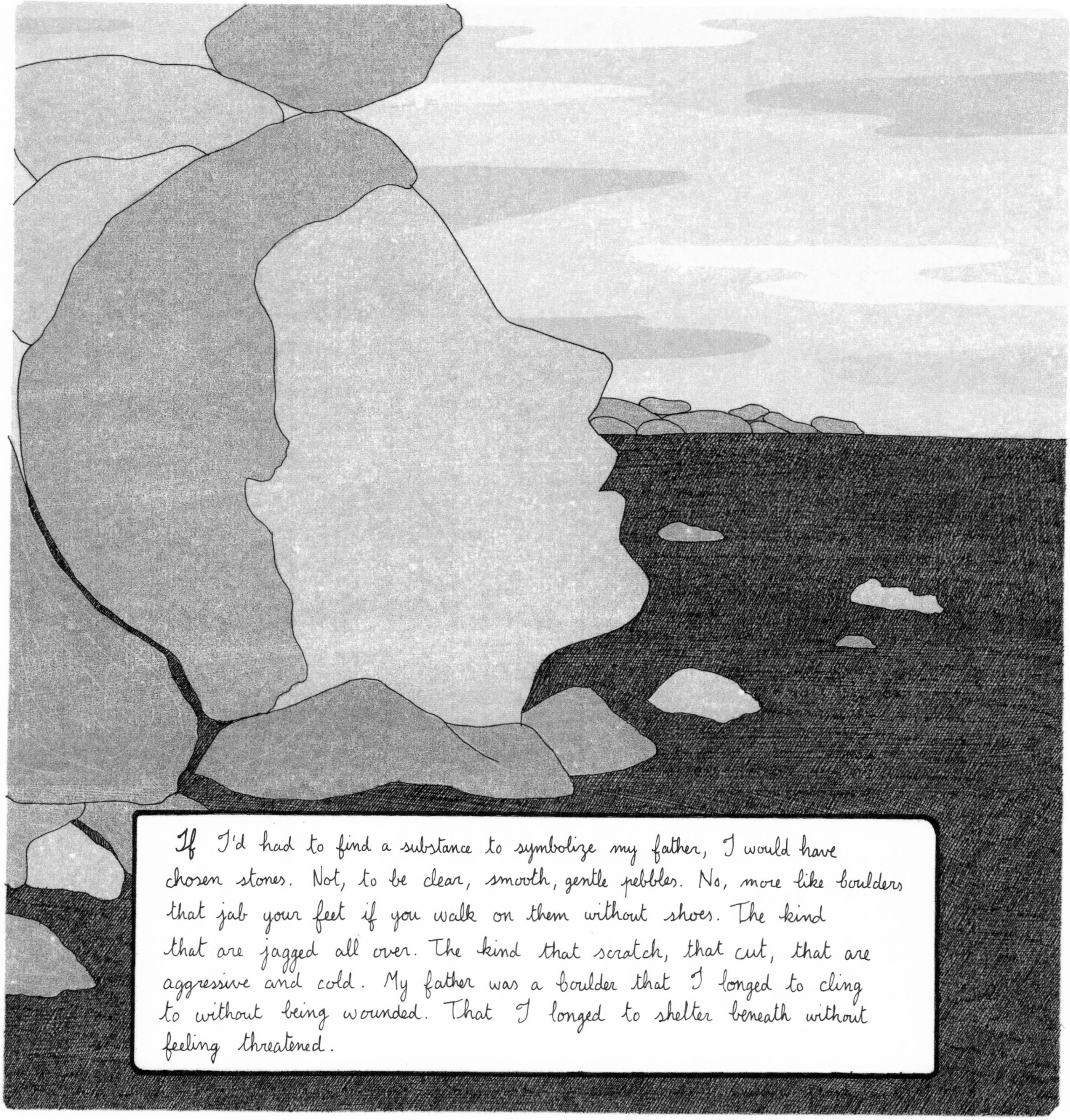
If I'd had to find a substance to symbolize my father, I would have chosen stones. Not, to be clear, smooth, gentle pebbles. No, more like boulders that jab your feet if you walk on them without shoes. The kind that are jagged all over. The kind that scratch, that cut, that are aggressive and cold. My father was a boulder that I longed to cling to without being wounded. That I longed to shelter beneath without feeling threatened.

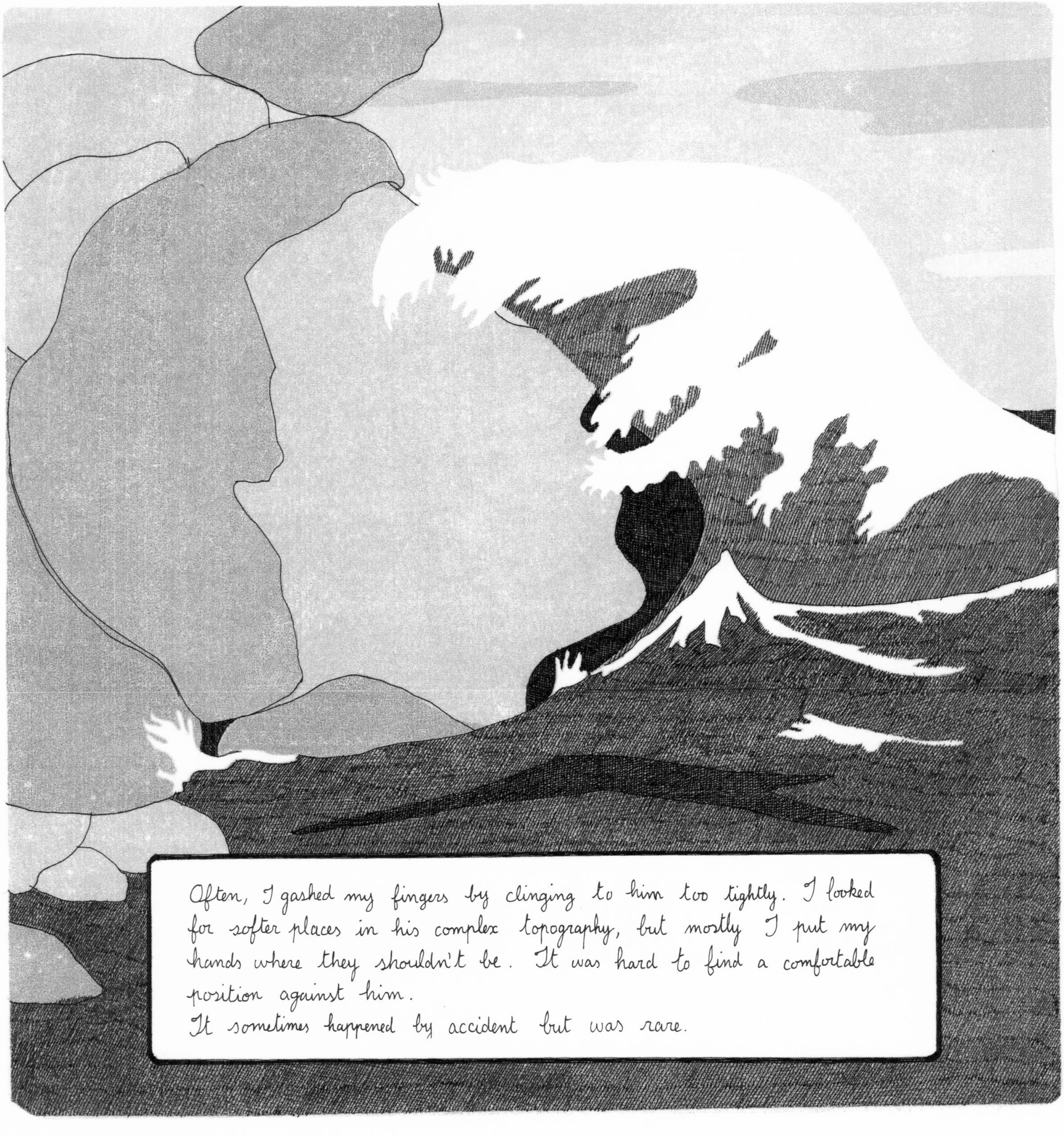
Often, I gashed my fingers by clinging to him too tightly. I looked for softer places in his complex topography, but mostly I put my hands where they shouldn't be. It was hard to find a comfortable position against him.
It sometimes happened by accident but was rare.

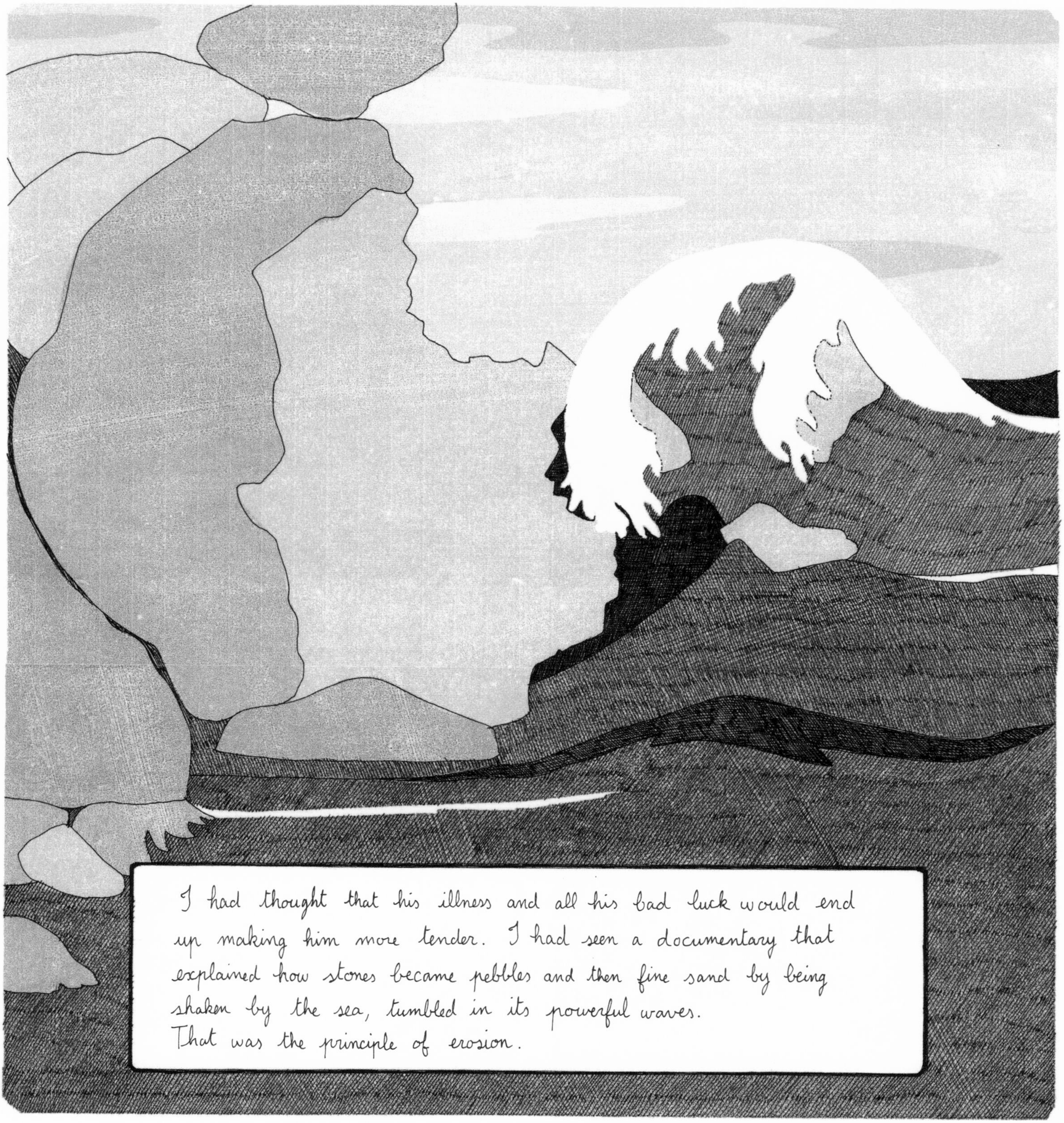
I had thought that his illness and all his bad luck would end up making him more tender. I had seen a documentary that explained how stones became pebbles and then fine sand by being shaken by the sea, tumbled in its powerful waves.
That was the principle of erosion.

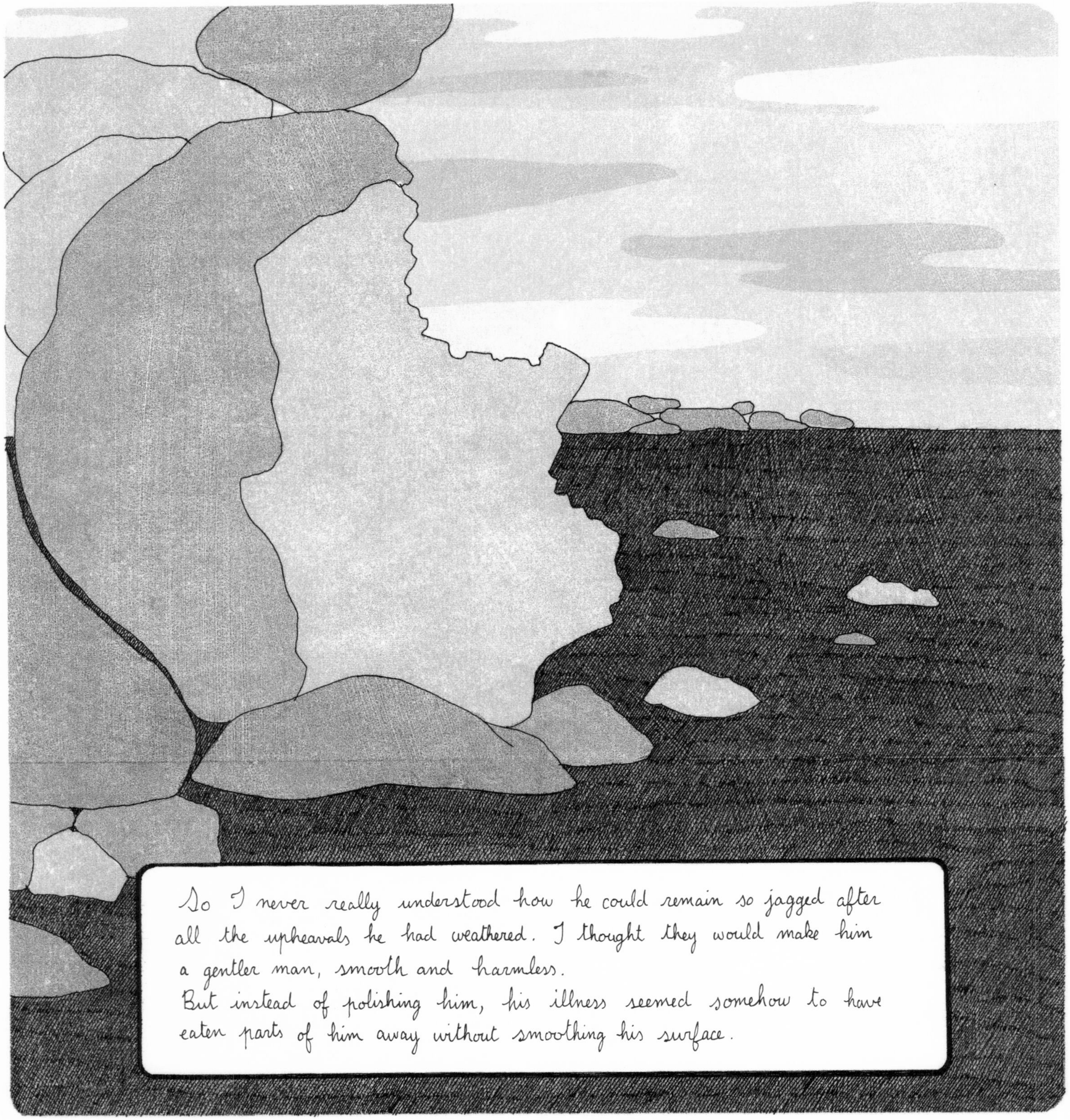
So I never really understood how he could remain so jagged after all the upheavals he had weathered. I thought they would make him a gentler man, smooth and harmless.
But instead of polishing him, his illness seemed somehow to have eaten parts of him away without smoothing his surface.

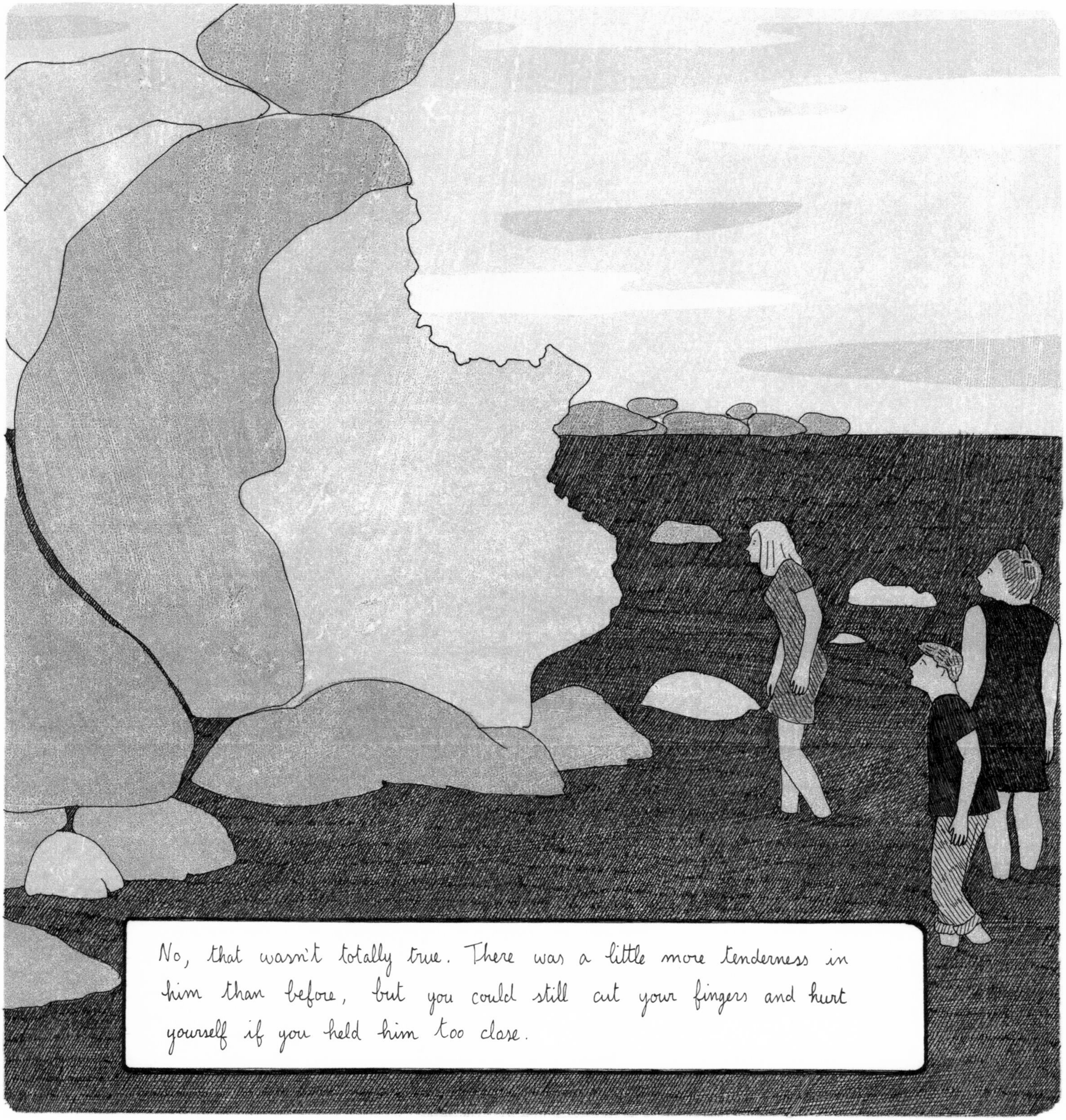
No, that wasn't totally true. There was a little more tenderness in him than before, but you could still cut your fingers and hurt yourself if you held him too close.

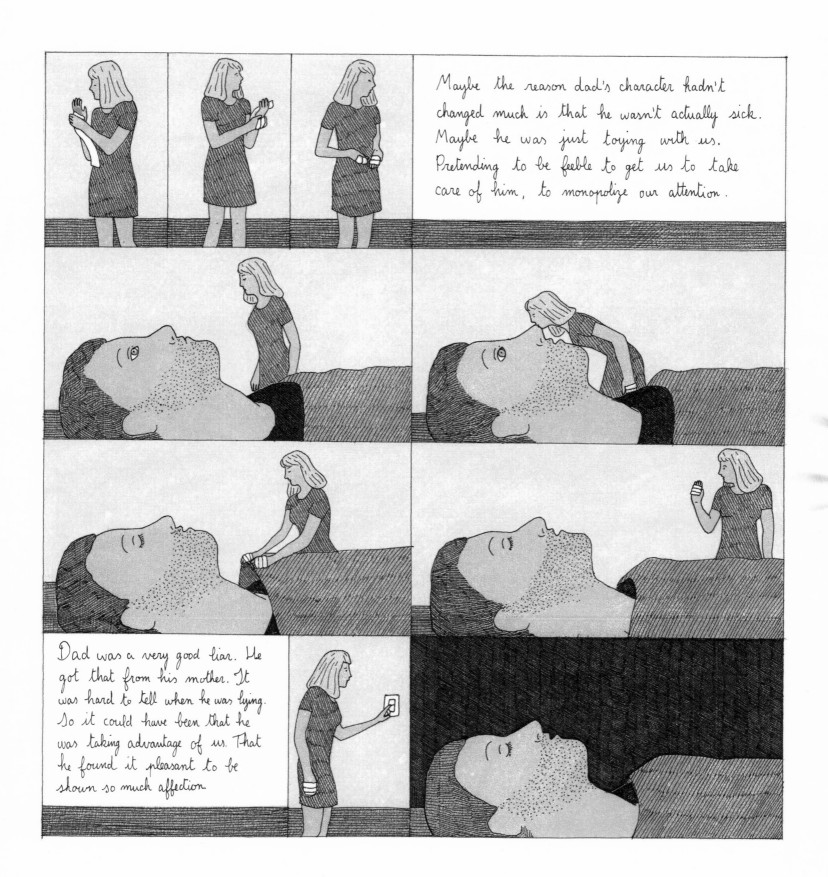

Maybe the reason dad's character hadn't changed much is that he wasn't actually sick. Maybe he was just toying with us. Pretending to be feeble to get us to take care of him, to monopolize our attention.

Dad was a very good liar. He got that from his mother. It was hard to tell when he was lying. So it could have been that he was taking advantage of us. That he found it pleasant to be shown so much affection.

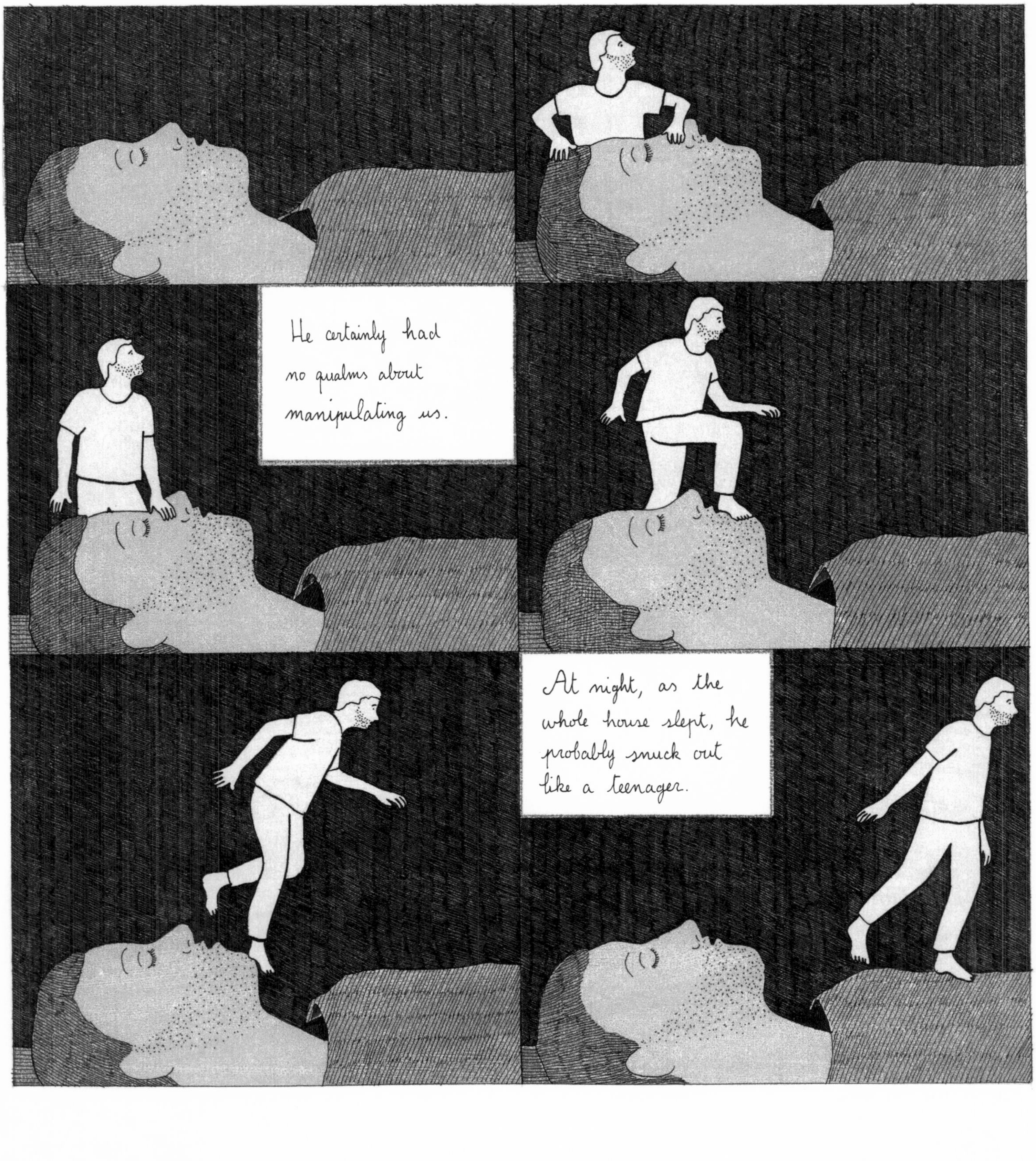
He certainly had no qualms about manipulating us.
At night, as the whole house slept, he probably snuck out like a teenager.

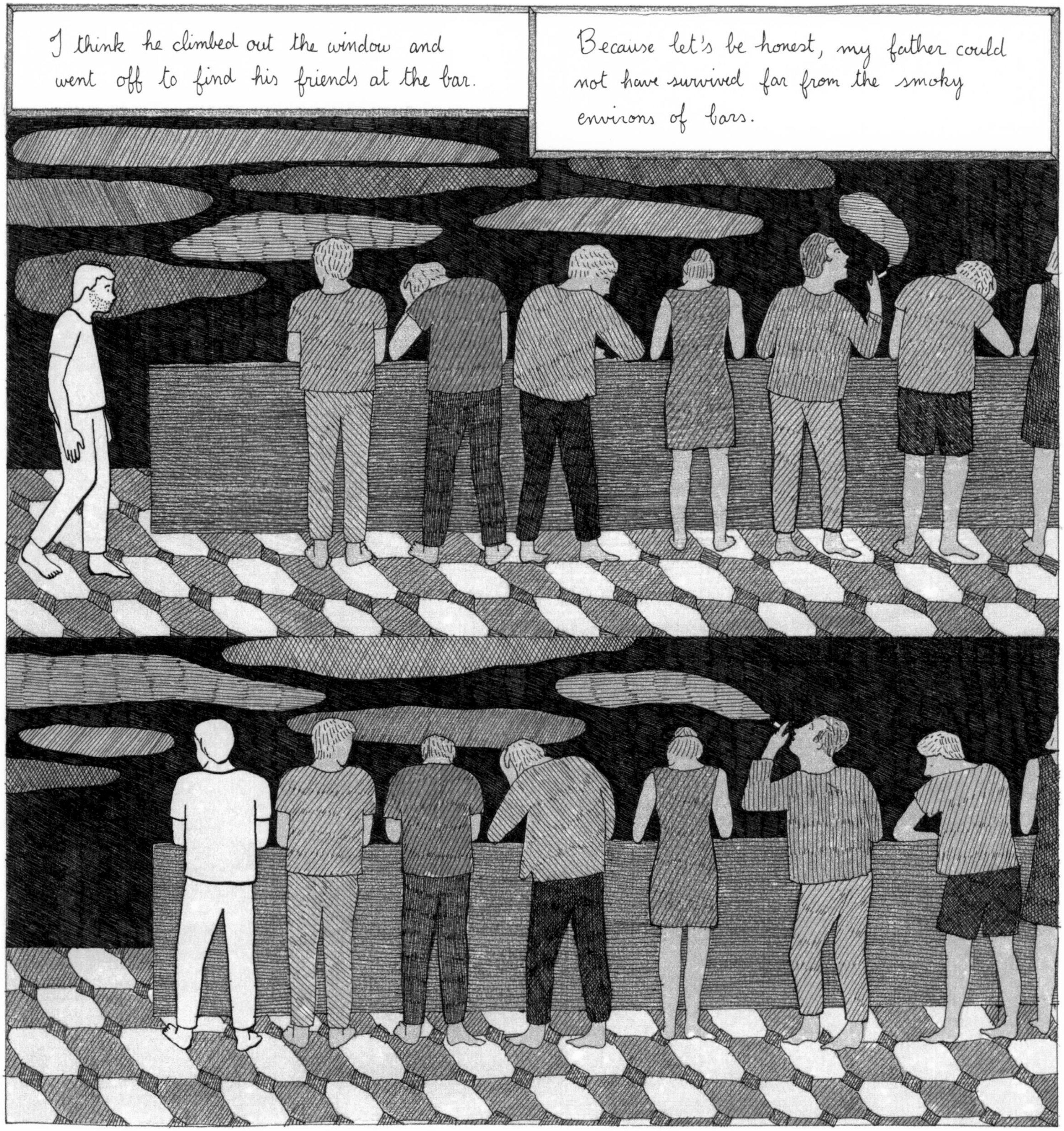
I think he climbed out the window and went off to find his friends at the bar.
Because let's be honest, my father could not have survived far from the smoky environs of bars.

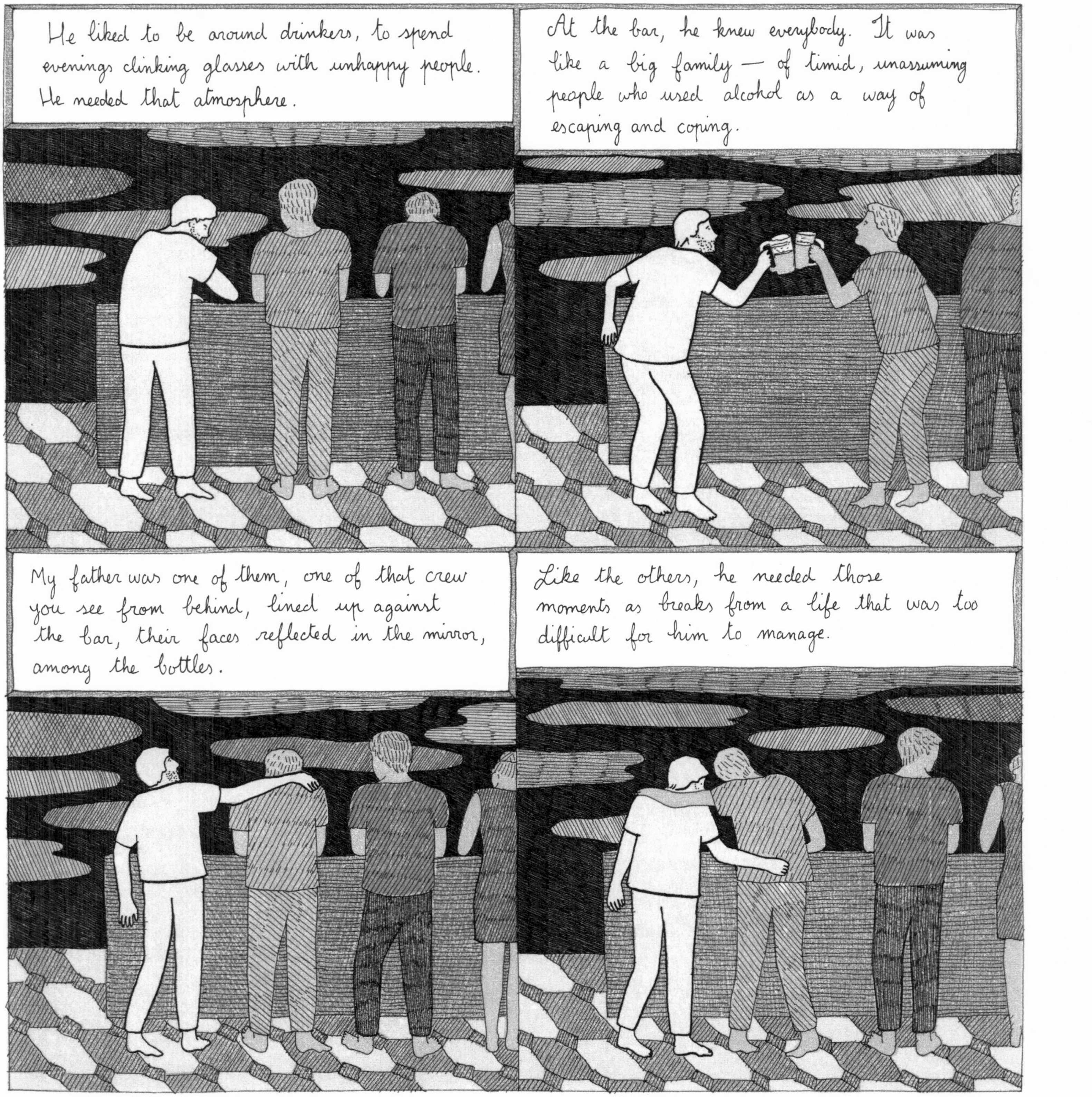
He liked to be around drinkers, to spend evenings clinking glasses with unhappy people. He needed that atmosphere.
At the bar, he knew everybody. It was like a big family — of timid, unassuming people who used alcohol as a way of escaping and coping.
My father was one of them, one of that crew you see from behind, lined up against the bar, their faces reflected in the mirror, among the bottles.
Like the others, he needed those moments as breaks from a life that was too difficult for him to manage.

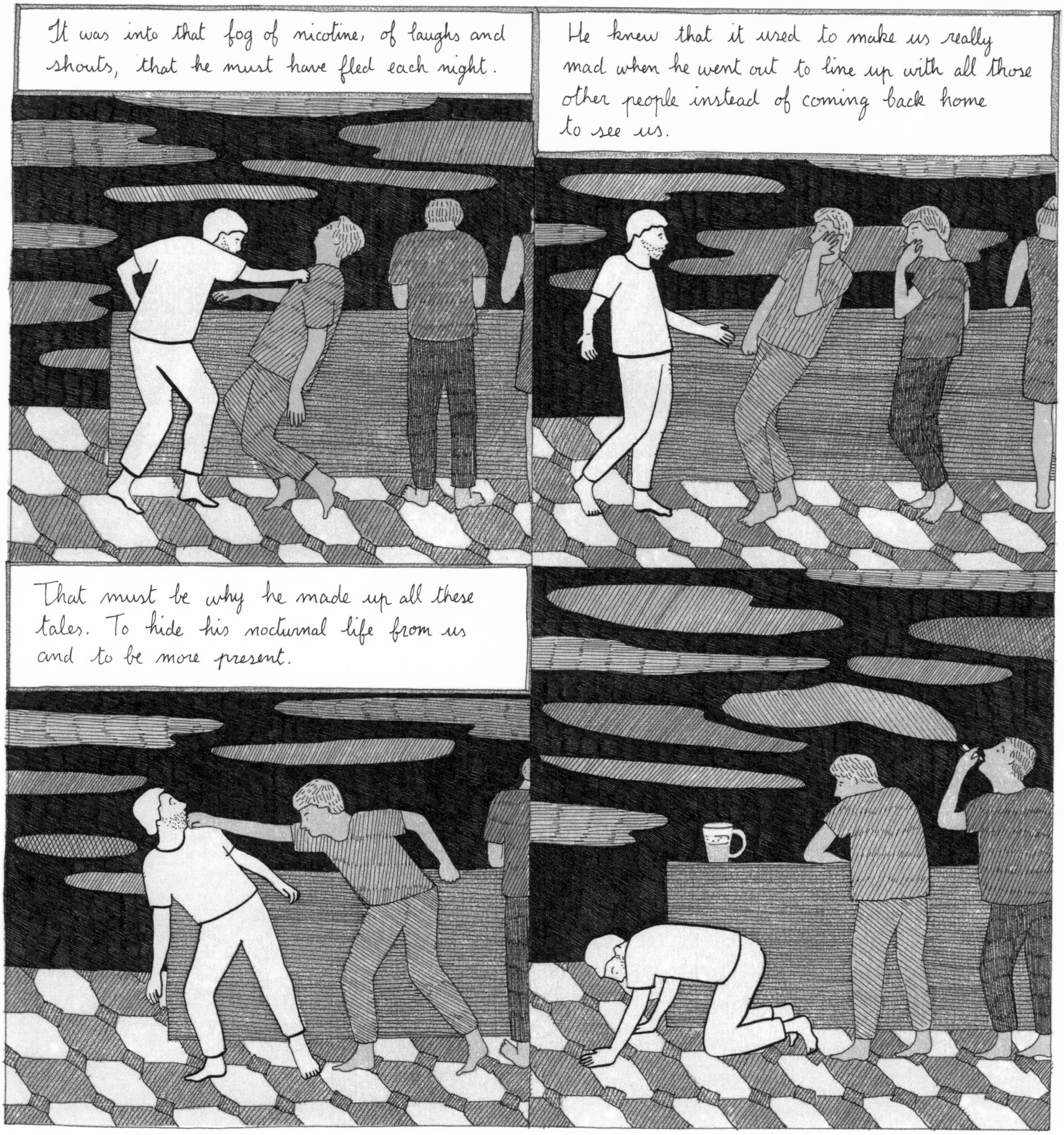
It was into that fog of nicotine, of laughs and shouts, that he must have fled each night.
He knew that it used to make us really mad when he went out to line up with all those other people instead of coming back home to see us.
That must be why he made up all these tales. To hide his nocturnal life from us and to be more present.

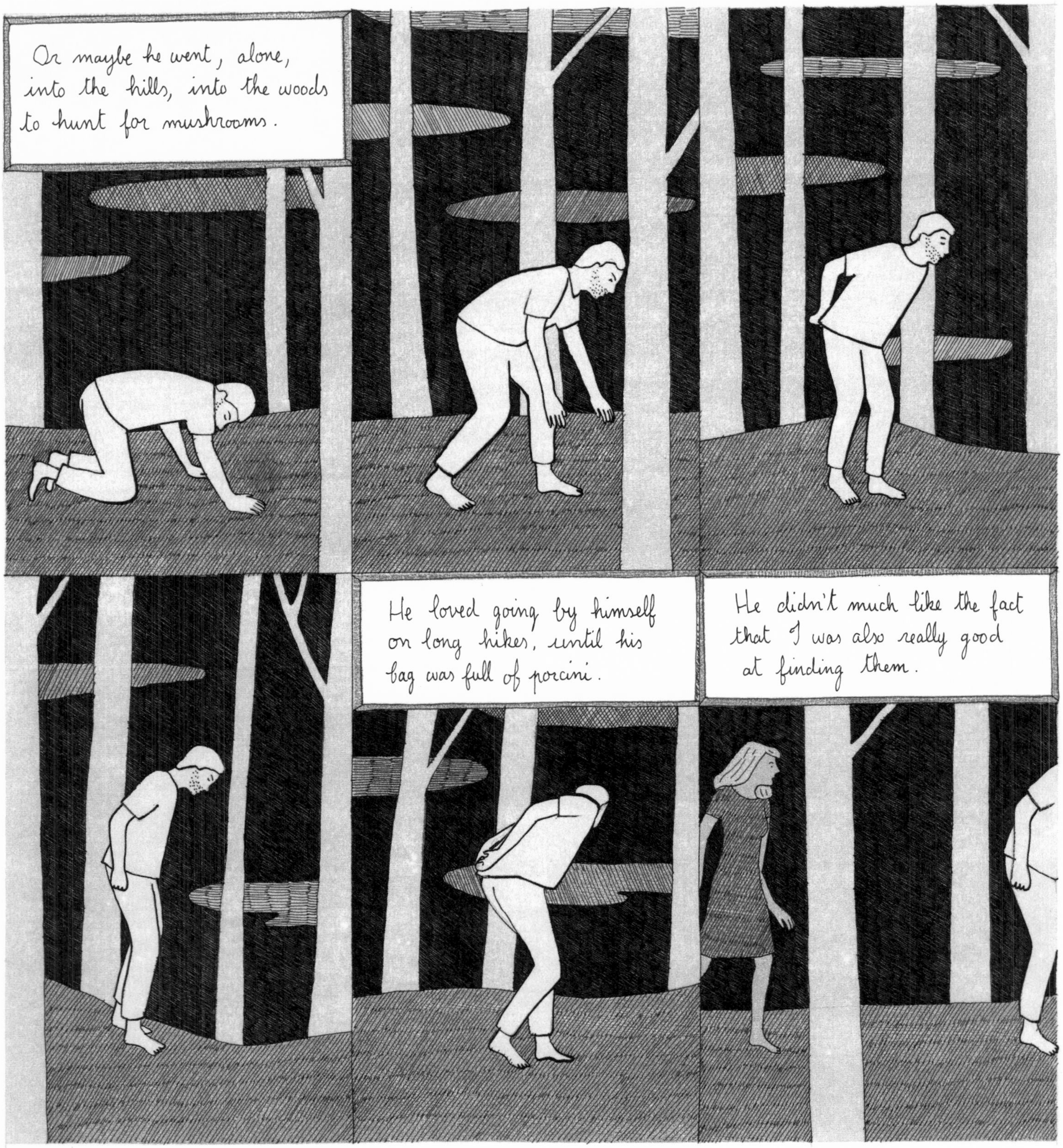
Or maybe he went, alone, into the hills, into the woods to hunt for mushrooms.
He loved going by himself on long hikes, until his bag was full of porcini.
He didn't much like the fact that I was also really good at finding them.

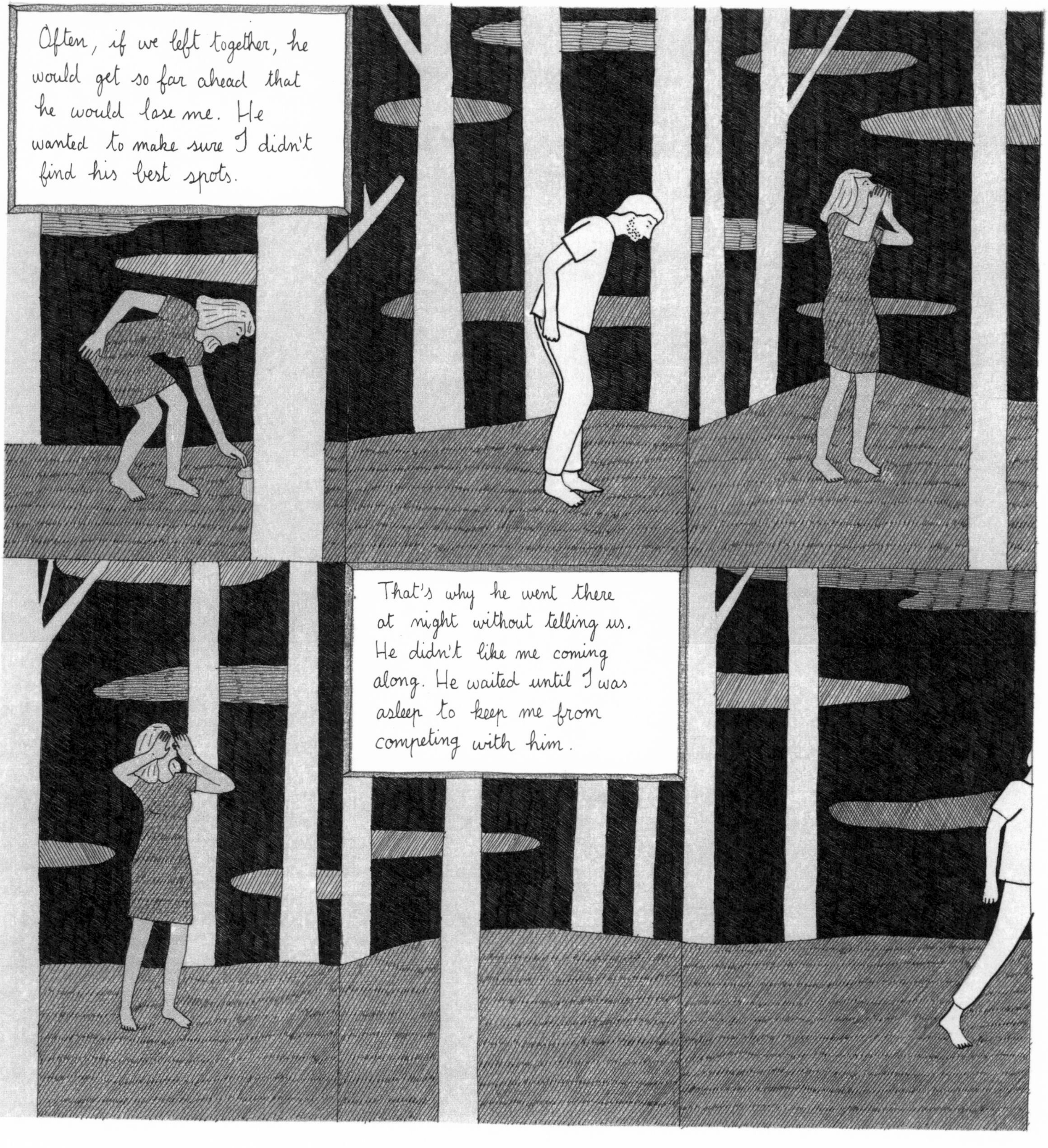
Often, if we left together, he would get so far ahead that he would lose me. He wanted to make sure I didn't find his best spots.
That's why he went there at night without telling us. He didn't like me coming along. He waited until I was asleep to keep me from competing with him.

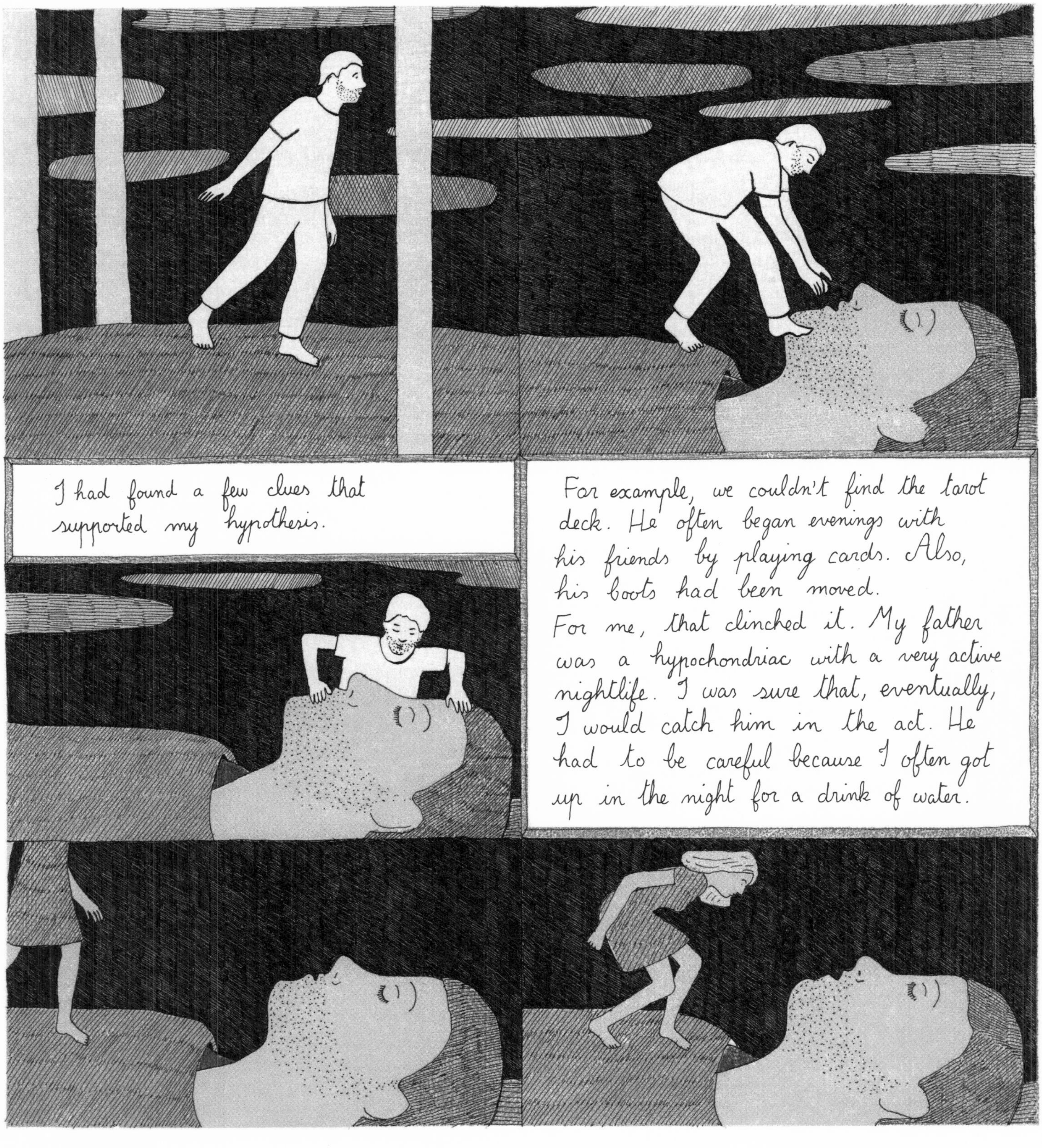
I had found a few clues that supported my hypothesis.
For example, we couldn't find the tarot deck. He often began evenings with his friends by playing cards. Also, his boots had been moved.
For me, that clinched it. My father was a hypochondriac with a very active nightlife. I was sure that, eventually, I would catch him in the act. He had to be careful because I often got up in the night for a drink of water.

IV

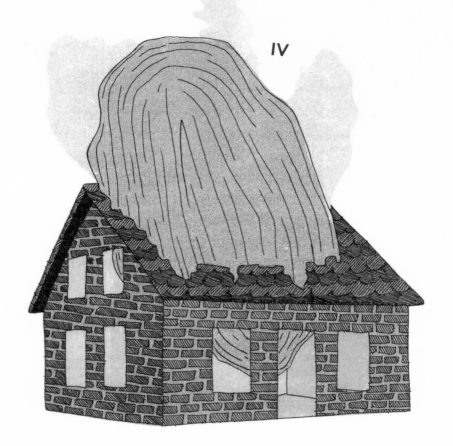

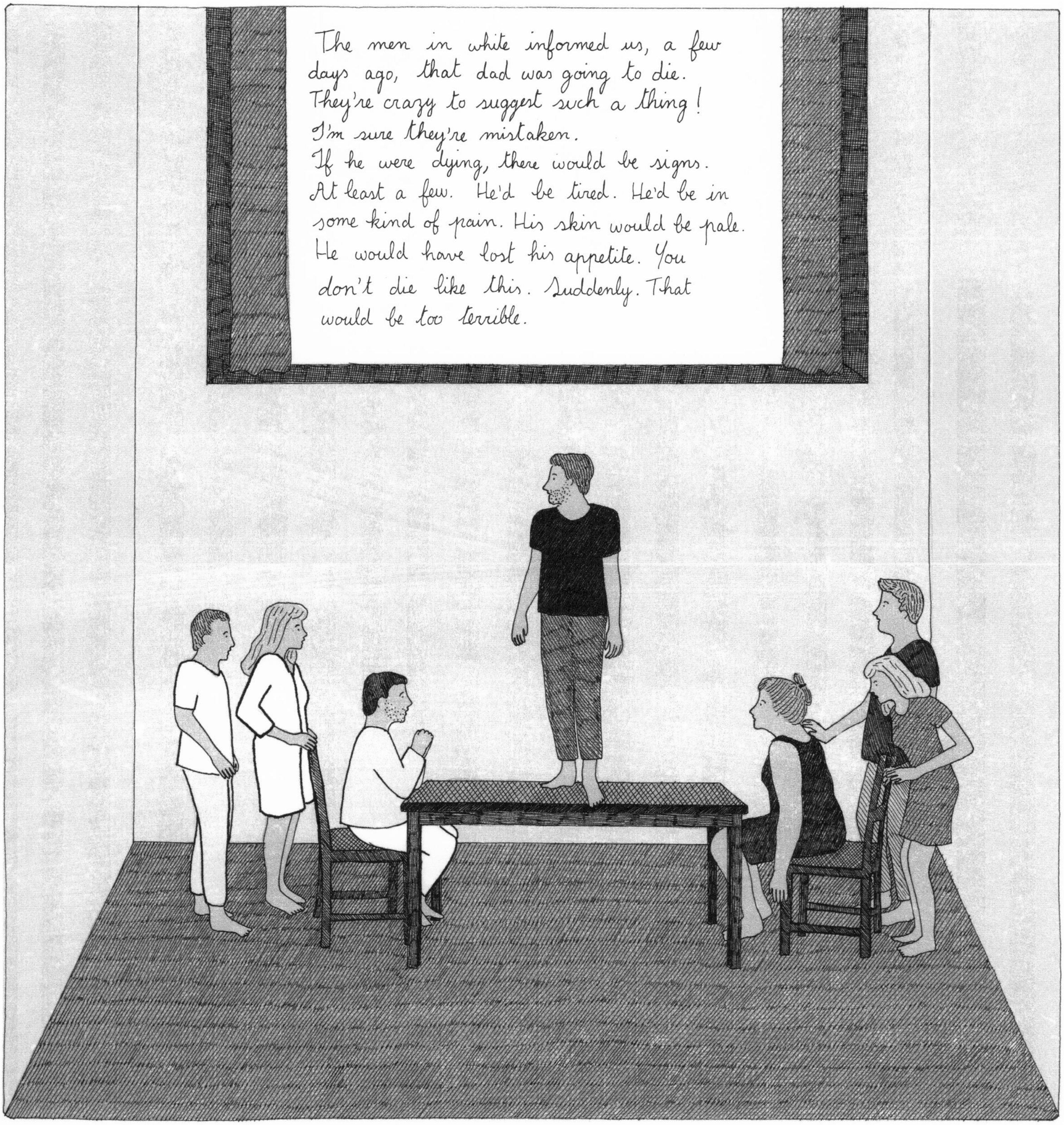
The men in white informed us, a few days ago, that dad was going to die. They're crazy to suggest such a thing! I'm sure they're mistaken. If he were dying, there would be signs. At least a few. He'd be tired. He'd be in some kind of pain. His skin would be pale. He would have lost his appetite. You don't die like this. Suddenly. That would be too terrible.

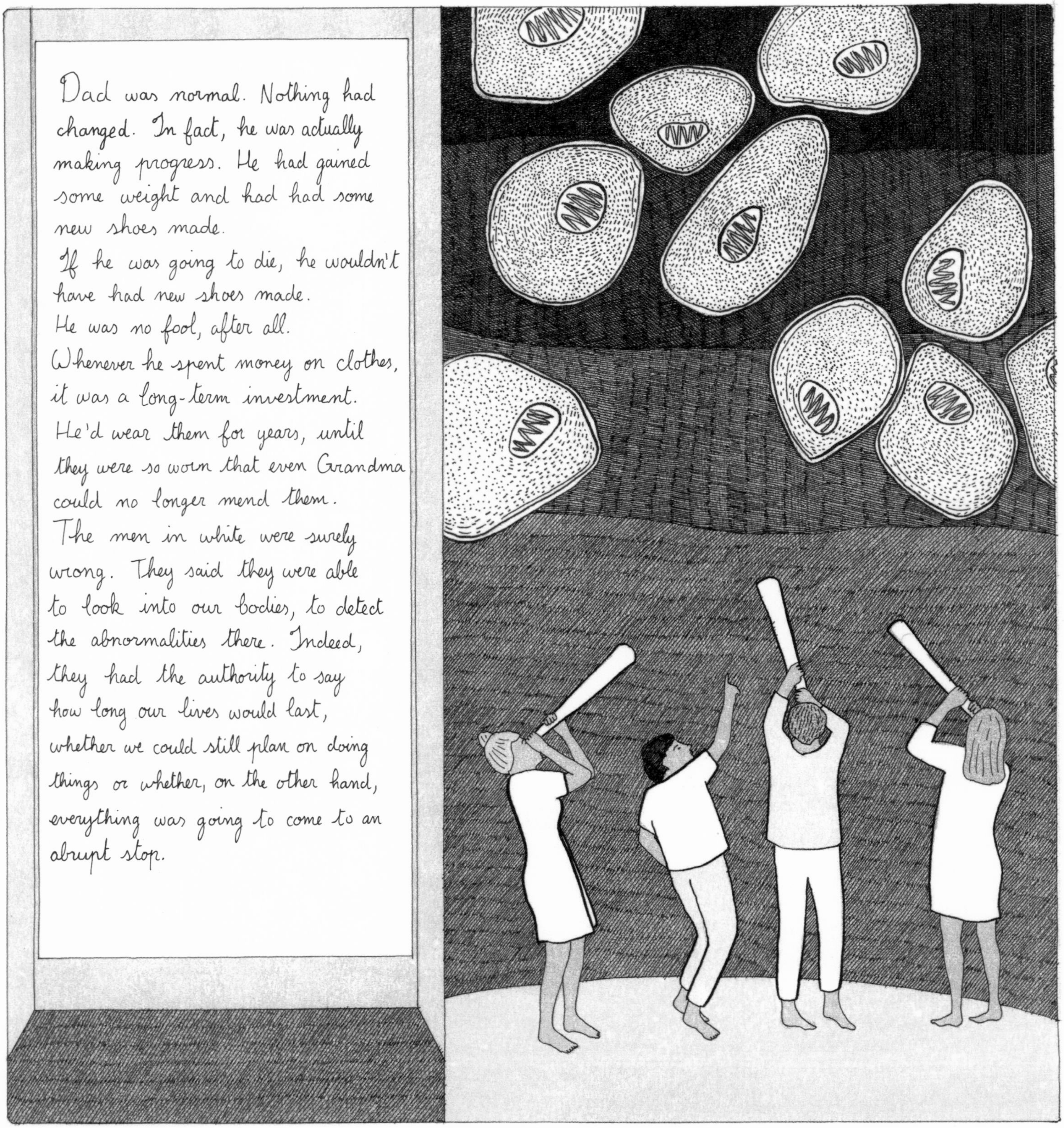
Dad was normal. Nothing had changed. In fact, he was actually making progress. He had gained some weight and had had some new shoes made.
If he was going to die, he wouldn't have had new shoes made.
He was no fool, after all.
Whenever he spent money on clothes, it was a long-term investment.
He'd wear them for years, until they were so worn that even Grandma could no longer mend them.
The men in white were surely wrong. They said they were able to look into our bodies, to detect the abnormalities there. Indeed, they had the authority to say how long our lives would last, whether we could still plan on doing things or whether, on the other hand, everything was going to come to an abrupt stop.

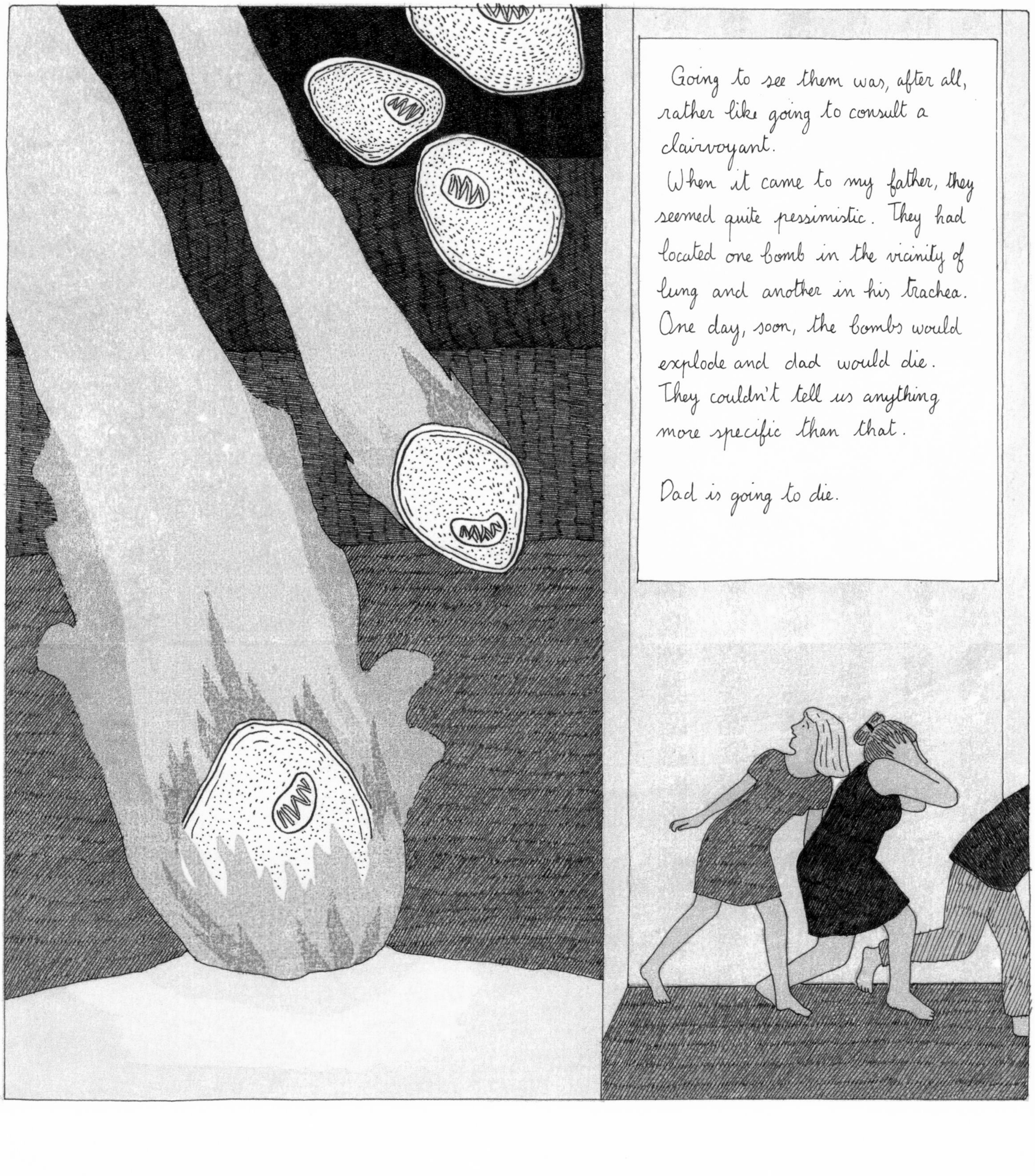
Going to see them was, after all, rather like going to consult a clairvoyant.
When it came to my father, they seemed quite pessimistic. They had located one bomb in the vicinity of lung and another in his trachea. One day, soon, the bombs would explode and dad would die. They couldn't tell us anything more specific than that.
Dad is going to die.

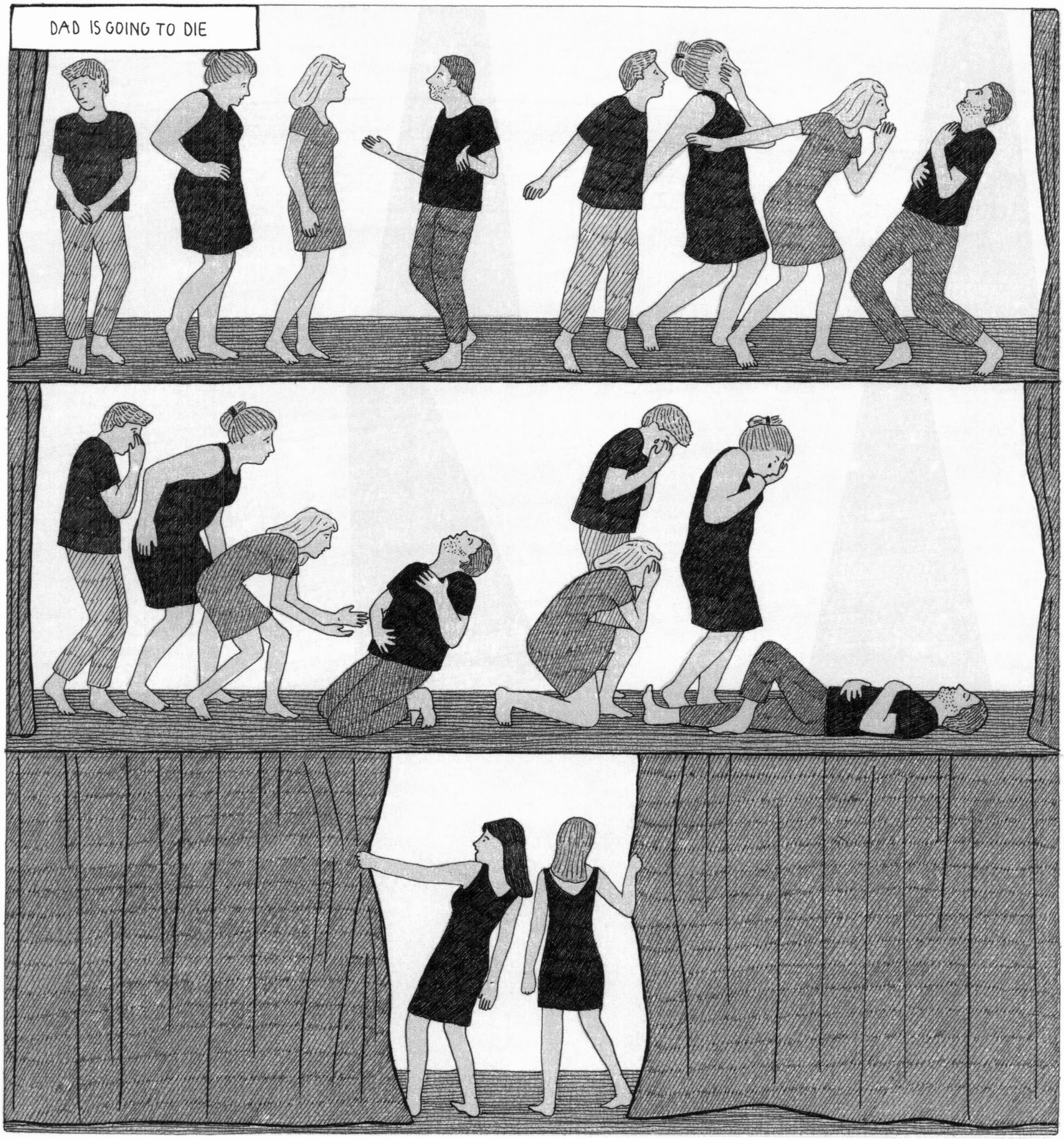
DAD IS GOING TO DIE

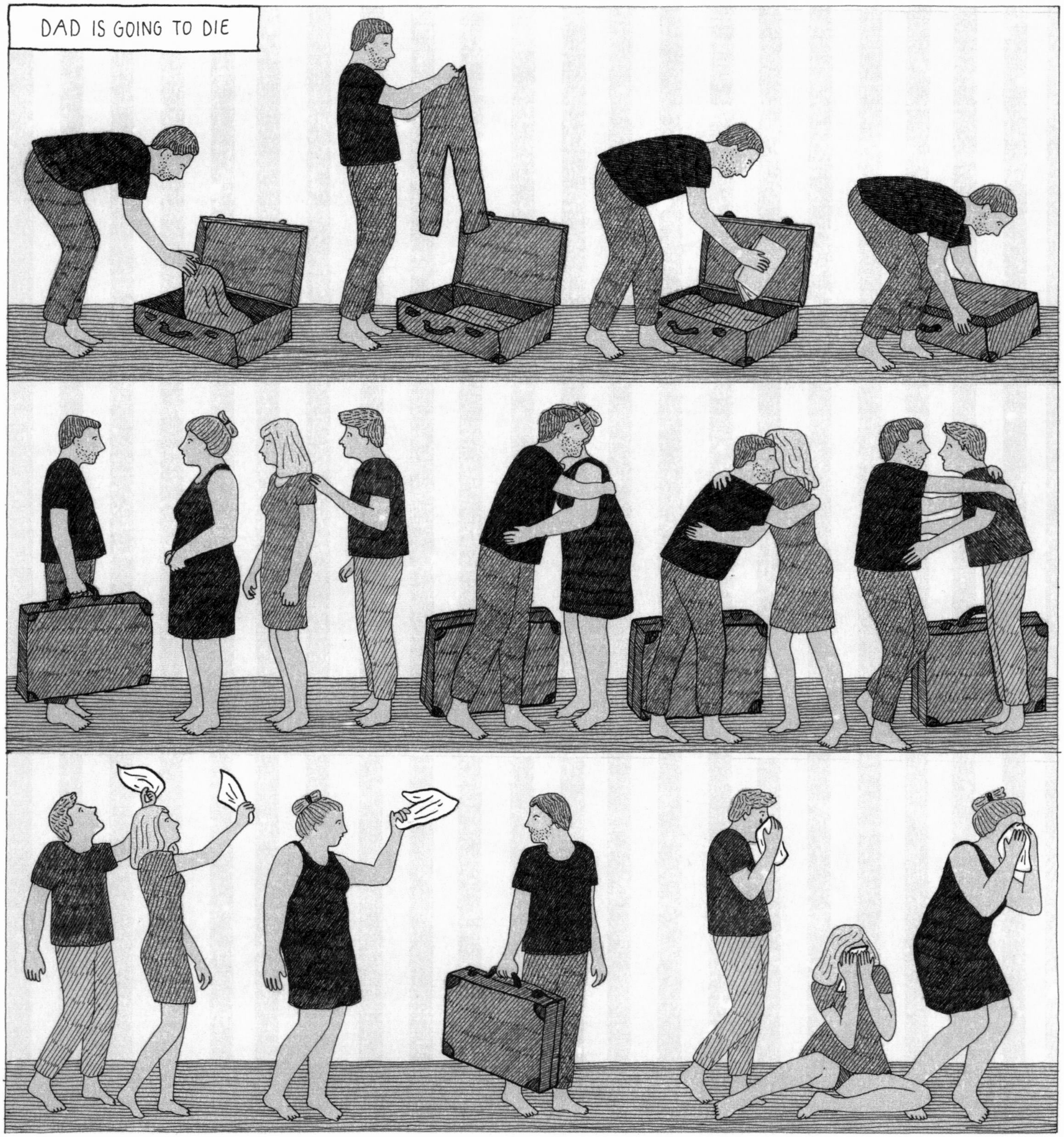
DAD IS GOING TO DIE

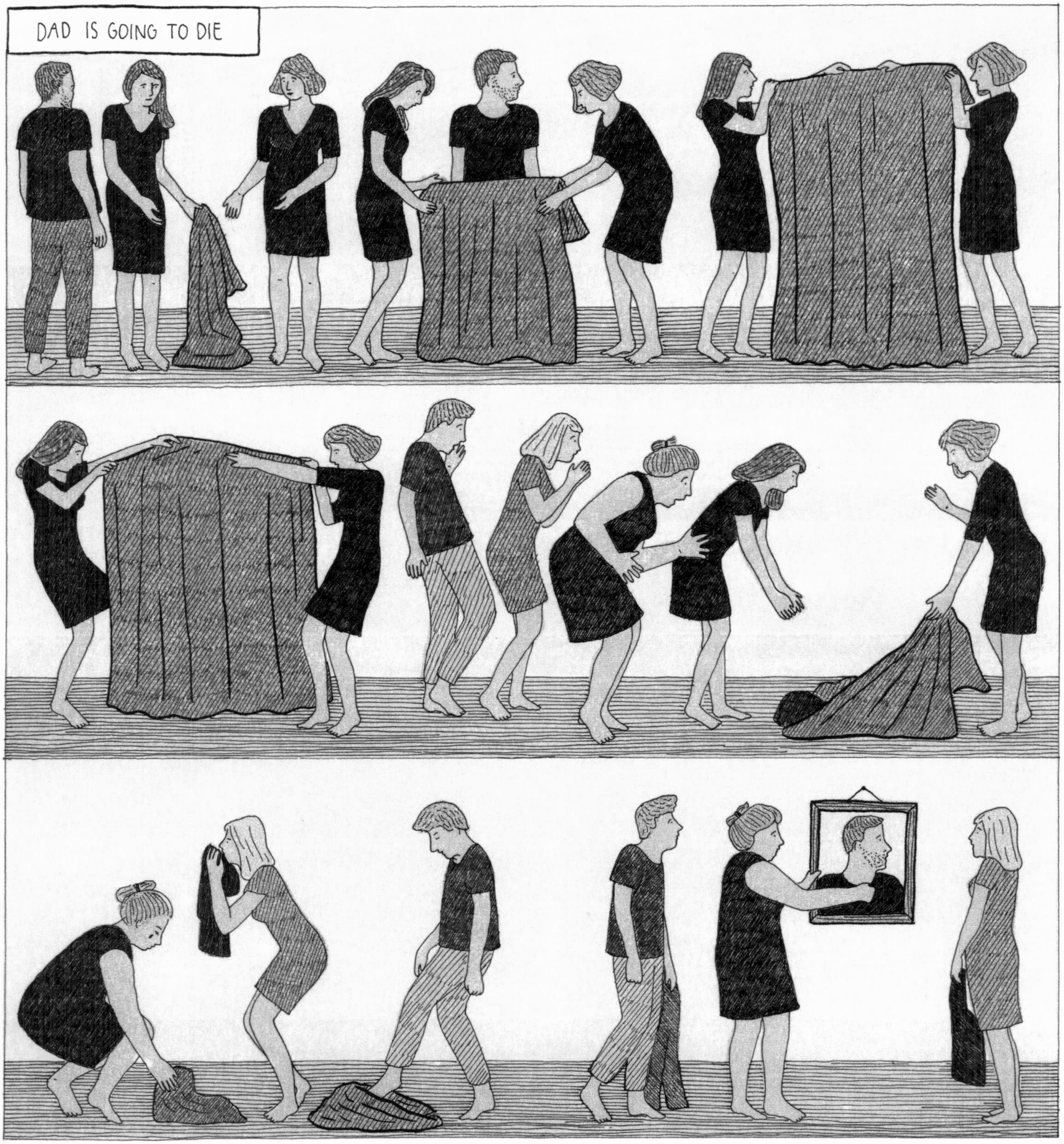
DAD IS GOING TO DIE

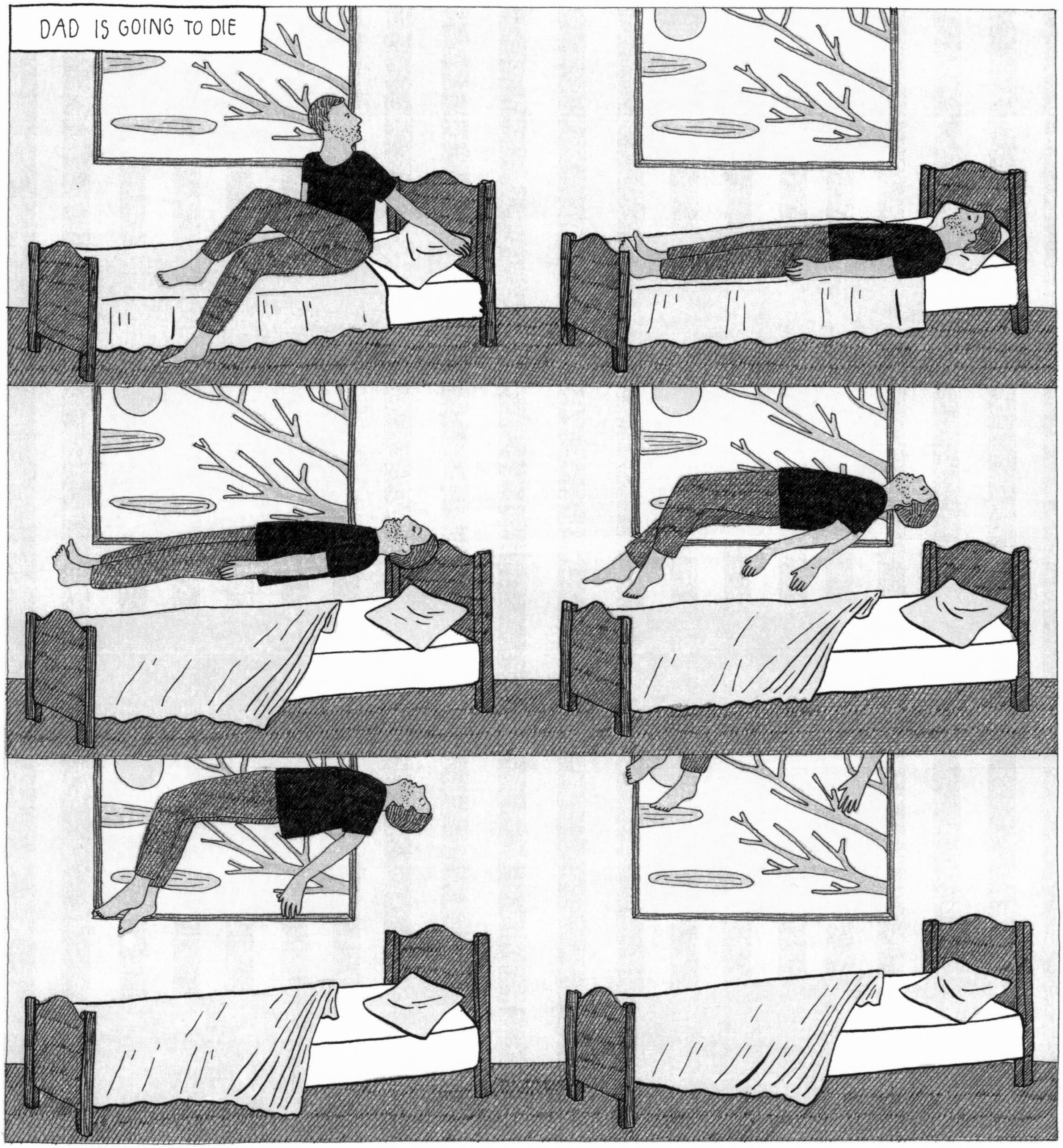
DAD IS GOING TO DIE

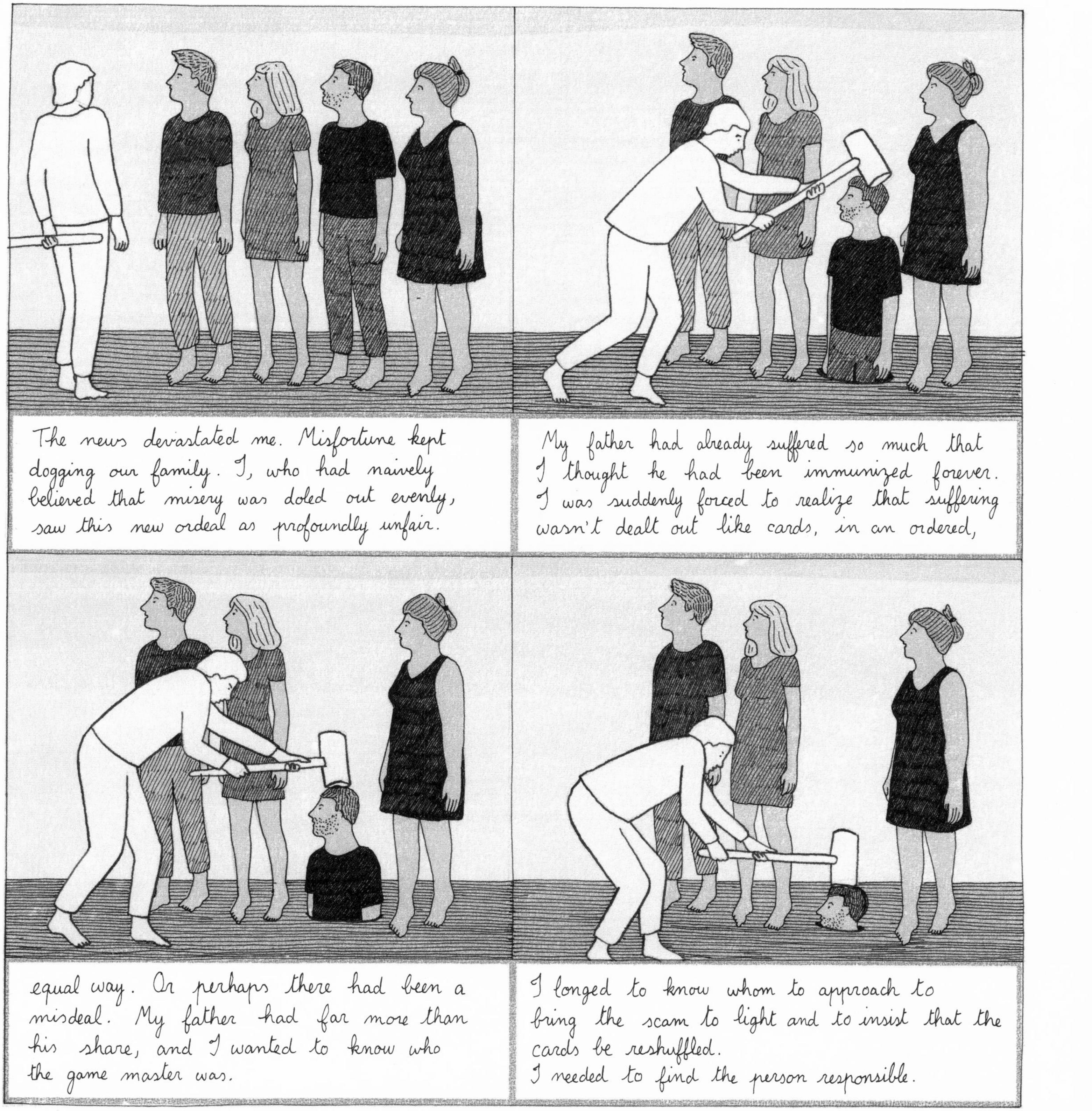
The news devastated me. Misfortune kept dogging our family. I, who had naively believed that misery was doled out evenly, saw this new ordeal as profoundly unfair.
My father had already suffered so much that I thought he had been immunized forever. I was suddenly forced to realize that suffering wasn't dealt out like cards, in an ordered,
equal way. Or perhaps there had been a misdeal. My father had far more than his share, and I wanted to know who the game master was.
I longed to know whom to approach to bring the scam to light and to insist that the cards be reshuffled.
I needed to find the person responsible.

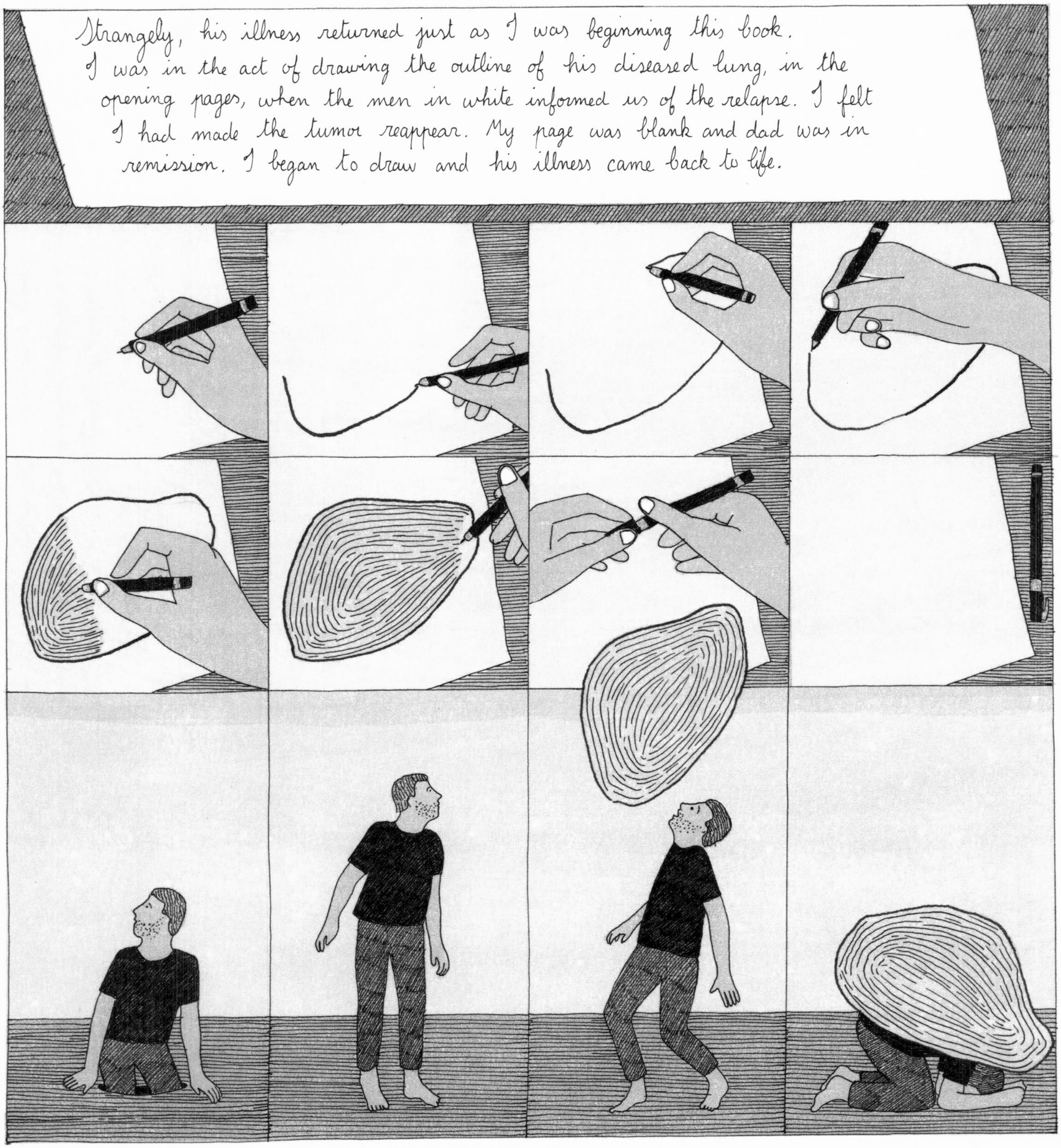
Strangely, his illness returned just as I was beginning this book. I was in the act of drawing the outline of his diseased lung, in the opening pages, when the men in white informed us of the relapse. I felt I had made the tumor reappear. My page was blank and dad was in remission. I began to draw and his illness came back to life.

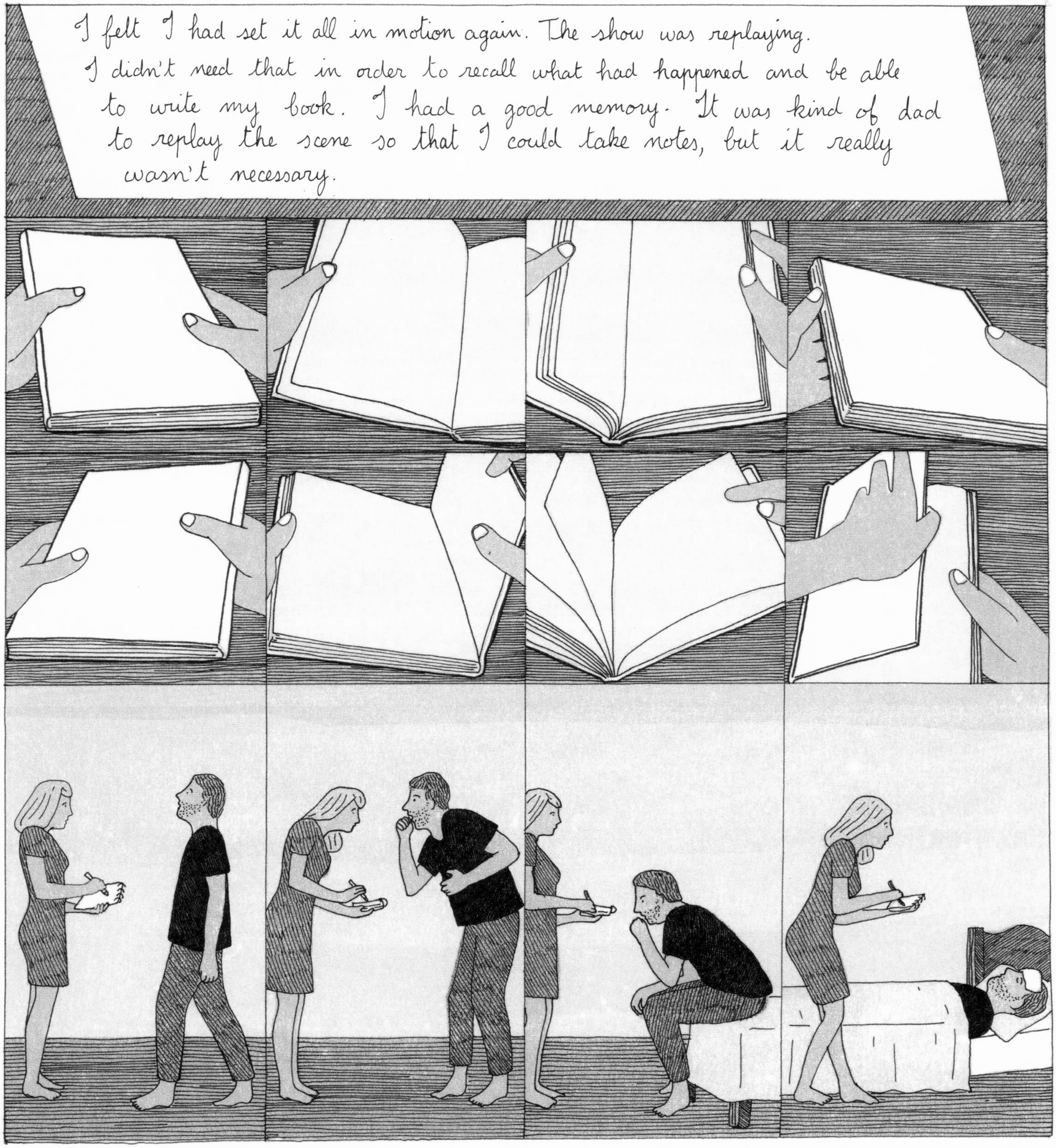
I felt I had set it all in motion again. The show was replaying. I didn't need that in order to recall what had happened and be able to write my book. I had a good memory. It was kind of dad to replay the scene so that I could take notes, but it really wasn't necessary.

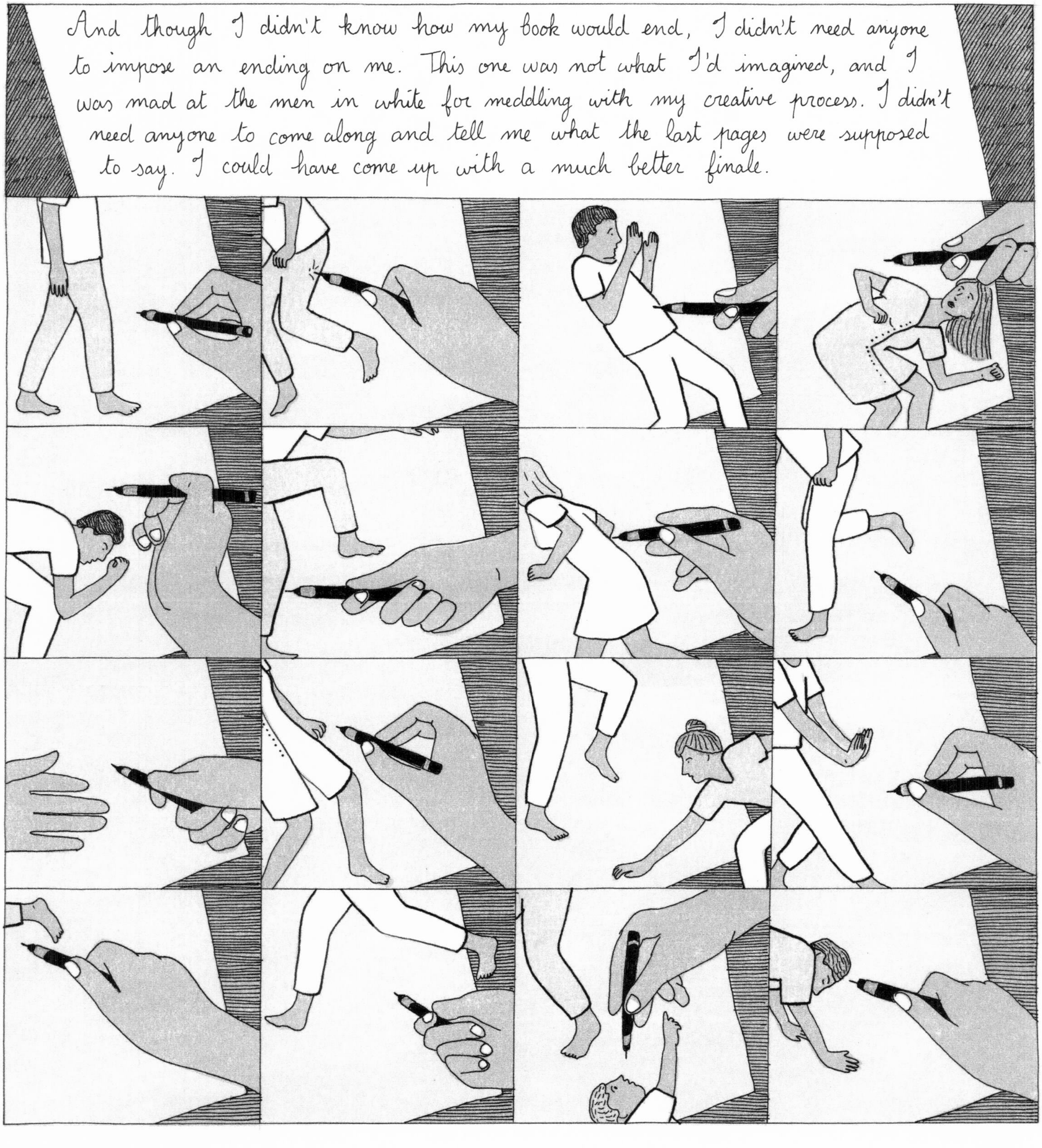
And though I didn't know how my book would end, I didn't need anyone to impose an ending on me. This one was not what I'd imagined, and I was mad at the men in white for meddling with my creative process. I didn't need anyone to come along and tell me what the last pages were supposed to say. I could have come up with a much better finale.

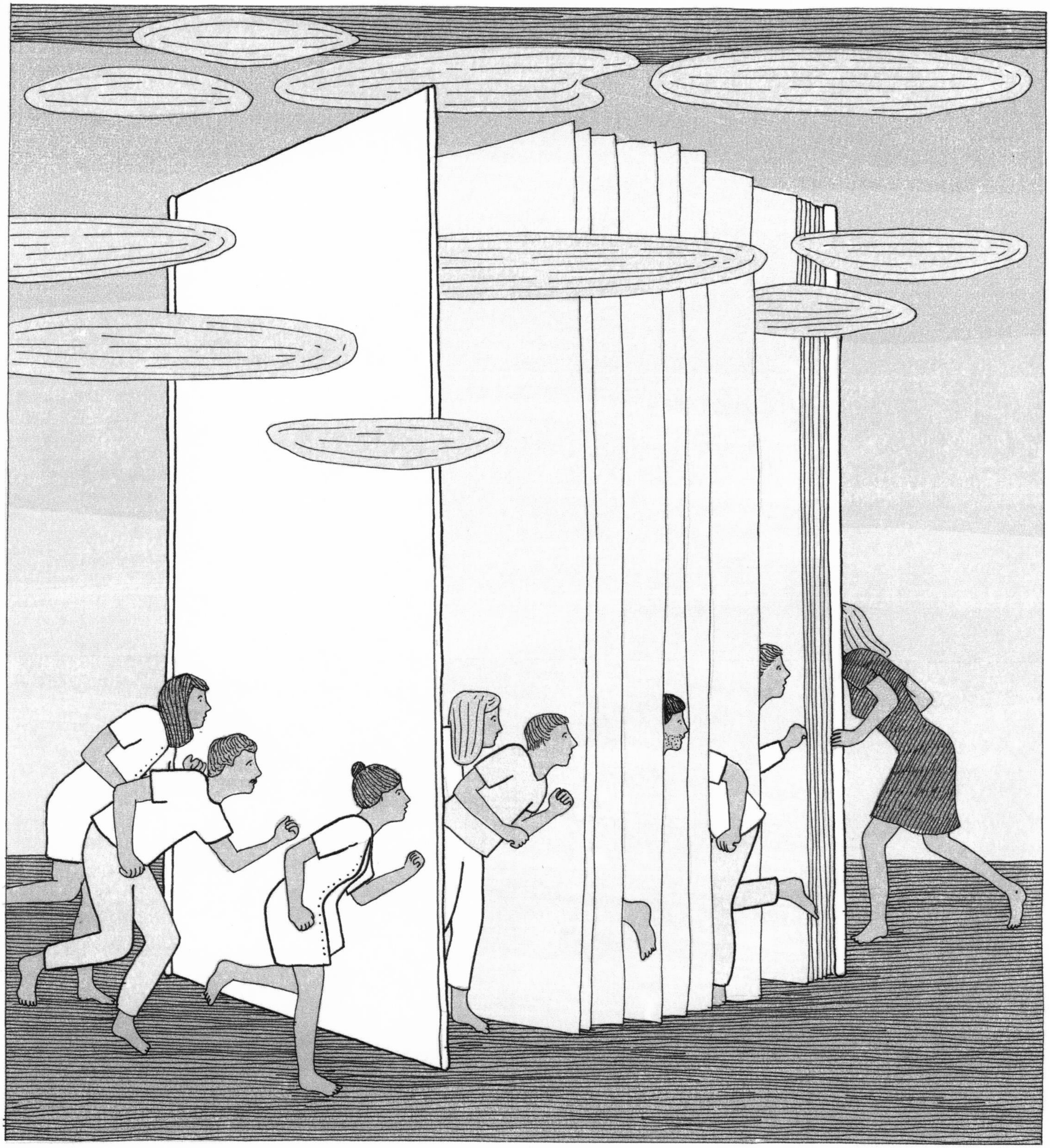

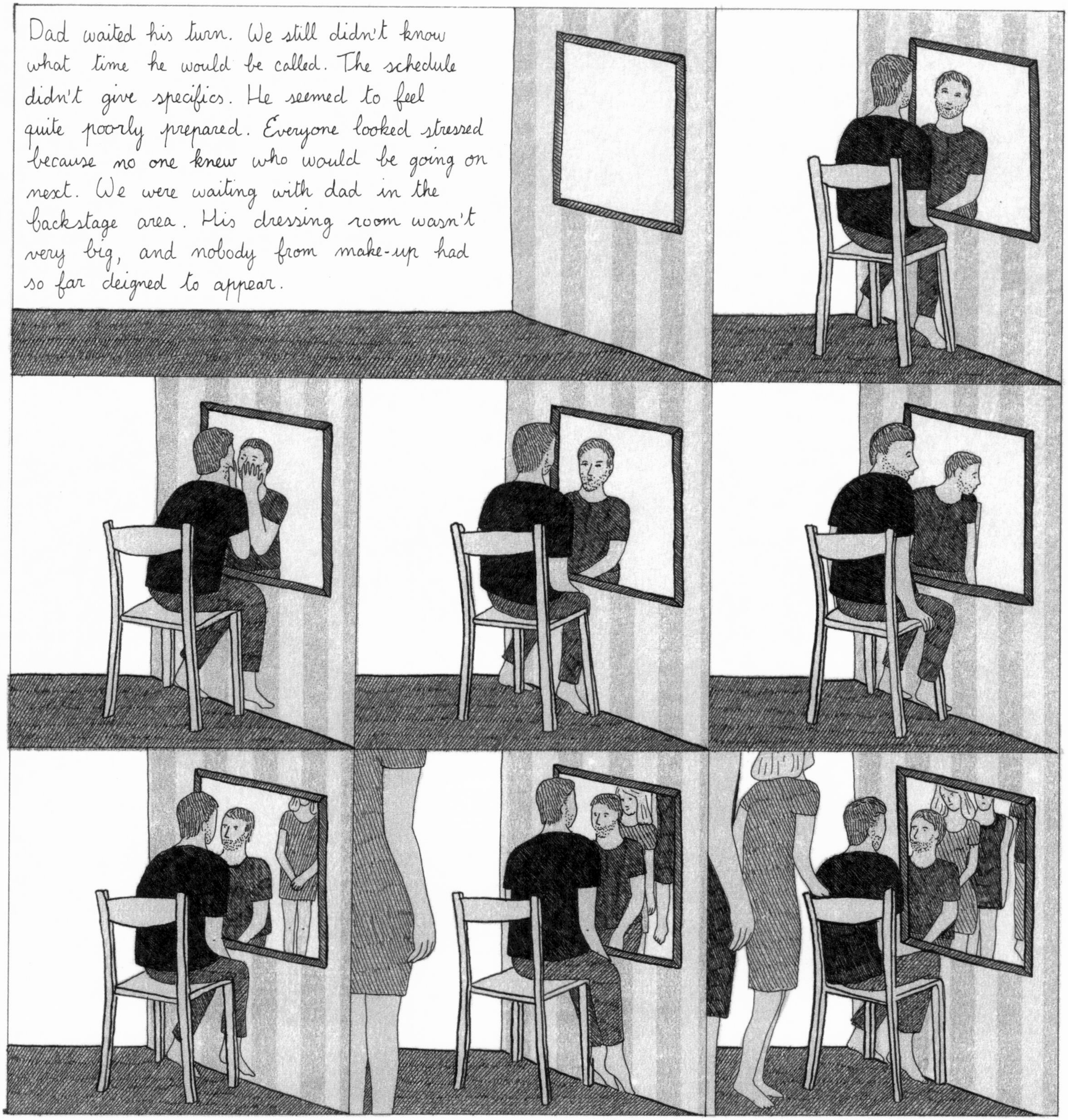
Dad waited his turn. We still didn't know what time he would be called. The schedule didn't give specifics. He seemed to feel quite poorly prepared. Everyone looked stressed because no one knew who would be going on next. We were waiting with dad in the backstage area. His dressing room wasn't very big, and nobody from make-up had so far deigned to appear.

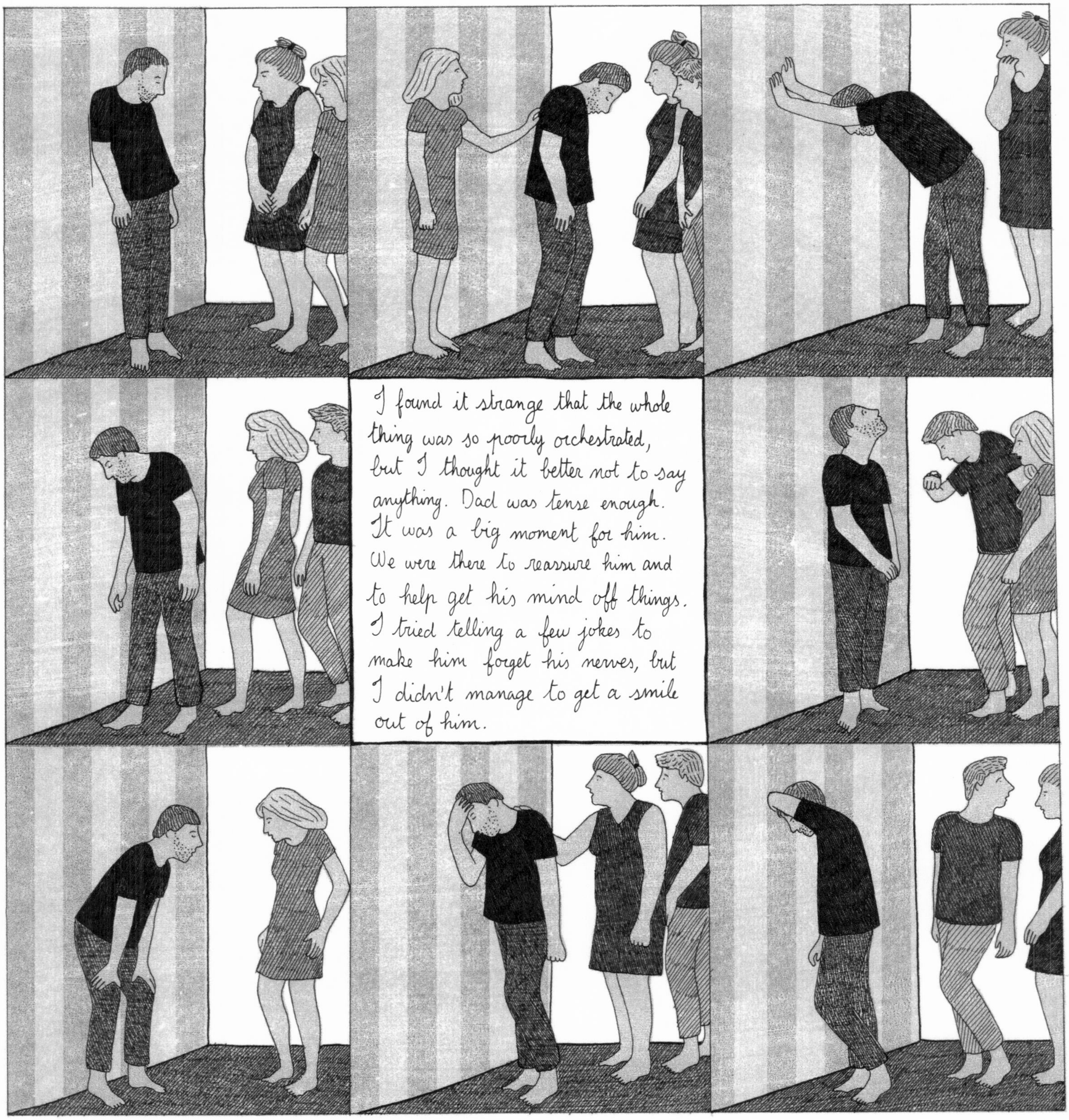
I found it strange that the whole thing was so poorly orchestrated, but I thought it better not to say anything. Dad was tense enough. It was a big moment for him. We were there to reassure him and to help get his mind off things. I tried telling a few jokes to make him forget his nerves, but I didn't manage to get a smile out of him.

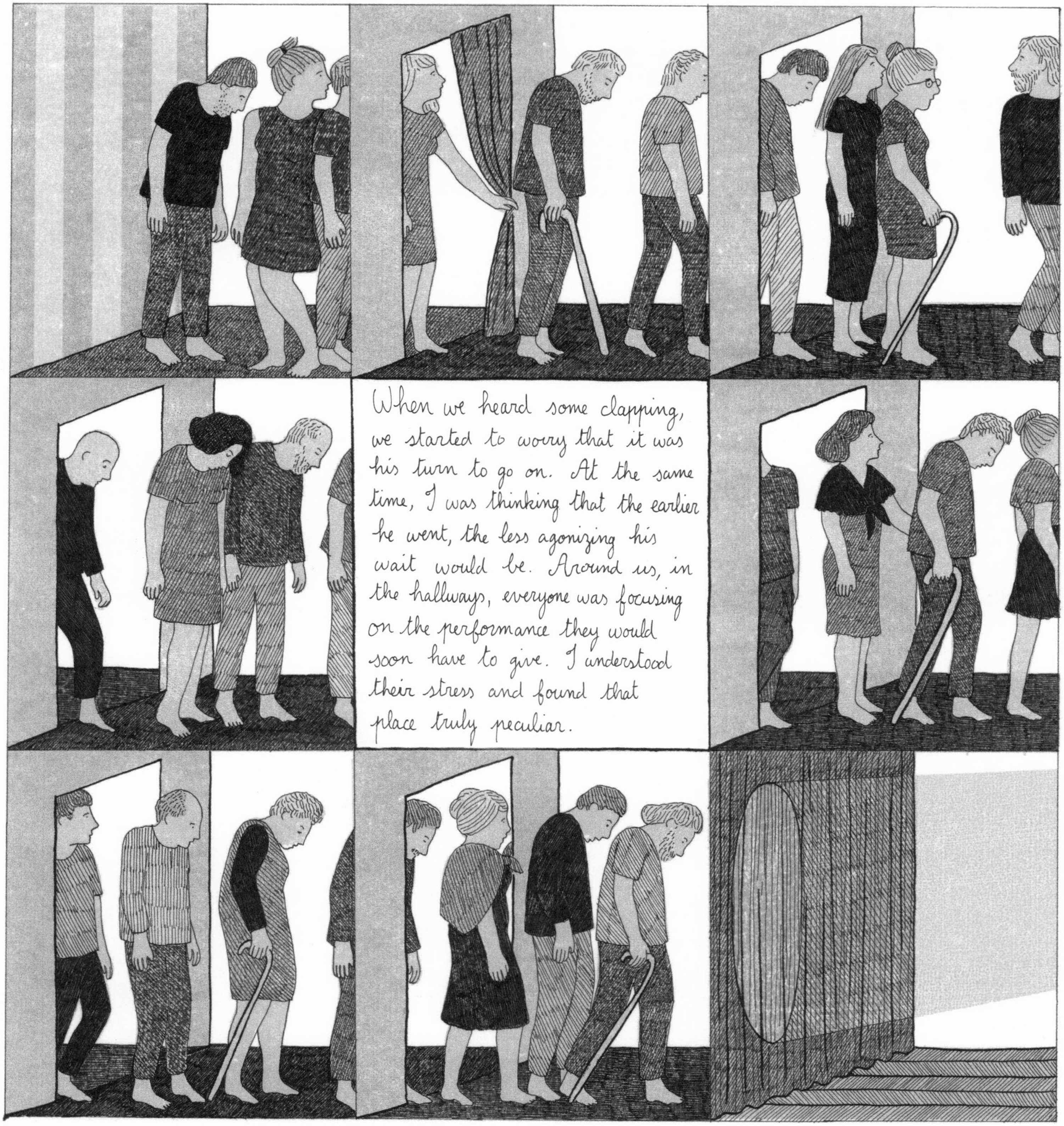
When we heard some clapping, we started to worry that it was his turn to go on. At the same time, I was thinking that the earlier he went, the less agonizing his wait would be. Around us, in the hallways, everyone was focusing on the performance they would soon have to give. I understood their stress and found that place truly peculiar.

Dad was anxious too. Mom was telling him he had nothing to worry about, that it would all go well, that he was ready, that he'd been rehearsing this for almost five years.

I added that, besides, everyone else was older and didn't seem as talented. He was quite young to have already been contacted. It was irrefutable evidence that he had what it took.

My brother tried to tell him that we would be proud of him no matter what.

But dad wasn't in much of a mood to chat and our words seemed barely to reach him. He was waiting for us to stop talking so he could focus. I would have loved to be able to hold him in my arms and take his hand, to encourage him, but I held back because he wasn't much of a toucher and I didn't want to irritate him.

The wait seemed interminable.

I even wondered if the organizer had forgotten about him. It was truly agonizing not to be given any information. You just don't make people wait like that.

It was ridiculous, and in his place I would have long since lost my patience.

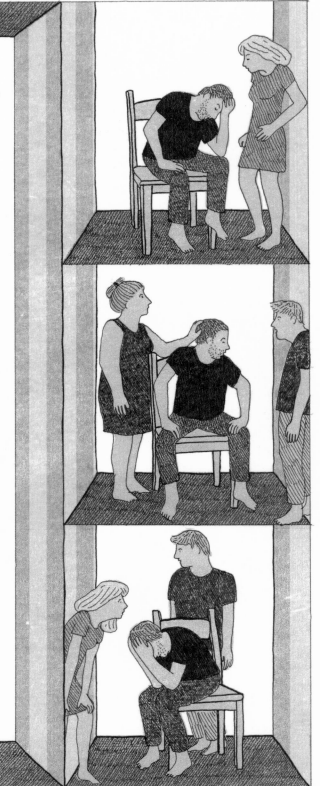

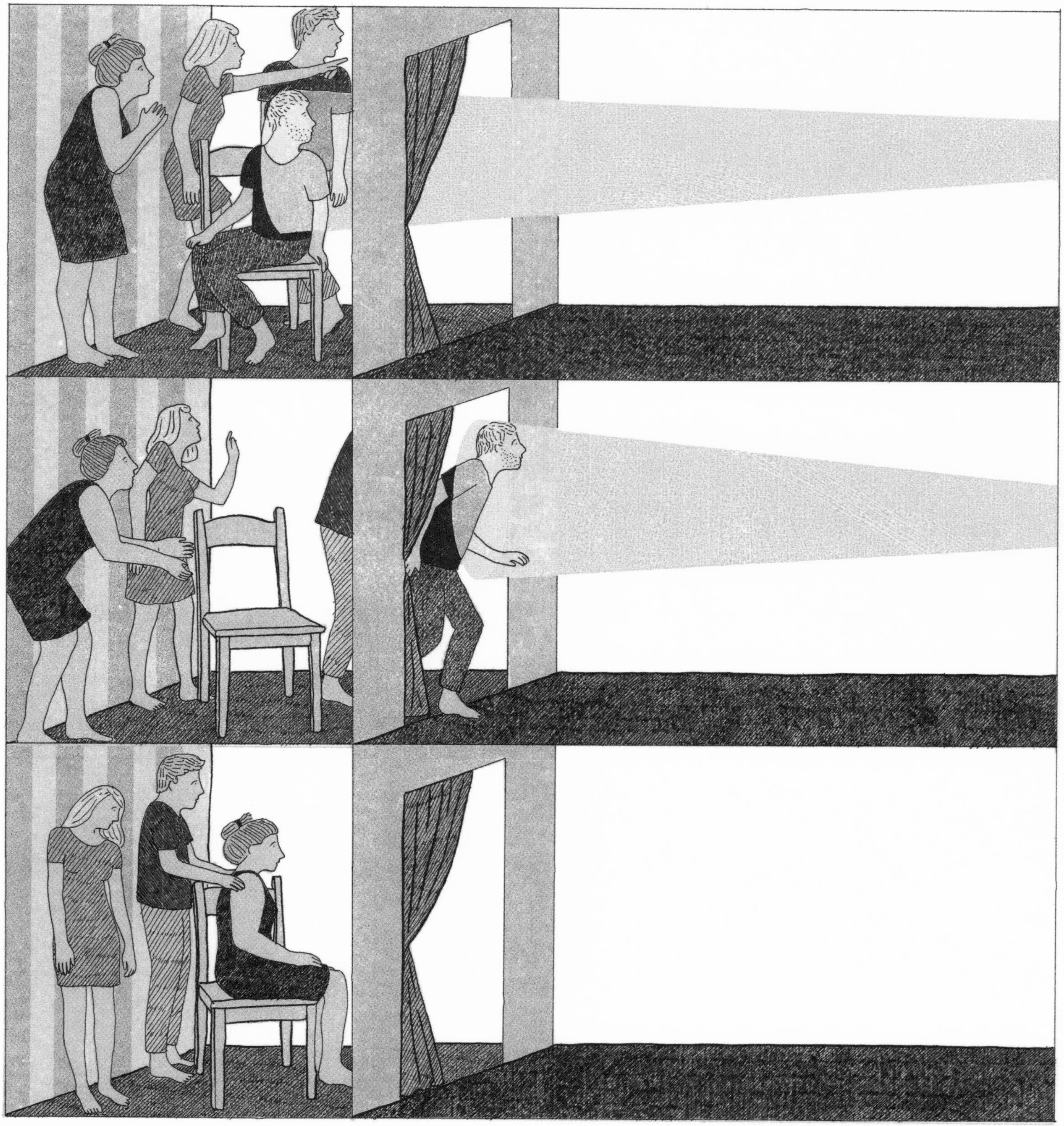